THE LIBRARY OF

HONESTY

UPRYS

ENERGY ECONOMY

Wentworth

Institute of Technology

About Island Press

Island Press, a nonprofit organization, publishes, markets, and distributes the most advanced thinking on the conservation of our natural resources—books about soil, land, water, forests, wildlife, and hazardous and toxic wastes. These books are practical tools used by public officials, business and industry leaders, natural resource managers, and concerned citizens working to solve both local and global resource problems.

Founded in 1978, Island Press reorganized in 1984 to meet the increasing demand for substantive books on all resource-related issues. Island Press publishes and distributes under its own imprint and offers these services to other nonprofit organizations.

Support for Island Press is provided by Apple Computer Inc., Geraldine R. Dodge Foundation, The Energy Foundation, The Charles Engelhard Foundation, The Ford Foundation, Glen Eagles Foundation, The George Gund Foundation, William and Flora Hewlett Foundation, The Joyce Foundation, The John D. and Catherine T. MacArthur Foundation, The Andrew W. Mellon Foundation, The Joyce Mertz-Gilmore Foundation, The New-Land Foundation, The J. N. Pew, Jr., Charitable Trust, Alida Rockefeller, The Rockefeller Brothers Fund, The Rockefeller Foundation, The Florence and John Schumann Foundation, The Tides Foundation, and individual donors.

About The Conservation Fund

The Conservation Fund works with public and private partners to protect land and water resources. Founded in 1985 as a nonmembership, nonprofit organization committed to entrepreneurial spirit and innovation, the fund targets specific priorities with a series of focused natural resource conservation programs.

American Greenways helps communities and states establish public and private open space corridors. The *American Land Conservation Program* of the Richard King Mellon Foundation, assisted by the fund, protects open space, wetlands, and wildlife areas of national significance. The *Civil War Battlefield Campaign* works to safeguard the nation's "hallowed ground" through acquisition and increased community awareness. *Public Conservation Partnerships* assist agencies by buying property, when it is on the market, for public open space. The land is sold to the agency when public funds are available. The *Freshwater Institute* develops economically feasible, scientifically valid, innovative approaches to protection, conservation, and wise use of freshwater resources. *Land Advisory Services* offer new ways to achieve conservation goals unattainable through traditional means.

Related programs support the conservation community through improved communication, increased resources, and greater public recognition. *Land Letter* and *Common Ground* newsletters report on legislation, news, and trends in natural resources and land conservation. *Giftlands* generates funds for conservation through taxwise donations of surplus non-conservation real estate. The *Alexander Calder Conservation Award*, established by the Union Camp Corporation, annually recognizes cooperation between business and conservation.

Donations from individuals, foundations, and corporations underwrite activities of The Conservation Fund, a 501(c)(3) organization. All contributions are tax deductible to the limit permitted by law.

Inside the
Environmental
Movement

Inside the Environmental Movement

Meeting the Leadership Challenge

Donald Snow
THE CONSERVATION FUND

Foreword by Patrick F. Noonan

Washington, D.C. □ *Covelo, California*

Text design by David Bullen

Library of Congress Cataloging-in-Publication Data
Inside the environmental movement: meeting
the leadership challenge / edited by Donald Snow.
     p.   cm.
    Includes bibliographical references and index.
    ISBN 1-55963-027-2 (alk. paper).—ISBN 1-55963-026-4
(pbk.)
     1. Conservation leadership—United States. 2. Conserva-
tionists—United States. 3. Environmentalists—United States.
4. Conservation of natural resources—United States—Societies, etc. 5. Environmental protection—United States—Societies, etc.
    I. Snow, Donald R., 1951–
    S944.5.L42I57 1991   91-20235
    333.7′2′0973—dc20   CIP

Printed on recycled, acid-free paper

Manufactured in the United States of America
10 9 8 7 6 5 4 3 2 1

Contents

List of Tables

Foreword

During the past two decades interest in conservation and the environment has grown at a remarkable rate. Broader public recognition has led to a dramatic increase in the number and size of the organizations dedicated to finding solutions for environmental problems and accomplishing conservation objectives. As we approach the twenty-first century, an estimated 10,000 conservation and environmental organizations protect wildlife habitat, provide recreational facilities, monitor toxic wastes, work for clean air, or lobby Congress. A number of large organizations like the National Wildlife Federation and The Nature Conservancy have annual budgets of nearly $100 million. A look at The Nature Conservancy provides a glimpse of the movement's growth. In 1969 the Conservancy had about 18,000 members and a staff of thirty. Now, the organization has over 600,000 members and a staff of over 1,300. Similarly, the number of the nation's land trusts has grown swiftly, doubling in the last decade alone. Today, the nation's 900 plus independent land trusts have a combined membership of over 750,000. Since the late 1980s, new land trusts have been forming on the average of one a week. Other organizations have similar histories of growth. All reflect the escalating concern Americans show for conservation and environmental quality.

The rapid increase in the size of the movement in recent years and the formation of new organizations have created opportunities for major advances. At the same time the opportunity has generated a pressing requirement to find, train, and employ individuals who are capable of exercising the effective leadership needed in an increasingly complex and challenging world.

The Conservation Fund was founded in 1985 to advance land and water conservation. Our approach is to look for common ground, to try new approaches, and to work in cooperation with the private sector, other nonprofit organizations, and public agencies to protect America's outdoor heritage. While we are involved actively in day-to-day conservation activities that range from helping states establish greenway systems to exploring entrepreneurial approaches to private-owner conservation, we also are committed to the long-term effectiveness of the movement. With this in mind, we began the Conservation Leadership Project in 1989.

When we started the Leadership Project, the impetus for this book, The Conservation Fund asked leaders currently in the nonprofit sector what needed to be done to increase the overall effectiveness of the movement. We wanted them to share their experiences and ideas. They did so in a series of telling, instructive, provocative articles that will be published by Island Press in a companion book, *Voices from the Environmental Movement: Perspectives for a New Era.*

The results of our extensive surveys and the comments of the eminent volunteer advisory panel for the project—representing government, academia, industry, philanthropy, and nonprofits— told us something more. They said that the leaders and managers needed for the future represented a new profession for which there was no established training, no university curriculum, no career path, and few standards. In short, we had ignored development of our most important asset—human capital.

Our advisory panel—distinguished by some of the best minds in the environmental field—urged us to ask the kinds of questions and gather the type of information that would establish the foundation for a new profession. At the same time, we sought to place the information in the context of the movement's history, accomplishments, and structure. The responses we collected provide a fascinating, insightful exploration of the conservation/environmental movement: its leaders and needs; its strengths and shortcomings. This storehouse of information served as the catalyst and underpinning for *Inside the Environmental Movement: Meeting the Leadership Challenge.*

Inside the Environmental Movement provides a unique in-depth look at people and organizations in the nonprofit environmental community. It probes the problems and highlights the areas where change is essential. As intended, the book does something else, too. The answers it provides and the questions it raises lay the groundwork for a new profession that crosses many traditional lines.

We learned that future leaders in this new profession need to be conversant with law, natural sciences, public relations and communications, human relations, resources management, marketing and fund-raising, and business management. And while the requirements are many, the resources and rewards—in the traditional economic sense—are often small. In one organization after another, respondents said they spent an inordinate amount of time and energy just trying to raise the funds necessary to survive.

Yet in spite of the lack of training, funding, and recognition, the accomplishments have been remarkable. The credit must be shared by the volunteers, who have been both leaders and workers, and the professionals. The question, however, is not what has been done, but rather what must be done. Never before have pressures been greater, and needs for collaborative action more urgent. The challenge—documented for the first time by *Inside the Environmental Movement*—is to address the organizational, educational, and financial challenges with better training, new partnerships, and new resources.

More important than the specific responses are two aspects of the broad survey. First is the interpretation of the charts and tables by Donald Snow, who as editor and project director spent a year refining, reviewing, and translating the volume of information to give it meaning and to make it useful.

But perhaps no element of *Inside the Environmental Movement* is more vital than the series of recommendations it contains. The panel of twenty-one leaders has carefully and thoughtfully shown what must be done to meet the challenges that we will face in the years ahead.

One recommendation is particularly telling. The panel confirmed that future success demands reaching out to embrace segments of the population that in the past have not been included within the movement. Too many times the issues of jobs and the problems of the cities are seen as separate from, or worse, compet-

ing with, concerns of environmentalists. Eliminating that conflict—
which exists more in perception than reality—is a key recommendation of the Leadership Project.

At the start of the project, we planned a modest report that would
outline a few critical issues. Thanks to the insight provided by
members of our advisory council, we were guided to much more. It
is our hope that this report will serve as the stimulus for private and
public conservation interests, for the academic community, and for
American business to begin the dialogue that is essential if we are
to improve markedly the effectiveness of the American conservation movement.

Patrick F. Noonan
President, The Conservation Fund

Preface

In March 1988, The Conservation Fund initiated a study of leadership development needs among conservation and environmental groups in the United States. We set out to determine whether the staff and volunteers of nongovernmental, nonprofit conservation organizations (NGOs) are being well enough prepared through academic and other training to meet the enormous challenges they face, including the seemingly mundane challenge of managing their own organizations. We hoped to assess the use and quality of existing programs designed to support the training and organizational development of conservation groups. We were curious as to whether conservation and environmental protection, as they are pursued by NGOs, require any unique or exceptional attributes of leadership; and we were hopeful that the organizational leaders themselves, both staff and volunteers, would offer an assessment of the environmental movement: From their point of view, where is the movement headed? What must leaders do to make themselves and their organizations more effective? This book presents the findings and conclusions of the Conservation Leadership Project.

As we began to define the Leadership Project and make our initial attempts to generate a national sample of organizations and their leaders, we began to encounter some slight resistance, though in the main the people we contacted were overwhelmingly supportive of the project and generous with their time. Still, there were a few who objected to the use of scarce foundation funds for the purpose of studying leadership in the American conservation movement. We took their objection as symptomatic. They asked the obvious question: Why should any organization receive funds to study the movement itself when the great issues of the moment demand immediate action? Why fund the army's library when soldiers on the front lines are starving?

The answer, of course, is at least as simple as the question: In any social and political movement, regardless of the issues being addressed, leadership is the key to effectiveness. Good leaders and healthy patterns of leadership create success; poor leadership—which is often the same as ephemeral leadership—causes failure and disappointment. Leadership, we believe, consists of a series of conscious acts. Leaders can be trained, and most of the skills of leadership are transferable.

We believe we found evidence for the claim that the most successful conservation and environmental organizations are those that deliberately nurture leaders and foster healthy patterns of leadership. They pay close attention to management and reward significant achievements in organizational development and efficient administration, as well as achievements in the substantive issues or activities. Indeed, in a healthy organization, it is very difficult to distinguish between good management and good leadership. Conversely, the least successful groups are the ones that ignore the long-term needs of their leaders. The language and attitude of good management are foreign to them; strategic planning (both short- and long-term) is often viewed as an unaffordable luxury. The pattern of fund-raising and development in these groups is hand-to-mouth; they hasten, willy-nilly, to fight the latest fires on the front lines of the cause and refuse to acknowledge the possibility that there may be a saner, perhaps a slower, way of operating. They tend to recycle leaders very quickly, often losing their most knowledgeable and effective people at about the time they have reached their stride. One might expect that these patterns of organizational behavior would be isolated among the newest and least mature groups of the environmental movement, but they are not. A surprisingly large number of groups whose origins reach back to the five years following Earth Day 1970—and some much older than that—have managed to survive using these very patterns of operation.

As we queried conservation leaders across the country, we were struck by the fact that the size or scope of the organization had little bearing on its record of effective leadership, though size is often a key determinant of the forms of leadership required and the tasks that challenge the leaders. Some of the largest and most well-established organizations we encountered were among the most poorly managed. Fraught with internal strife, poor morale, wasted resources and opportunities, they lacked a clear vision of their mission and scope, possessed no methods for evaluating effectiveness or efficiency, and could not clearly recount their record of undeniable achievements. Some of the smallest groups we encountered were virtual models of excellent management; their leaders had adopted processes and developed systems and skills that were exactly right for the long-term needs of their developing organizations. They possessed clear track records and honest methods of evaluation, and they carried rich institutional memories that allowed them to learn from past mistakes. Characteristically, they paid close attention to, and spent money and time on, the development of their leaders.

While the foregoing speaks to the condition of the relatively well-established, staff-run organizations of the movement, we did not neglect the emergent groups, usually run by volunteers, and those rare examples of long-established organizations (twenty years old and older) with no paid, professional staff and only the minimum of administrative apparatus. We located leaders of numerous all-volunteer groups and asked them many of the same questions we asked the professionals and board members of the staffed organizations. In the process we ran across some remarkable stories: all-volunteer groups that raise more than a million dollars annually to support some program or facility dear to their members' hearts; volunteers who have worked for more than thirty years with an organization they founded and still manage; emerging leaders who have taken a single environmental issue in their own neighborhoods and turned it into a national campaign, joining forces with other local leaders far away and finding support for their cause in the highest levels of government. For some of these great spirits of the movement, questions about organizational management and development truly seemed moot. And some of them told us so.

As we performed our research, we encountered many of the

biases and interorganizational tensions one is apt to find within any
social and political movement. There is in some quarters, for example, a strong sentiment favoring volunteers, who are sometimes
seen as the only righteous leaders, unsullied with the mercenary
impulse to "do it for pay." In this view of activism, paid, professional
staff are suspect—persons to be watched, and preferably con-
trolled, lest they run off with the agenda and make it their own. We
suspected, when we heard such sentiments expressed, that they
were most likely the result of some very sour relations with current
or former staff, especially in organizations where staff leadership is
a recent phenomenon. We also found a tendency on the part of
professional staffers to pay overweening respect to the volunteers
in their own organizations. Rarely did we hear the professionals
denigrate any volunteers, even in strictest confidence, though the
reverse seldom held true: Some volunteers seemed to feel that the
professionals had "stolen" their movement, and said so at every
turn. Perhaps these tendencies are the inevitable fallout from a
social-political movement that, in the words of historian Stephen
Fox, "began as a hobby and became a profession."

While there is clear recognition of the crucial role that volunteers
play among the conservation NGOs, there is just as clear a widespread sentiment that the environmental movement has benefited
from the increased levels of professionalism that one now finds in
every quarter and that arises principally through the involvement of
paid staff. Most of our respondents—both volunteer and professional—overwhelmingly rejected the notion that the environmental
movement has become "too professional" in its outlook, operations
and makeup. Indeed, most felt that it is not yet professional
enough, that even greater levels of skilled management and expertise in the substantive issues would help the movement rise to the
challenges ahead.

The obvious questions left for anyone advocating an increased
capacity of leadership among the conservation NGOs relate to
training and preparation: How should professional and volunteer
leaders be trained in order to meet the new, unprecedented challenges of the 1990s and beyond? Are the existing centers for training and support adequate? If not, how can they be improved? To
begin to answer these questions, we used written questionnaires

and interviews to query the leaders of academic programs designed to train conservation and environmental professionals. We wanted to assess the health and future direction of the more than 400 U.S. academic programs in natural resources, environmental sciences, environmental studies, forestry, and related fields. We knew that a great many of those programs, like many of the NGOs, were partly the creation of the original Earth Day and the massive burst of environmental activism that came to the fore during the early 1970s. We wanted to find out to what extent they serve the NGOs, training staff who can meet the challenges of managing nongovernmental organizations or offering midcareer training in which NGO leaders can participate.

We also surveyed a sample of nonacademic programs and organizations that offer in-service training, management support, and other forms of organizational enhancement to conservation NGOs. Several of these were located in the NGOs themselves in the form of in-house training for staff and board members and volunteers, but the majority were found among nonprofit consulting agencies outside the conservation-environmental movement.

By now our biases should be evident. We believed, as we initiated the Leadership Project, that natural resource conservation and environmental protection are very long-term goals and that the organizations attempting to achieve them must be designed for longevity. They therefore should encourage among their leaders a lifelong commitment, not necessarily to any one organization but to the cause of conservation and the enterprise of effectiveness. They should always be searching for new leaders and new forms of leadership. We believed that neither the professionals nor the volunteers are in any sense the preeminent leaders of the movement, but rather that movement organizations ought to use both as effectively as they can—and indeed that most cases of extraordinary effectiveness can be traced directly to the conscious fusion of professional and volunteer talents.

We also believed that in most instances of solving contemporary problems, leadership is more about teamwork than it is about great feats of individual initiative. Increasingly, great leaders submerge themselves with others; they build great (though not necessarily large) institutions, and through those institutions they perform pioneering and innovative work. To study leaders and leadership out-side of the organizational context where they usually occur is thus both futile and misleading. We wanted to study environmental and conservation leaders where they are to be found, and that took us into their organizations.

In the case of worldwide natural resource conservation and pres-ervation, the risk of failure cannot be endured. It is possible that the survival of thousands of species, including the human species, depends on the development of dynamic, permanent leadership within the worldwide conservation movement and the ability of that leadership to make conservation and environmental protection into matters of first importance in governance, social justice, and hu-man enterprise. Conservation leaders in the United States are crit-ically important in creating an effective global movement, because the United States is the birthplace of institutional conservation as we know it today. The success of the movement here at home should thus be of concern to all.

The Conservation Leadership Project is not about issues, but about people and organizations. Environmental issues do not take care of themselves. They emerge because people identify them and are moved to act upon them; they are resolved because people have somehow learned how to marshal the resources—the time, the hu-man energy, the knowledge and information, the public opinion, and the money—to resolve them; they linger, some of them seem-ingly forever, when the people who care cannot marshal those resources or do not know how to put them to effective use. Con-servation leadership today is no longer a matter of merely alerting the populace to the problems we create through insensitive man-agement of resources; it is now about mass mobilization, the careful formulation of policy, good science, good government, and a mas-sive realignment of ethics and economics. National polls tell us re-peatedly that people are ready for leadership in conservation, but are conservationists ready to lead? That was the central question of our study.

Acknowledgments

We wish to express our deepest gratitude to the distinguished members of our advisory council who volunteered their valuable time and expertise: Lamar Alexander, Wallace Dayton, Thomas Deans, George F. Dutrow, George T. Frampton, Jr., Jerry F. Franklin, Ralph E. Grossi, David F. Hales, Jean W. Hocker, Charles R. Jordan, Jack Lorenz, Gerald P. McCarthy, Lyle M. Nelson, Donal C. O'Brien, John C. Oliver, III, James Posewitz, Nathaniel P. Reed, Henry R. Richmond, Daniel Simberloff, Hubert W. Vogelmann, and Norman K. Wessells. Similar thanks to go to the hundreds of working conservationists who participated in this study.

We offer special appreciation to those who made the Leadership Project possible, and whose foresight and generosity continue to support the work of conservation and environmental protection organizations. The Compton Foundation, The Ford Foundation, Hanes Family Fund, The William and Flora Hewlett Foundation, George Frederick Jewett Foundation, Morgan Guaranty Trust Company of New York Charitable Trust, Curtis and Edith Munson Foundation, The Pew Charitable Trusts, and the Town Creek Foundation all generously supported this project. Grants from The Pew Charitable Trusts and the Munson Foundation made it possible to publish the results of the study in two volumes.

Three individuals deserve special recognition. Laurie L. Hall, Dr. Joe W. Floyd, and Jean McKendry made truly exceptional contributions on behalf of the Conservation Leadership Project.

We also thank the staff of Canyon Consulting for their skillful and supportive help in administering this challenging project.

Finally, we offer our thanks to Barbara Dean and Barbara Youngblood, our editors at Island Press; the staff of The Conservation Fund, especially for the enthusiastic support of Kiku Hoagland Hanes; and to Jack Lynn, who served as executive editor for The Conservation Fund. Their keen eyes caught many of the errors we missed and their judicious and professional work has made this an infinitely more readable and useful book.

Patrick F. Noonan
President, The Conservation Fund

G. Jon Roush
Senior Associate to the Project

Donald Snow
Project Director and General Editor

Executive Summary

The Conservation Leadership Project of The Conservation Fund, Arlington, Virginia, surveyed over 500 conservation leaders nationwide to gain their views on the future of the conservation-environmental movement and the need for enhanced training of movement leaders. The study focused on the staff and volunteers of nongovernmental, nonprofit conservation and environmental organizations (NGOs) and leaders of academic and in-service programs designed to train natural resource and environmental professionals. Data were gathered through six components of the study:

1. A staff questionnaire administered to the CEOs of 516 conservation and environmental groups in forty-nine states. Two hundred and forty-eight leaders responded. The questionnaire explored leadership training needs, the use of various management tools, and attitudinal questions related to the future role of the NGOs in solving environmental problems.

2. Follow-up interviews with 30 NGO staff leaders that allowed project staff to gain deeper insight into the issues revealed by the completed questionnaires.

3. A volunteers' questionnaire that examined leadership issues and training needs among the trustees and other volunteers who serve conservation NGOs. This questionnaire was administered to 305 volunteers nationwide. One hundred and sixty-one responded.

4. An academic programs questionnaire administered to 390 schools, departments, and interdisciplinary programs that train natural resource and environmental professionals. Responses came from 141 academic leaders. The questionnaire examined the role

of the academic programs in preparing leaders for service in the NGOs and other settings that employ environmental professionals.

5. A report on in-service training and support programs that documented the activities of thirty-seven regional and national centers offering staff training, management support, fund-raising assistance, coordination of internships, training for work in international settings, and other forms of instruction and support for staff and volunteers of conservation organizations.

6. A twenty-one-member national advisory council that guided the direction of the research and helped project staff frame research questions pertaining to leadership in the American conservation-environmental community. The council was comprised of NGO, academic, and government leaders in conservation. It met regularly during the planning and research phases of the project and contributed its own insight and originality to the study.

The Challenge

The Conservation Leadership Study observed that many of the leading ideas, as well as much of the effective advocacy, for environmental policies and programs have arisen historically from the nongovernmental, nonprofit conservation organizations. The NGOs have long played a unique and crucial role in the evolution of effective environmental policy and programs. They have often created and maintained the conditions for reform through effective research, mass communication, lobbying, agency monitoring, litigation, and various forms of direct action (both political and nonpolitical). Their financial independence and their direct adherence to the dictates of their cause and their constituents have allowed NGOs to serve as effective conservation advocates, with remarkably little embarrassment, throughout the twentieth century.

However, the environmental challenges that lie ahead in the 1990s and into the coming century will require extraordinary new leadership of a kind rarely seen in the American conservation community. The new mandate for leadership demands that virtually every institutional sector of American life—education, government, business, public communications, and the not-for-profit sector—become deeply engaged in solving environmental problems.

The NGO conservationists must and will lead in this endeavor. In order to do so, they must learn to dissolve the self-imposed boundaries that isolate them from other sectors of economic and educational enterprise. Historically, they have relied on the government—chiefly, the federal government—to manage most environmental problems. But, clearly, the national government's ability to do so is now severely strained. The next stage in conservation and environmental leadership will be to create the conditions whereby major environmental issues can be resolved through local and state-based initiatives, initiatives developed in the private sector, and enriched education of the electorate beginning in early youth.

Simultaneously, issues that are national and international in scope and character must be resolved by redoubling efforts in the appropriate policy arenas. The new initiatives will not be tied exclusively to the promulgation of new public policies; rather, they will be a blend of public policy, private initiative, and public communications.

Findings

The Leadership Study found a movement with an astonishing number of capable leaders who have done great things against great odds. Unfortunately, we are squandering that leadership in organizations that too often are not up to the challenge. They are chronically undersupported; their staffs are not trained or prepared to help convert the conservationist ethic into an effective national-international ethic; their boards frequently lack the diversity of expertise to ensure that they work toward greater horizons of issues development, membership and financial development, volunteer recruitment, and effectiveness in the policy and economic arenas. The conservation-environmental movement is fraught with xenophobia and internecine strife. These are its most debilitating features.

In their day-to-day operations, many conservation-environmental groups are so busy struggling with finances, overbearing work loads, and staff teetering on the brink of burnout that they can hardly find the time or the will to look for long-term solutions to their problems. Two crucial solutions are especially underused:

planning and training. Caught up in crisis management, organizations defer long-range planning. The catch-22 is that with better planning, they would have fewer crises. The average CEO of a conservation nonprofit has no formal training in organization management, yet spends virtually no time engaged in leadership or management training or other forms of in-service education. Similarly, the boards of NGOs receive little training in the duties, roles, and techniques of board membership. Most conservation leaders learn organization management in the school of hard knocks. The majority of conservation groups are perpetual management experiments.

Nor do they learn from each other. Staff leaders complain of personal isolation and a sense of stagnation. They see (and help create) very few opportunities to cross organizational boundaries and meet with their peers in other groups to exchange expertise and work on joint strategies; they see even fewer opportunities to meet with policymakers, government officials, and business representatives in order to negotiate new strategies for environmental protection. Yet it is precisely through these kinds of encounters that new initiatives of environmental leadership could often emerge.

When NGO conservation leaders look to academia for help, they see a very discouraging picture. While about one-third of the academic natural resource programs offer in-service training opportunities, nearly all of these are designed for midcareer professionals in government service, consulting firms, and corporate environmental programs. Training for service in the conservation NGOs is an afterthought for most academic programs, and while the field of nonprofit management is burgeoning at many American colleges and universities, conservationists will soon learn that practically none of those programs fits very well with nonprofit organizations designed to create social change. Even fewer of them will be able to train effectively in the arcane management of conservation efforts, where science, the humanities, policy, and law meet in a uniquely holistic setting. There are many nonacademic training programs offering a variety of support services to conservationists, but there is no independent national organization dedicated to training and retraining effective conservation NGO staff and volunteers.

With little or no training and support, conservation leaders have necessarily focused on building and maintaining their organizations as best they can but often without the benefit of sound planning. But that emphasis has its costs. Managing for the bottom line has allowed the leaders of many large, prestigious conservation groups to become virtually divorced from their own memberships. Many organizations have accepted the financial support of a check-writing membership without questioning the severe constraints that come with such an approach. Although most organizations are proud to declare that they are membership-based, too few of them possess or use strategies to empower, activate, or even help them listen to their members.

Practically none of the mainstream conservation-environmental groups in the United States—regardless of location, scope, or size—works effectively with or deliberately tries to include people of color, the rural poor, the politically and economically disenfranchised. Using tried-and-true demographic profiles to build membership and donor support, the American conservation movement seems to have abandoned the people who bear the greatest brunt of environmental assault. The makeup of the vast majority of conservation NGOs clearly demonstrates this abandonment. The leadership of the environmental movement stands as an obdurate white-male island in the middle of the work force increasingly populated by women and people of color. This is a most peculiar condition for a movement that is so firmly rooted in the tradition of American social change.

In the Recommendations section of this book (chapter 6), the Conservation Leadership Project calls for the creation of new, decentralized training centers designed to assist conservation leaders. But there are many other recommendations as well. What they point to is the overarching need for leaders to rethink many of their assumptions about environmental effectiveness and the makeup and operation of effective organizations. Many of the patterns of operation that have made the flagship conservation groups so successful will prove to be impediments to the new leadership that must emerge if environmental reforms are to continue—and, indeed, if new issues of unprecedented magnitude are to be addressed. These will be hard lessons for the leadership of conser-

vation and environmental groups; but the movement has always at-
tracted extraordinary leaders who place their cause ahead of self-
interest. It will be these leaders who take the findings of this study
and transform them into effective change—change that must begin
within the context of their own organizations.

Inside the Environmental Movement

Chapter 1

Introduction

Conservation began as a hobby and became a profession. . . . The first public alarms about endangered wildlife, trees, rivers, and wilderness were raised by enthusiasts like Muir who might take a firmly practical ground in arguing their cases but who acted ulti-mately from a love of unspoiled nature. . . . So it went: Audubon Society members would cite the useful role of birds in controlling insects, but they most cared about birdsong and the flash of color on the wing. Within a few years these avocations turned into jobs and conservation was transformed. Forestry became a profession more intent on board feet than esthetics; wildlife protection was lodged in a government bureau responding to political lobbies and gun com-panies. Embarrassed by its sentimental origins, conservation aimed to be a science.[1]

—*Stephen Fox*, John Muir and His Legacy

The growing professionalism of conservation throughout the twentieth century was by no means confined to government bureaus or societies of foresters. "Official" conservation-ists employed by government might have been increasingly attached to careers as professional resource managers, but another kind of professionalization was occurring simultaneously among the non-governmental organizations. As historian Stephen Fox rightly points out, membership-based advocacy groups—almost without exception born of the amateur tradition of volunteer conserva-tion—were busy adopting the characteristics of professionally managed businesses. Necessity dictated that they must. The phenomenal growth in membership experienced by wildlife groups in the first quarter of the century forced organizations to hire staff and begin to adopt sophisticated techniques of organizational management. In conservation's early days, there were no few struggles over the managerial abilities of the new professionals who came to staff the youthful organizations of the movement; several were fired by their boards for incompetent or despotic behavior.

The tendency toward professionally managed conservation groups has continued unabated. Debates continue over how much professionalism is good for the environmental movement. Some of the people we interviewed or surveyed decry the apparent tendency for conservation groups to "hire from the outside" as they seek managers to run increasingly sophisticated organizations. Others complain that organizations have become overrun with lawyers who lack the political courage and scientific curiosity of the Leopolds, Marshalls, and Muirs. Still others seem to yearn for a vanished, golden era of amateur righteousness, when conservationists were employed for their zeal, persistence, and charisma rather than their ability to manage sophisticated fund-raising campaigns or make prudent decisions over whether to build a new headquarters. The good old days, in the minds of some, seem to have been a moment long ago when Great Conservationists stalked the earth, fighting the epic battles more or less alone and unfettered by the nettlesome details of an organization.

Yet such a moment probably never existed. Virtually from its birth, the American conservation movement has been comprised of *organizations* that the great leaders helped to spawn. The fact that many early conservation leaders seem to outshine their own organizations—not to mention their seemingly lesser counterparts today—is more a testimonial to the way history is written than an accurate reflection of how social movements progress. People are intrinsically more interesting than organizations. Historians brighten their writing with the incandescent lives of great women and men, who seem somehow to grow more luminous with time. Beneath the selective lamps of history, the great and departed are bound to shine more brightly than their living counterparts, who still survive to make both enemies and errors. Social movements progress, however, not only with the heroic leaps of great individualists, but also on the slow-plodding backs of organizations. The John Muirs, Bob Marshalls, and Aldo Leopolds were rare, visionary persons, and their individual achievements are not to be discounted. But neither should we overlook the contributions of the early Sierra Club, The Wilderness Society, and the Ecological Society of America, where the ideas of these great men took hold and swelled with political force.

Indeed, for most practical purposes it is futile to try to examine conservation *leadership* as if it could be divorced from conservation *organizations*. Even John Muir without the Sierra Club might have been just a voice in the wilderness—an influential voice, to be sure, but not one that could have effectively mobilized the mass of support needed to designate parks and preserves against a Congress increasingly thirsty for commerce to close the Western frontier. In today's policy arena, organizations are even more important. Says John Gardner: "The first thing that strikes one as characteristic of contemporary leadership is the necessity for the leader to work with and through extremely complex organizations and institutions."[2] American pluralism insists with increasing force that we do our political bidding through institutions, so much so that even the most grass-roots campaigns of mass mobilization, if they survive, tend eventually to seek their place upon the institutional bedrock. The process is familiar enough: Ad hoc, inchoate groups of volunteers harden into chartered organizations, which, if successful, evolve over time into long-standing, stable institutions.

There are some who deplore the institutionalization of American conservation, and who would say that the impulse to hire professional staff is the first fatal mistake of any young group. These proponents of the amateur way seem to want to keep organizations perpetually frozen in their youthful state—organized and run exclusively by volunteers, unsullied with the mercenaries who desire to become professional staff, divorced from any sense that the work of conservation and environmental protection might, for some, actually constitute a career. Said one prominent national leader we interviewed: "The thing I always tell people, especially leadership people, is to be careful not to become professionals." In this view, professionalism is bad because it inevitably blunts political activism.

Yet as conservationists have proven time and again throughout this century, there is no one way to be effective. The solitary John Muir helped found the Sierra Club and became its first president against his own instincts because he sensed the power of collective action—and power was exactly what Yosemite needed. Bob Marshall chose to work from both within and without: As a career employee of the Forest Service, he pushed relentlessly for the wilderness concept; simultaneously, he was a founder of The Wilderness Society and a tireless champion of this fierce, young organization dedicated to the protection of wild lands. Rosalie Edge spent decades as an Audubon volunteer—and a fly in the ointment of its professional leaders who, in her view, favored the revenues from gun companies over the welfare of birds. Aldo Leopold was a professional's professional. His scientific rigor and skepticism helped keep his colleagues in the early wilderness movement credible and on track while he continued to expound ecologically based management of game species. The reclusive Rachel Carson changed the world with a book.

Diversity and multiplicity, not uniformity, serve conservation as well as nature. Conservationists have never been of a single stripe, and need not be today; over the past century, they have endured because they have adapted to circumstance. They have taken their place among other professionals partly to ensure their own and their movement's longevity and effectiveness. Indeed, a healthy conservation movement will continue to be a volatile mixture of amateurs and professionals, youth and old age, dedicated volunteers and equally dedicated careerists. There is nothing wrong with the impulse, the passion, to want to be a conservationist for life, and to be paid and respected as a professional in pursuit of a conservation career.

Yet there is a paradox here: For social and political movements to remain dynamic, the organizations that comprise them must strive to maintain the spirit and vigor of volunteerism even as they become increasingly professional in their management. It is often the active corps of volunteers and amateurs who keep organizations from becoming tired old bureaucracies. So the contemporary environmental movement is engaged in many efforts to nurture the volunteer grass roots. Well-established organizations do so through deliberately planned training and recruitment programs. Every national organization with any sort of field program understands the value of volunteers in creating healthy chapters and affiliates; and they all rely exclusively upon volunteers to serve on their boards. New organizations arising at the neighborhood or community level nurture volunteer leadership virtually by definition: Most of them are comprised exclusively of volunteers, at least in the beginning. If these groups are to succeed and survive, the volunteers must learn to lead, and they must teach others.

But fostering the leadership capabilities of volunteers is not enough. In particular the young environmental organizations, still filled with the fervor of righteous activism, often need a healthy dose of business and management acumen. Many of them have teetered on the brink of bankruptcy for a decade or more; they have relied upon a seemingly endless stream of committed activists, both volunteer and professional, to steer them through controversy and financial hard times. Their only endowments are human ones: They have borrowed on the interest of the most deeply committed. Perhaps because the endowment has been so productive, they have paid less attention to adding new capital in the form of fresh recruits trained as leaders. There is reason to question whether this pool of human capital will continue to be available, in adequate numbers and with adequate skills, for conservation NGOs.

Clearly, leadership in conservation varies with the setting. While some attributes of leadership seem to remain fixed regardless of the conservation setting (or indeed, whether the setting is conservation at all), others vary greatly depending upon the sector. The leader of a professional association faces demands that are quite different from those faced by the head of a statewide land trust. The CEO of a well-established, national lobbying organization with scores of staff fields a different set of challenges than those presented to the head of a neighborhood group fighting a hazardous-waste facility. Leaders must be viewed in their organizational contexts. Organizations must be examined for ways in which they themselves provide institutional leadership within the movement—and their manner of facilitating, or impeding, the individuals who try to lead them. Do they liberate or frustrate emerging leaders? Do they manage their affairs as much as possible through the effective use of teams? Do they possess ways of lightening the burden on their principal officers—staff or volunteers—by spreading responsibility? Do they *develop* volunteers or merely use them up, discarding them as the key issues reach resolution? Examined outside of the organizational setting in which it occurs, the concept of leadership readily degenerates into a useless abstraction; discussions about it easily trail off into high-sounding but facile statements and recommendations. In conservation, as in most other fields, the leader and his or her organization cannot be separated without peril of losing the sense of the whole.

Yet the whole of American conservation is not easy to grasp. This is a movement that is, after all, about a century old. It is comprised, at one end of its chronological spectrum, of sedate, venerable organizations where the word *activism* is seldom used and, at the other end, of exuberant, infant groups still smoldering like hot steel from their origins on the anvil of politics. Comparing the leadership attributes of these two cousins in the conservation family is like comparing the qualities of two precocious children, one an accomplished classical dancer, the other a junior high linebacker.

Still, there are many common threads. Conservative and radical conservationists continue to work in symbiosis across the United States. Radical environmentalism expressed through political channels often makes more centrist arguments all the more appealing; groups that carefully "use the system" confess that their cause is usually aided by those that attack the system. While there are fierce intramovement debates over the very meaning of the word *conservation*, and while the environmentalists, preservationists, and classic conservationists fight over the correct labels to identify the philosophies guiding their work, all who are involved in environmental protection and natural resource conservation have much more in common than they have differences. And they are all dependent upon healthy patterns of leadership to ensure their success.

When we initiated the Conservation Leadership Project, we outlined five broad sectors in which conservation leadership could be studied: (1) governmental organizations (federal, state, and local), (2) nongovernmental, nonprofit organizations (the NGOs), (3) aca-

demia and other centers of training and support, (4) private philanthropy, and (5) natural resource–oriented businesses. We did not
have the resources to study leadership in all five sectors; we chose
to examine primarily the NGOs (both the paid, professional staff
and the volunteers) and secondarily the academic and training centers with respect to the extent to which they help foster and support
leadership among the NGOs. The Leadership Project thus left
ample room for further studies.

We chose to focus on the NGOs for several reasons. First, the
environmental movement continues to be a relatively cohesive social and political movement comprised of a vigorous and growing
throng of organizations. There are probably more than 10,000 nationwide—most of them small, locally focused groups of volunteers—with more being set up every day. In many areas now,
organizations founded upon causes other than conservation (such
as civil rights, social justice, economic empowerment, feminism,
and peace) are turning increasingly toward environmental protection, for they have learned over time that many of the issues they
care about are often expressed through patterns of exploitation—
of both human and natural resources. As more and more citizens
become alarmed over the rapid depletion of natural resources, as
more of them are exposed to the hazards of pollution and poorly
planned development in their own areas, and as they continue to
be deprived of opportunities to participate in decisions affecting
their lives, they will continue to create NGOs to fight for conservation and environmental protection.

The environmental movement is healthy and growing; we felt it
could benefit from a stronger tradition of consciously building its
own leadership.

Second, we believe that many of the best ideas, most of the leading policy initiatives, and nearly all of the public advocacy in conservation have originated historically among the NGOs. There is
no reason to believe that the importance of the NGOs has been or
will be much diminished by the institutionalization of environmentalism throughout society. New environmental initiatives will continue to emerge from the NGOs, and indeed the NGOs will be
increasingly important in finding solutions to the vexing problems
we face today.

Third, conservation and environmental organizations offer myr-

iad opportunities for citizens to participate in their own government; indeed, in some regions of the country they provide the
definitive link for such participation. Conservation is not only about
resource protection, preservation, and science; it is also about good
government. Since long before Earth Day, conservation NGOs
have been among the leading champions of citizen participation,
open government, and access to information. Conservation NGOs
are worth special attention because of the crucial role they play in
our civic and public affairs. Without them, our political life would
be much poorer.

Finally, no matter how important the conservation NGOs continue to be, they remain chronically undersupported and must thus
continue to make optimum use of their limited resources. Academia prepares many students for work in the resource agencies and
businesses, but almost no academic programs pay serious attention
to the needs of those who wish to serve through careers in conservation NGOs. Moreover, the other sectors of conservation tend to
have much stronger traditions of in-service and midcareer training—as well as the money to take advantage of it. The NGOs appeared to us to lag far behind in resources for, and often interest
in, the conscious development of leaders and leadership. Through
the Leadership Project, we believed we might be able to identify
some cost-effective strategies for enhancing the leadership capabilities of conservation NGOs in all regions of the country.

A Thousand Different Threads

Even John Muir's genius for invention could not have
conjured up or predicted the astonishing proliferaion of conservation and environmental groups since the original Earth Day. No one
yet has accurately assessed the total number and array of these organizations nationwide—let alone worldwide—and doing so would
daunt the ablest computerphile: Groups emerge, merge, and disappear daily. Sudden coalitions of convenience or necessity tumble
together, win or lose, on the issue that sparked their merger, then
disband. Social-change organizations that never before struggled
with environmental issues—indeed, some that once opposed
them—have found new life in the social justice arguments that

have always underpinned conservation and environmental protection. Whether in New England or the Rockies, Florida, California, or Alaska, citizens continue to invent myriad forms and hybrids of conservation groups, all recognizable as contributors to the environmental movement even if competing organizations sometimes refuse to claim one another as allies. Keeping up with it all is virtually impossible. States with well-developed networks of environmental organizations are fond of publishing directories, then uniformly lamenting the incompleteness or outdatedness of them in the hour following publication. The difficulty is compounded at the national level. The National Wildlife Federation's *Conservation Directory,* the most sophisticated attempt to catalog national conservation organizations, inevitably suffers from omissions and errors. It is like trying to catalog a meteor shower.

One trouble with keeping tabs on conservation NGOs in the United States is that the overwhelming majority of these groups are all-volunteer operations in which the leadership tends to be fluid, hard to identify, sometimes seemingly nonexistent. Groups rise and ebb with the energies of their founders, or the second, third, or fourth generation of leaders who emerge to assume control. The majority of conservation leaders are not carefully trained for their jobs; they assume responsibility for running an organization because of a moral or political imperative and a deep personal commitment. Their records as budding conservation professionals are not recorded at the local college or university; there is no scorecard of their accomplishments as leaders, except in a box full of press clippings or a plaque at the entrance of a local nature preserve or in the minds of the other, similarly motivated people with whom they have worked. The organization's affairs over time are hard to chronicle because, in many cases, no one is left after a dozen years to remember when or how the group emerged, or why it turned away from this issue and toward that. Keeping tabs on the affairs of these groups, in some states at least, would thus be nearly a full-time job. Given the paucity of resources available to the groups themselves, it's little wonder no one seems eager for the job of merely keeping track of them all.

To any student or chronicler of the movement, the vast number of emerging organizations is intriguing, and it grows more so when one asks exactly what constitutes an environmental or conservation group. For the traditional organizations, with their ideological roots planted firmly in the turn-of-the-century debates between Pinchot and Muir, the answer is simple. Any group whose principal mission is to foster the wise, sustained use of natural resources for human need, enjoyment, and betterment ought to be understood as a conservation group. Along with a plethora of wildlife, forestry, water conservation, and land-use organizations, certain trade associations, educational institutions, natural resource consumer groups, and even natural history museums and zoological gardens might fall within this definition. Still, it must be remembered that many groups that were spawned long before Earth Day endured sweeping transformations when the nation suddenly awakened to the environmental crisis as it was perceived around 1970. Several of the old-style wise-use groups became oriented more toward preservation and environmental protection, even if that meant less emphasis on the conventional use of resources.

Preservationist groups would seem equally simple to define: As their tag implies, they stand for the maintenance of natural living systems intact and as whole as possible, usually under the aegis of special protective designations, whether public or private. They are the makers and maintainers of nature parks, preserves, refuges, wilderness and primitive areas, coastal zones and waterways, ecosystems or natural areas prized for their biological diversity or their ability to provide a sustaining habitat to threatened or endangered species. The question of *use* among these groups seems troubling only to those who lose sight of the meaning of *preservation.* It means the maintenance of a natural living system as nearly as possible in its natural or pristine state so that it can go on doing what it has done on its own for thousands or millions of years. Obviously, it might sometimes need help from human hands if it is to do so. Thus, management is as strong a concept for the preservationists as it is for the conservationists, but the goals of preservation management may be quite different or even opposed to the conservationists' goal of sustained use.

Even environmentalist groups—whose emergence historian Stephen Fox dates to around 1966—have now taken on a fairly distinctive definition. For the most part they profess "environmental protection" as their primary goal; that definition, imprecise as it sounds, becomes quite clearly delineated in practice. Environmentalist groups fight the pollution of land, air, water, and sometimes workplace. They concern themselves (increasingly, it seems) with the contamination of food and the poisoning of living creatures through various human-caused assaults. They attack resource management practices that they view as environmentally destructive and are often the leading critics of public land management agencies. They usually share the preservationists' concern with maintaining whole ecosystems and are often among the leading advocates for wilderness areas, refuges, and nature preserves. Yet preservation is not necessarily their principal motivation; indeed, many environmentalist organizations, while supporting the concept of preservation, do not pursue it as a matter of policy.

None of this is meant to suggest that environmentalist organizations are uniformly managerial-technocratic in their approach to environmental problems, for the environmentalist camp is the broadest and most varied of all. It includes, for example, a strong component of preservation-oriented "deep ecologists," bioregionalists, and other philosophically oriented people who object to what they perceive as the more-technology approach to problem solving. These environmentalists suggest that technology itself lies at the root of most environmental problems, which they view as deriving from a flawed set of ethics. In their view, modern technology incarnates a shortsighted philosophy of human dominion that permits people and societies to destroy the biological foundations of their own and other species' survival.

The environmentalist camp must also claim some of the animal rights organizations, especially those that oppose some forms of sport hunting or the slaughter of fur-bearing animals. That these groups find themselves at odds with many of their conservationist cousins bears testimony to the richness of multiplicity of the overall movement.

Environmentalist organizations are often hybrids of the philosophies of conservation, preservation, and the newer emphasis on pollution, human health, and environmental protection, particularly in urban and developing areas. They often focus on pollution abatement and control, try to foster appropriate technologies, and speak at least part of the language of bioregionalism or deep ecology. That the latter language tends to remain "soft" in their publications and pronouncements gives testimony to their understanding of the nature of political credibility. Indeed, the philosophical labels often seem to slide around willy-nilly; there are many instances of organizations with multiple programs crossing all the boundaries between conservation, preservation, and environmentalism. The reason is simple: Contrary to what many of their critics say, conservationists are pragmatic problem solvers above all else; they tend to look for workable solutions first and the correct philosophy later.

The philosophical splits within the environmental movement are all too evident to many who have tried to study it; indeed, it is easy to make too much of these splits, forgetting in the blizzard of contested philosophies that the entire movement is comprised fundamentally of organizations concerned with the question of humans' use of nature. It is easy, especially for righteous newcomers, to lose sight of the fact that all of these groups share a common plight that thoroughly eclipses their differences with one another: namely, that they must compete for the public's attention across the full spectrum of world issues, among which resource conservation and environmental protection still seem arcane to many. Conservationists of all stripes can hardly afford to forget that until a very short time ago they were considered by many to be the pleasant oddities of American politics, sitting off together in their eccentric corners of nature appreciation and rattling on about parts per billion and allowable cuts and reclamation standards until the world's eyes glazed over. Now that they have finally gotten the international attention that they have sought for so long, they might not know what to do with it.

Operationally, at the level of organizational structure, focus, and purpose, the environmental movement is even more diverse than it is philosophically. It is at the operational, not the philosophical, level that we find the most useful distinctions in discussing issues of conservation leadership. At this level, we find at least eleven different kinds of conservation, preservation, and environmental groups. We also find that the careful distinctions separating these groups are often blurred, and that groups very often work in informal synergy, combining talents and efforts to resolve specific issues in specific settings. The following list borrows and takes off from the Training for Environmental Groups study of The Conservation Foundation, performed in 1983.[3] It is intended only to describe very broadly the types of NGOs that comprise the contemporary movement.

Types of Conservation and Environmental Organizations

SMALL, ALL-VOLUNTEER, ISSUES GROUPS. Normally operating at the local level, these groups tend to be young, institutionally immature, and driven by the energy released from a single public dispute. A small corps of highly motivated volunteer leaders serve as the founders and organizers; usually they view the core issue as one of self-interest or even survival. Having annual budgets of usually less than $20,000 and thus being unable to afford paid staff, these groups are often ephemeral, disbanding or radically refocusing once the original issue is resolved. The lexicon of empowerment and social justice often typifies the language of these groups. They are often less likely to be purely environmentalist or resource-oriented, but are very likely to protest the absence of citizen representation in important public decisions. The members or adherents of these groups are often those who feel disenfranchised from the prevailing economic and political system. The organization is thus best understood as an instrument for political empowerment.

Interestingly, there are now dozens of examples of nontraditional environmental groups and programs springing up all over the country, many of them resembling these all-volunteer associations even though their founding issues might not have been environmental issues at all. These are among the groups that some have labeled "the new environmentalists" to distinguish them from the so-called "establishment environmentalists" of the mainstream. What makes them nontraditional is that their approach to environmental problems is almost exclusively political rather than scientific or technical, and they are often led and populated by minorities, the poor, and the disenfranchised—hardly the traditional core of conservation throughout the century. These groups are becoming an increasingly potent force both in the environmental movement and in American politics.

SMALL, QUASI-VOLUNTEER NATURALIST GROUPS. These are likely to be run for many years by a corps of dedicated volunteers and may or may not have paid, professional staff. Most likely, the group focuses all of its efforts on interpretive and educational activities related to a single species and its habitat, or an established natural area. The group may also be a political advocate, lobbying before legislatures or national or international commissions to alter practices that damage the species or habitat it is organized to defend. These groups are often long-term operations with fairly stable budgets and memberships. The key volunteers or paid staff members who run them are frequently affiliated with universities; regardless, the leaders tend to be highly educated, highly motivated individuals. These groups can be fairly sizable operations with budgets running into the hundreds of thousands or, in rare instances, millions of dollars. Most often, however, they are of modest means, capturing less than $100,000 per year from memberships of several hundred to several thousand.

RECREATION AND SPORTING CLUBS. Rod and gun clubs once dominated the American conservation movement, and still do in some states. On the national scene, several large, notable organizations more closely resemble "grown-up" rod and gun clubs than they do any other type of conservation organization. The small versions of these groups attract members who share an interest in protecting game species and habitats defined roughly by a geographical region. Members rely on the club for social activities. On the national scene, these organizations employ hundreds of professional staffers who organize local affiliates in support of certain well-defined types of game species: ducks, trout, bass, walleyes, whitetails, elk, and so forth. Among the national groups there is usually no clear geographic focus, but a strong emphasis on protecting habitat. The small versions are usually low-budget and run entirely by volunteers; the large adaptations are in some instances among the largest and most sophisticated private conservation concerns in the world, using a wide range of financial and transactional tools to preserve habitat and see that it is managed well by the appropriate agencies. These groups are usually dominated by members who enjoy the "taking" of wild animals and argue for it in the context of an often broad and sophisticated understanding of resource conservation in which humans act as surrogate predators.

STATE-BASED OR REGIONAL ADVOCACY GROUPS. In some states, these organizations serve as umbrellas or coordinating councils for many conservation groups that unite in order to influence sate government. Often, however, these groups are independent, grass roots membership organizations that serve no coordinating function. Some of them work from a regional (substate-level) platform but maintain strong representation before state governments as well. Typically, these groups lobby and monitor state, local, and federal agencies, and serve as advocates across a broad range of conservation issues of interest to their members; their breadth is a distinguishing characteristic. They usually have paid staff and budgets ranging from $60,000 to over $1 million, depending on the maturity and location of the organization. Board members tend to represent the grass-roots membership and keep strong reins on the organization's activities and staff. Where these groups work well, they are often a nearly ideal mixture of amateur, grass-roots conservationists and professional activists whose work on staff often involves roughly equal shares of policy, law, science, and organizational management.

EDUCATION, RESEARCH, AND POLICY-DEVELOPMENT CENTERS. Often these are not membership organizations but rather policy-research centers served by a self-appointed volunteer board and a professional staff. They tend to investigate global, international, national, or regional issues and are among the newest arrivals on the scene of American conservation. Typically, they are grant- and patron-funded and might also make substantial income from the sale of publications and other products, or from research contracts with agencies or businesses. Budgets vary widely, usually beginning at around $100,000 and soaring to beyond $10 million per year. These organizations occupy a specialized niche in the environmental movement. Many of them arose to fill the gap in policy-related information and analysis created by the overwhelming focus on political activism among most environmental groups. They serve activists and others by providing credible information and helping to frame the public debate.

LAW AND SCIENCE GROUPS. Like the policy-development centers, these groups are relatively recent creations. They arose largely to advocate the enforcement of new environmental laws and policies, and they tend to limit their arena of activity to the highest levels of decision making: the courts, administrative law boards, sometimes Congress or the legislatures. They operate from a strong motive to create precedent-setting test cases. While many of these groups have memberships, members are typically inactive "check writers" who belong because they support the organization in principle and not for any participatory benefits of membership. The boards tend to be self-appointed, to some degree honorary, and increasingly prestigious. The staff is often a high-powered mixture of lawyers, scientists, and economists—a staff of bona fide technical experts whose job is to challenge the knowledge and data of the experts who are protecting the interests of corporations and government agencies. These organizations rely less on rhetoric and broad-scale public education and more on winning major cases and precedent-setting agency appeals. Increasingly, states with a very active corps of conservation groups are beginning to establish their own versions of these groups, often in the form of a nonprofit "public interest law clinic," which handles environmental law. At their best, these groups keep a sharp legal and technical edge on the environmental movement; they are often the enforcers.

SMALL NATIONAL AND INTERNATIONAL MEMBERSHIP GROUPS. Several dozen conservation organizations—not all of them located in Washington, D.C., New York, or San Francisco—fall into this category, which is perhaps the most difficult one to define. These groups can be of any age within the conservation spectrum, but most tend to be younger organizations, dating back to no earlier than 1970. They have memberships numbering in the thousands or tens of thousands and budgets that reach as high as about $5 million. Some of them are splinter groups from larger, older organizations that at some point suffered a board-level crisis leading to a faction breaking off. Others are simply new, national organizations out competing for members and philanthropy in an increasingly choked conservation market. Some of these groups are the "radical" counterparts of their more staid and established cousins on the national scene. They variously lobby, litigate, monitor federal and state agencies, work the news media, and publish newsletters and reports of interest to their members. Many of them operate much like the independent state-based organizations discussed above, with grass-roots-flavored boards and staffs comprised primarily of professional activists.

LARGE NATIONAL AND INTERNATIONAL MEMBERSHIP GROUPS. These elder statesmen of the national conservation community typically have memberships in the hundreds of thousands to millions, annual budgets ranging from $5 million to $100 million and, in many cases, local chapters or affiliates scattered across the country. They usually work on a broad variety of issues such as wildlife preservation, wilderness management and designation, public lands management, pollution control, or energy conservation. Most operate multiple programs, each administered by a staff with specialized expertise: One program provides services to members, including educational materials and field experiences, while another lobbies Congress, another litigates, and still another manages an array of educational publications or products. In some instances, staff are hired to develop substantive programs focusing on a single but very broad issue that takes them out into the field to work with the chapters and affiliated organizations. Examples of such issues might be Alaskan wild lands, offshore drilling, old-growth forest protection, or acid-rain abatement. Membership involvement within these organizations varies greatly. Some groups have members who are fundamentally inactive subscribers to the organization's periodicals; others have highly sophisticated membership recruitment and training programs, operated through chapters or affiliates; several have both kinds of members—the highly active and the inactive, sometimes with the ensuing tensions between the two being expressed through the board. These organizations have sometimes been called the flagships of American conservation.

REAL ESTATE CONSERVATION GROUPS. An increasingly important and popular component of the conservation community is the land or species conservation group that primarily uses the tools of real estate exchange to accomplish its objectives. These groups are now so numerous that we place them in their own category, though in many respects they cut across several of the profiles above. At the local and regional levels, these groups are usually land trusts attempting to preserve undeveloped tracts of private or public land for some very specific purposes—greenways, agricultural natural area or species preservation. Organizations at the state, national, and international levels use a variety of transactional tools ranging from outright purchase to easements, land trades, and debt buy-outs as incentives to preserve biologically rich habitats. Some of them have highly sophisticated science programs designed to identify rare species and other biological elements in the United States and abroad, and to test various scientific theories on nature-preserve design and ecology. Some of the groups have memberships, but member activity varies widely. Invariably, however, these groups learn how to leverage capital—sometimes massive amounts of it—to accomplish their property-oriented objectives. Lobbying and litigating are sometimes used, but usually to accomplish very narrow objectives related to land or species preservation. For the most part, these organizations do not join with their cousins in conservation to work on a broad range of controversial issues. They prefer a very narrow focus.

PROFESSIONAL SOCIETIES. Professional conservation societies resemble those affiliated with other professionals: They promote research and sponsor publications and forums to discuss research. They usually employ a staff to produce journals and organize conferences; budgets vary widely depending on membership size, dues, and sales. Often these groups are affiliated with universities that have strong programs in the natural resource disciplines. Their research and publications are variously used by advocacy groups; in some instances, they are critical to the success of efforts to craft conservation policy.

SUPPORT AND SERVICE ORGANIZATIONS. As conservation and environmental groups proliferated following Earth Day, their organizational problems grew in pace with their memberships. In various parts of the country, management and fund-raising support groups surfaced to serve conservation NGOs and other kinds of nonprofit organizations. While few of these could be described as conservation groups per se, their efforts to assist conservationists are often crucial. Some of these support groups help devise substantive strategies and tactics, as well as provide advice and counsel in such matters as organizational planning, fund-raising, membership and board development, and staff training. They usually perform their services for fees, but the fees are often kept low through the device of philanthropic subsidy—grants and donor support from funders who have a strong interest in the long-term survival and health of conservation groups.

The conservation NGOs as we find them today constitute a broad, kaleidoscopic enterprise that has the attributes of a maturing social and political movement but that still manages to spawn new organizations at an astonishing pace. The various organizations are arrayed across a complex spectrum of interests crosscut by time, experience, and the fortunes of politics. There are very telling differences among them—differences that become especially apparent when one begins to examine them with respect to the forms of leadership and management they require.

Among the types of groups broadly outlined above, one finds a pattern of evolution common to social and political movements. Organizational success brings a kind of maturity that not everyone in the movement considers healthy. The righteous fervor and radical action pursued by youthful, activist organizations gradually gives way to a more settled and predictable approach to issues and organizational problems. Systems grow to replace the more direct and volatile forms of decision making within the organization; growth engenders bureaucracy. In the case of the conservation and environmental movement, these changes in approach have tended to take on a decidedly technical-scientific flavor. Given the nature of many environmental issues, as complex and scientific as they are, this is not surprising. As organizations grow and mature, the raw politics of environmentalism are tempered with the more methodical approach offered by legal, scientific, and economic experts. Groups start out serving as passionate firebrands of advocacy, but they often simmer down in later years. The world as they perceive it grows more complex; they come to value compromise and negotiation. In Barry Commoner's terms, they take the "soft political road."[4] To some, these settled organizations of the movement appear stodgy, self-aggrandizing, overly cautious, even unethical in their studied refusal to adopt a more radical tone. Yet they act as they do probably because moderation has served them well. In moving toward the center, they have broadened their appeal, gained new members, and increased their influence among the agencies they set out to change. They have begun to value, and consciously address, longevity.

As the evolution from the inchoate to the institutional occurs, new kinds of leadership are required. Leaders who stay aboard through the long and often halting periods of transition find that they must evolve, too. They must develop new skills, relinquish some control to trusted allies, and break old patterns of management. They must determine the things they do well and hand over the rest to people with other skills and interests. Leaders of successful organizations accommodate change by changing. The ones who cannot are often left behind.

Diversification usually accompanies growth and, indeed, it is necessary in order for growth to occur. One distinguishing characteristic among the many conservation organizations we studied is the degree to which they embrace diversity. Successful organizations are often those in which diversification for the purpose of strengthening business operations consists of a series of conscious acts. The leaders realize at some point that new blood is needed on the board—not just new faces and energy, but different skills and interests. They make efforts to ensure that the board evolves from a group of peers comprised mostly of distinguished volunteer activists to a diversified team with the combined wisdom to guide the many operations of the organization, including its financial and business dealings. The staff, if there is one, undergoes a similar evolution. The organization itself—and not merely the issues or substantive agenda—becomes the object of conscious, strategic planning. The group begins to fashion its substantive campaigns less in terms of ideology and impassioned calls to action at any cost and more in terms of challenges that require the marshaling of resources and that in turn will put resources back into the organization. The casualness of volunteers is replaced with the businesslike formality of professionals. Not everyone likes it.

Yet diversification among conservation and environmental groups is oddly narrow, hewing as it often does to the strategic purposes of enhanced financial power or increased credibility among agencies and businesses. Practically none of the established movement organizations has successfully reached out into multicultural America to recruit people of color, the rural poor, the disenfranchised. For a movement whose leaders profess the gospel of mobilizing mass support in favor of political and economic change, the environmental movement remains profoundly undiversified in its racial and cultural composition. Some organizations have proven themselves more willing to diversify by courting corporate leaders than by making alliances with civil rights leaders. The obdurate whiteness of the environmental movement—reaching back, again, to the early conservationists—is one of the greatest challenges facing its leaders.

The Factiousness of a Dynamic Movement

Conservationists have always had their critics, both within and outside of the movement. If anything, the criticism is louder today than it has ever been, perhaps because the issues have become so formidable and pervasive, and the movement itself has achieved substantial influence. Some of the strongest recent voices of condemnation are most concerned about the increasing institutionalization of environmentalism: It has become, in the minds of many, entirely too mainstream.

The voices that decry the loss of passion in the contemporary environmental movement are complaining, in effect, about the perceived eclipse of the amateur, volunteer tradition among many of today's more settled organizations. They see that as conservation and environmental protection have become increasingly institutionalized, conservationists and environmentalists have gradually become less strident and (some would say) less bold. Pragmatism, credibility, and organizational growth have become the watchwords of the mainstream movement. Many organizations long ago outgrew their origins as small groups run exclusively by committed idealists; they have become professionally managed businesses operated by teams of highly trained specialists in law, economics, science, and policy. Many have adopted direct-mail campaigns as their primary—or exclusive—approach to membership recruitment. Their appeals to grantors and other funders have become extremely sophisticated. They have fought hard to establish their respectability as lobbyists, policy advocates, agency watchdogs, and in some cases land managers—and they aren't about to give it up by engaging in radical action.

Critics often seem to forget that the many changes wrought among the movement's organizations since Earth Day have come in response to the increasing power and success of the movement itself. The daunting complexity of most environmental issues demands an increasing level of sophistication among the organizations that tackle them. It also calls for a more careful and systematic linkage of skills among the various sectors of the movement. The national-international organizations themselves have evolved internally to reflect these trends. Among the larger, more settled components of the movement, single-issue organizations, once common in conservation, are now nearly extinct. Most groups operate multiple programs, planned strategically to address various levels of government or business while simultaneously being broadcast to the public in efforts to recruit. Statewide and regional groups increasingly resemble their national and international counterparts with respect to programmatic complexity, though their patterns of membership and staff recruitment are often very different. The intricacies of organizational management have likewise intensified. Competition for scarce funds and members has required the adoption of sophisticated new marketing strategies, which in turn force issues-oriented organizations to seek new kinds of managers. By the mid-1970s, many of the brand-new environmental groups spawned by Earth Day had already learned the limits of relying on charismatic, inspirational leaders as the sole means of gathering adherents and filling coffers. The trail by then already lay littered with the carcasses of dead, dying, or stagnant organizations—victims of the inability to learn the intricacies of nonprofit management.

The increasing complexity of both issues and organizational management has led larger organizations to develop more complex and specialized organizational structures. In those groups, lines of authority have become departmentalized, with issues of substance being led by professionals in policy, law, and science and issues of organizational business being left in the hands of management specialists. Still, the majority of conservation groups cannot afford such specialization. Most have no paid staff at all; dedicated volunteers act as both board and staff. Among the smaller groups that have professional staff, responsibilities cannot be so well divided. These groups are more likely to be managed by a team of three to five staff whose responsibilities all cross the nebulous boundaries between issues and business, and whose job descriptions (if they have any) are by no means simple and clear-cut. The smaller organizations often increase their technical firepower by reaching outside: They recruit volunteers or paid consultants who are the same kinds of specialists now employed by the larger groups. In so doing, they mimic their more prosperous counterparts at the national-international level but save the fixed costs.

Although they have added to the richness and diversity of the environmental movement, these changes in operations and focus cause understandable tensions. There are many critics from within, and the issues they raise often cut to the quick of how movement organizations behave relative to one another.

Perhaps the most difficult dispute within the modern environmental movement—and the one pressing hardest upon its leaders—revolves around the use and empowerment of members and volunteers. In an article entitled "The New Environmentalists," Robert Gottlieb and Helen Ingram argue that

> a new kind of environmentalism is gradually coming to the fore in the United States. It is a grass-roots, community-based, democratic movement that differs radically from conventional, mainstream American environmentalism, which always had a strong nondemocratic strain.[5]

The authors contend that mainstream environmental organizations, buoyed by their successes in formulating new regulatory and management programs through the 1970s, have become increasingly reliant on "lobbying, litigation and 'science' to achieve their objectives, creating in the process a kind of cult of expertise."[6] In so doing, they have managed to remove themselves from the direct concerns of grass-roots citizens and their own members, relegating them to the status of check writers acquired through sophisticated direct-mail campaigns. During the Reagan years, according to the authors, the mainstream environmentalist groups grew further apart from the grass roots. Their technical-bureaucratic approach was often rewarded by funders and people in power: "They were congratulated by policy makers . . . on their growing maturity, reasonableness, and sound management."[7] They also garnered the reward of substantial numbers of new members—often because of the administration's hostility to environmental reform. From the inside, it appeared that they were doing everything right.

Meanwhile, a new environmental movement was growing up vigorously among the very grass roots that the mainstreamers had all but abandoned. The new environmentalists, according to Gottlieb and Ingram, are concerned primarily with the urban, industrial environment. The leaders of the new movement argue that protection of scenic resources and wildlife and efforts to regulate or manage pollutants without abating them are not enough. The battle must now be taken to the new ground of the local community; fundamental decisions relating to development and industrial production must be subjected to democratic control, not managerial-executive control that mainstream environmentalists tend to support.[8]

The authors claim that mainstream leaders have divorced themselves and their organizations from the new, grass-roots environmentalists. Indeed, some environmental leaders now regard the grass-roots movement as a potential threat to their newfound respectability as reasonable negotiators. As heirs to their conservationist forerunners' deference to expertise, establishment environmentalists are embarrassed by the lack of scientific sophistication in the grass-roots movement.[9]

Gottlieb and Ingram thus see the new environmentalists breaking away from their mainstream counterparts, just as the original environmentalists of the Earth Day era broke away from the conservationists. Interestingly, they see the split in the movement deepening because of issues related to decision making and control of environmental policy—issues that are more germane to democratization and empowerment than they are to the technicalities of environmental protection.

As we performed our research, we found similar concerns in every region of the country, though the staff and volunteer leaders we encountered—insiders all—usually put a different spin on the issues of decision making and empowerment. Many leaders are concerned with the processes of decision making within their own organizations. Leaders of national-international organizations are grappling with the difficult question of involvement and activism among memberships that have grown vastly beyond the dimensions of a neighborhood or community grass-roots group. They acknowledge that their organizations continue to display embarrassing elitist qualities, and that they are missing large, important constituencies.

Many leaders of state and local groups, even those that remain close to their grass-roots origins and have memberships that are smaller and much more accessible, share similar concerns. Despite their small size and scanty resources, many are as sophisticated as their national counterparts in their ability to perform legal and policy analysis. They, too, have successfully lobbied new environmental programs into place at the level of state government and like the national groups that Gottlieb and Ingram criticize, have entered into the next layer of the environmental debate—the layer that thrusts them into the thick of regulatory standards, scientific management objectives, compliance, and negotiation. These are not issues that can be easily or competently addressed through direct-action politics or mass-mobilization campaigns.

Yet, in very significant ways, Gottlieb and Ingram's analysis ignores these intermediary conservation groups. Many of them represent precisely the fusion of grass-roots activism and professional expertise that Gottlieb and Ingram seem to feel is now lacking in the national mainstream organizations. Year after year, they have proven that volunteers, working closely with a small coterie of professional staff, can craft extremely sophisticated and effective public policies without entering into any "cult of expertise." Some are virtual models of participatory decision making. That these groups tend to share the homogeneous whiteness of their national counterparts is a concern to them, however, and many of their leaders are also working to diversify.

State and local leaders have an additional concern that is related to empowerment: They often feel a lack of support from their counterparts on the national-international scene. The strongest critics see the large, national groups engaged in a heated competition for members, funding, and organizational growth—a competition that diverts them from successful involvement with state, local, and grass-roots groups in matters of importance to all. National conservation leaders readily profess that the battle now must be taken to the state and local fronts, but the state and local leaders who have been on those fronts for nearly twenty years often wonder when the rhetoric will lead to action. The existence of field programs among national organizations is not necessarily beneficial to the local, grass-roots groups.

These issues are now on the minds of many conservation leaders, but most prefer to couch them in positive terms. Rather than casting the environment movement as a movement divided—at war with itself over fundamental strategies of empowerment and polarized between national and local levels—they see that it might be more productive to look for ways to combine the talents and resources of organizations at various levels in pursuit of common goals, and many organizations are doing so quite successfully.

The groups that can afford lawyers and well-trained technicians are certainly welcome allies among the grass roots, provided that their approach is respectful and that they understand the nature of the issues as they are perceived by local citizens. Technical expertise is often the critical element missing from grass-roots campaigns. The grass-roots groups that emphasize democratic process and social justice can bring new political vigor to larger organizations seeking the means of empowering their own members. They can also provide the critical link for national-international organizations seeking to work effectively at the state or local level. This kind of exchange of talents is already happening, to be sure, but much more can be done to link the levels of the movement effectively to one another. We will revisit this issue in Chapter 4.

The National Conservation Mosaic—Many Pieces Are Missing

It is increasingly difficult to isolate environmental issues at any particular level of policy-making. Most national environmental issues ultimately reach the local level; and there is plenty of evidence that success in the national arenas of policy and management does not necessarily translate to good conservation or environmental protection "on the ground."

This translation works best among those states that have their own rich fabric of local and state-based advocacy organizations arrayed across a broad spectrum of issues. The existence of a long-lived and successful "coordinating council" with a paid staff and a grass-roots board is a good indicator of whether a given state has a rich enough corps of environmental activists. In most states where they occur, these coordinating councils often arose from the need to enhance the representation of many local conservation organizations before state legislatures and administrations. The councils are themselves NGOs, usually with boards of directors comprised at least in part of representatives from the member organizations that belong to the council. Examples of such groups include the Washington Environmental Council (in Seattle), the Ohio Environmental Council, and the Wyoming Outdoor Council. The very demands giving rise to a statewide or regional coordinating council suggest a willingness to recognize and engage in synergy: Organizations can share expertise, knowledge, and power; they often find opportunities to strategize together to resolve issues that no one or two groups could resolve alone. In states where a professionally staffed coordinating organization is missing—still the majority of states—chances are good that the environmental NGOs remain relatively weak; there is little opportunity for synergy either because too few organizations and skills exist to create it or, in rare instances, because one or two large organizations have managed to "clear the market." In those states, we discovered, the environmental movement is often just getting started; it resembles the condition of more active states twenty years ago, when citizens were just catching on to the fact that through tiny, seemingly powerless organizations, they could have enormous leverage on environmental policy.

States with a weak corps of activists need help. They are usually places where environmental policy remains poorly developed, where state agencies struggle and routinely fail to meet federal pollution standards, where the state has not adopted its own strong environmental standards, and where the public's awareness of environmental issues is dim. Ironically, in many such states—most of them rural and agricultural in character—local and national wildlife organizations are very strong. But this is not enough to meet the many and broad environmental challenges faced by every state. Leaders across the country should be concerned with these blank spots on the map of American conservation. They should be willing to help weave together a solid blanket of environmental policy, combining the best of federal and state initiatives and the organizational acumen it takes to foster their implementation. To refuse is to perpetuate an even greater parochialism than now exists in the environmental movement, and parochialism—not hostile government officials—may be the movement's worst enemy.

The Need for In-service Training

Our research clearly demonstrates the need for more training among the staff and volunteers of the conservation NGOs. In the broadest terms, the leaders of large, successful organizations need to find their way back to productive contact with the grass roots. They need to demonstrate an understanding of the complexities of the environmental movement as it exists outside of Washington, D.C., New York, and San Francisco. Often they would benefit from seeking out opportunities for collaboration with their counterparts at the state, regional, and local levels.

Among conservation and environmental groups, there are two brands of grass-roots movement. The national organizations with highly developed field programs commonly lead an active cadre of well-educated and successful "doers." No one can deny the legacy of hard-won victories they have bequeathed America. They have used their influence, skills, and prestige for thousands of local victories.

Yet with few exceptions, their memberships do not include significant representation from America's disenfranchised, who are hard at work building their own grass-roots movement quite apart from the influence of the mainstreamers. The divergence between these two movements jeopardizes either one's chances for making conservation or environmentalism a truly national concern.

Conservation leaders of state, regional, and local organizations still struggle mightily with most aspects of business management. Too many of these groups stagnated at the membership levels they attained over a decade ago and, ironically, they remain stagnated at a time when many national and international organizations are growing at astonishing rates—in some cases adding over 25,000 members per month.[10] National interest in environmentalism continues to explode, yet many of the established local groups—the coalitions and membership-based groups that have been around for nearly two decades—somehow remain unaffected. Too many local groups, both new and old, have only the most rudimentary grasp of strategic planning and board and staff development to help achieve financial stability and improve membership and donor recruitment. The data show a strong link between internal diversification and organizational success. Yet many struggling organizations seem xenophobic, frightened of diversification, and threatened by persons whose views and skills seem alien. Although their leaders complain about their lack of money, time, and staff, they resist the diversification that could help solve their problems.

Unfortunately, we discovered, academia is not at all well equipped to help develop leadership among the NGOs. There are practically no academic programs in natural resources, conservation, or environmental science that pay close attention to the peculiar needs of NGO professionals. Understandably, academia responds to its own market: Students want to be trained for the more stable, better-paying jobs in industry and government. The NGOs employ comparatively few professionals, and typically under far less secure circumstances. With respect to midcareer training, academia is even less prepared to be of much help to conservation NGOs. There are few colleges and universities offering midcareer training for conservationists at any level; of the programs that do exist, very few have cogent applications to the NGO setting.

The burden of in-service training is now being shouldered by the NGOs themselves—the largest among them being able to afford their own in-house programs—and an assortment of management consulting firms, nonprofit management support groups, and training seminars and programs offered through traditional and nontraditional education centers. Some conservation professionals are finding good programs for training and skills development, but for most, especially those in the rural states, the opportunities are slim to nonexistent. The conservation-environmental community needs its own midcareer training programs, tailored to the particular needs of its leaders. Programs must be designed for both staff and volunteers, and they must focus at least in part upon creating new opportunities for synergistic work among various organizations.

The Enormous Challenges Ahead

Conservation leaders now face unprecedented challenges. Economic progress will come to be measured increasingly in terms of environmental quality. It is very likely that in the midst of all the changes and reorientations, leaders of nongovernmental conservation groups will have an increasingly powerful voice. The NGOs, in the United States and elsewhere, will be called upon as never before to provide new ideas, new strategies and solutions to turn back the clock as much as possible on the egregious effects of climate change, transborder pollution, and the various forms of contamination that threaten individuals, cities, and whole nations. Conservationists and environmentalists must begin to ask themselves whether they and their organizations are prepared for such challenges. They have lived so long in the shadow of national and local debate, seemingly far out of the mainstream issues of economic growth, war and peace, human rights and social justice, that their position on the center stage of world politics must seem strange indeed. Now at the helms of their undersupported and embattled organizations, they are rushing into the limelight. There is a serious question as to whether they can meet the great challenges ahead.

We will now turn our attention to what the leaders of American conservation had to say about their movement and what must be done to make them more ready to lead.

Chapter 2

Staff Leadership

Many writers on leadership are at considerable pains to distinguish between leaders and managers. In the process leaders generally end up looking like a cross between Napoleon and the Pied Piper, and managers like unimaginative clods. This troubles me. I once heard it said of a man "He's an utterly first-class manager but there isn't a trace of leader in him." I am still looking for that man, and I am beginning to believe that he doesn't exist. Every time I encounter an utterly first-class manager he turns out to have quite a lot of leader in him.

—*John Gardner,* On Leadership

In every quarter of the country, the great diversity of the conservation movement persists. It remains a crazy quilt of liberals, conservatives and radicals, monkey-wrenchers and mediators, idealists and pragmatists, homemakers and lawyers, scientists and activists, volunteers and professionals. Increasingly it is guided by paid professional staff who exert more and more influence through the offices of more and more sophisticated organizations. Nationwide, there is an inexorable thrust toward turning volunteer conservation groups into professionally managed organizations. For better or worse, success in conservation is often tied to a young organization's ability to afford paid staff, hybridizing them with the healthy corps of volunteers who founded and managed the original organization. The ability to hire and maintain a staff shines as an emblem of, and often accompanies, organizational success, and almost no one says of an organization that has lost all its paid staff and reverted to a group of volunteers that it has succeeded.

The rise of professional staff among conservation NGOs was and is a significant development for the movement; it has brought about myriad benefits. Regardless of their size, staffed organizations tend to achieve a greater degree of institutional stability and longevity than their all-volunteer counterparts. Paid staff often help create the conditions for successful organizations—organizations that can expand the horizons of their activities, plan and execute strategies over the long term, and take their place as a prominent feature of the political landscape where they operate. Moreover, paid staff perform vital services for the movement as well. They often seem to multiply an organization's capacity to assist other conservation groups and efforts. Staff can help others organize and launch new groups, lighting the path with their own experience. They can help keep the records of many conservation efforts that transcend those of their own organization, and thus help maintain the "conservationist history" of a given place or political arena. Moreover, the presence of a strong, professionally led conservation group can make an enormous difference in states with little natural tendency to adopt conservation policies. The mere presence of a professional organization helps make politicians more responsive to conservation issues—or prepare to tell the electorate why they are not.

States with a strong corps of staffed conservation groups are usually those with the best, and most, environmental policies. Often in those states the local, regional, and statewide organizations are able to maintain an effective coalition, usually through the offices of a staffed organization that coordinates the lobbying and other statewide advocacy efforts of many groups. These states, too, are more likely to send environmentally minded politicians to Congress; they provide the key support to place and keep them in office. The paid, professional staff of the conservation movement are increasingly crucial to the development and further reach of the movement into larger, more powerful constituencies—and into the major institutions that control the fate of natural resources.

But the foregoing, as we discovered throughout the study, is an arguable point of view: There are many conservationists and environmentalists who denigrate the importance of professional staff among the NGOs. These critics often set up a dichotomy between "the professionals" and "the volunteers," and they view these two camps of leadership in opposition rather than cooperation. They see the professionals as a threat to amateur hegemony, and often seem to feel that while volunteers work purely from the motive of altruism, paid staff are apt to become mercenaries capable of selling out their organizations to the lure of Mammon merely to protect their own jobs. To many who see their movement in these stark terms, the very notion of professionalism within the ranks of the NGOs seems repugnant. At best, staff are to be tolerated as a necessary evil.

The majority point of view, however, is altogether different. Most volunteers and professionals alike view their respective roles as cooperative and synergistic. They see each other as working to maintain the passionate heart of volunteerism within the well-oiled machinery of a competently managed organization. They do not think that organizations necessarily need to choose between passion and competence; indeed, they recognize that most conservation staff still bring the commitment and passion of volunteerism to their roles as managers and staff leaders, and that the best ones shine as the most effective and inspirational catalysts for volunteer action.

Still, emergent groups must grapple with the new demands placed on their organizations when they decide to hire, or increase the size of, a professional staff. The hiring of staff most often leads to a divestiture of control, as well it should. Staff members, like volunteers, must be empowered if they are to perform at their peak. Yet many small organizations, still wedded to the ideals and ideas of an all-volunteer association, have no concept of what it means to empower staff. In these groups—and there are many—the professional staff act as if they were merely secretaries to the board. They spend too much time wading through factional disputes among powerful but narrow voices on the board, and too little time carrying out the real responsibilities imposed by substantive programs and campaigns. Those volunteers who find themselves unable to empower their staff and learn to share levels of responsibility in a productive, well-planned synergy probably should not have a staff at all. For them, a staff will create nothing but trouble; the group will find itself spending most of its energy on its own internal warfare until the sources of the trouble resign. By then, it's often too late.

Staffed organizations also have to face the burden of increased fund-raising; they must decide what kinds of benefits to offer and what kinds of personnel policies make the most sense; they face compliance with regulatory standards and must file new forms with federal and state agencies; and they must learn how to manage the inevitable and healthy split of responsibilities between a board and a staff. The organization is no longer managed by a committee of peers; it probably now exhibits the bifurcated management of the small nonprofit corporation, where responsibilities must be divided between the board as policy-making body and the staff as implementer. The board must learn to stay out of the staff's way and vice versa. For this to occur, a new level of formality will probably come into play, and some of the old-timers will not like it.

If the organization eschews the hiring of a staff, then it faces the familiar dilemma of the all-volunteer group: namely, how to maintain vitality in a setting where all the work is freely given and no one's job is on the line based upon performance. Only a very few all-volunteer associations survive for more than a dozen years; most are defunct in two or three. Hundreds, perhaps thousands, of American conservation groups have faced the decision to hire professional staff, and many more new ones will face it soon, just as the earliest conservation groups had to face the same decision at around the dawning of the century. Those organizations that faced it successfully are still around today; the rest are now names in obscure books of the movement's history—or, more likely, they are altogether forgotten.

As we embarked on our study of professional leadership among the conservation NGOs, we were very much aware of the hidden tensions that inevitably exist between paid staff and their volunteer directors (or trustees). We were careful to examine the question of delegation of authority within organizations, and were we especially curious about the issue of accountability: How does the board assess the level of a staff's performance? To what extent do various organizations rely on systems of evaluation to ensure rigor and consistency? Whether NGOs are managed in ways that foster rather than impede leadership was the central question we tried to answer through an examination of organizations with paid, professional staff.

Our premises were simple. First, we observed that organizations with paid staff were relatively stable and permanent; unlike many volunteer associations, they are unlikely to disband or lose viability once the founding issue is resolved. Second, their relative stability puts them in a position to influence public decisions and events over a long period of time; their leaders thus have an opportunity to exercise a form of public leadership that is distinctive in American democracy: the so-called third-sector leadership offered by nongovernmental, nonprofit organizations. Third, in influencing public affairs, longevity counts. Deliberate efforts to develop and nurture conservation leaders should aim for the long term; in most cases, the NGOs should manage their affairs in ways that encourage their leaders to stay, if not in any one organization then at least within the conservation movement. Fourth, progressive leadership in the American conservation and environmental movement has almost always come from the nongovernmental sector. NGOs offer liberties of thought, action, and personal independence that are enjoyed to a far lesser degree in governmental agencies; they are free to tell the truth as they see it, and their leaders thus can exert the maximum leverage of public advocacy. Fifth, effective organizations are those that excel at external communications. Sixth, good management and good leadership, while not identical, are closely intertwined. Poorly managed organizations tend to stifle emerging leadership as they bear evidence of its lack at the helm. Finally, given the magnitude of their goals and tasks, the most effective conservation NGOs are those that learn to leverage their resources; conservationists are constantly at risk of being overwhelmed by institutions with far greater resources and influence.

Method

The Conservation Leadership Project sought to identify in all fifty states organizations with paid staffs, and to assess the needs of existing staff leaders within their organizational contexts. We tried to determine the midcareer training and development needs of these leaders and the key needs of their organizations. Moreover, we wanted to assemble a body of information on the state of the conservation movement nationwide in order to make recommendations to funders and other providers of support as to how the movement could be improved through efficient and effective placement of resources, including training and personnel development.

Recognizing that conservation advocacy and education occur on many levels, from local to international, we sought to assemble a sample representing the full range of conservation activities among the NGOs. In order to qualify for the sample, each organization had to

- raise its own funds through one or more kinds of sources.
- employ at least one paid, professional staff person (or a volunteer leader who acts in lieu of paid staff) who discharges the same responsibilities and uses the same authority as an executive director or president.
- accept as an organizational identifier one or more of the following terms: *conservationist, preservationist, environmentalist,* or *educational.*
- operate as a nongovernmental, nonprofit organization (but one that is not a college, university, or school in the usual sense).

The original sample contained 516 organizations; each state (except Nevada, where, at the time we circulated the questionnaire, we could find no staffed organizations) was represented by at least three organizations with paid staff. In instances where states lacked a sufficient number of independent conservation NGOs, we selected field offices or state offices of national organizations operating in those states. The very large sample of organizations in the Washington, D.C., area is a reflection of the importance of the capital as a worldwide center for activity among the NGOs. Still, a few D.C.-area groups represented local, not national or international, constituencies.

Table 1 presents the number of organizations in the sample by state.

With respect to their primary geographic scope of operations, the 516 organizations in the sample were selected to represent all

TABLE I   Staff Questionnaire Sample—Number of Organizations
Sampled in Each State and Number Responding to
Questionnaire

	Number in Sample	*Number Responding*
Alabama	7	3
Alaska	15	8
Arizona	13	8
Arkansas	4	3
California	36	11
Colorado	14	11
Connecticut	5	3
Delaware	3	2
District of Columbia	63	27
Florida	10	3
Georgia	7	0
Hawaii	6	3
Idaho	5	2
Illinois	16	2
Indiana	6	3
Iowa	7	5
Kansas	4	3
Kentucky	7	1
Louisiana	7	7
Maine	4	3
Maryland	11	10
Massachusetts	15	10
Michigan	17	17
Minnesota	7	7
Mississippi	11	2
Missouri	5	3
Montana	16	10
Nebraska	4	4
Nevada	1	1
New Hampshire	8	3
New Jersey	6	3
New Mexico	9	6
New York	24	11
North Carolina	4	2
North Dakota	4	2
Ohio	6	4
Oklahoma	3	2
Oregon	10	6

TABLE 1   (*continued*)

	Number in Sample	Number Responding
Pennsylvania	19	10
Rhode Island	3	2
South Carolina	8	5
South Dakota	3	1
Tennessee	4	0
Texas	9	1
Utah	6	4
Vermont	9	3
Virginia	24	10
Washington	9	6
West Virginia	4	0
Wisconsin	9	4
Wyoming	9	6
Ontario, Canada*	1	1
Puerto Rico	1	1
Totals	518	265**

*Two non-U.S. groups were included in the staff survey. They apparently received questionnaires forwarded to them by acquaintances in the United States. Upon examination, their completed questionnaires appeared appropriate to include in the data, since these groups work on issues similar to those found in the United States and have organizational structures and policies that closely resemble those of U.S. NGOs.
**While 265 responses were received, only 248 were deemed valid. The remainder were not tabulated due to various factors. Some arrived too late to be included; others were illegible; still others duplicated information already provided from the same offices of the same organizations.

levels, from international to local. The most common focus among the organizations was national (185 organizations or field offices). A state focus was the next most common (150 organizations).

Table 2 presents a summary of the organizations in the sample according to their geographical focus.

The surveying instrument used to query the chiefs of staff of these organizations was a fifteen-page mailed questionnaire. Two hundred and forty-eight respondents (48 percent of the original sample) returned completed questionnaires. (A sample questionnaire is included in appendix A.)

Questions fell into five categories: personal identification; per-

TABLE 2   Staff Questionnaire Sample—Primary Geographical Focus
of Organizations

	Number of Organizations	Percentage of Sample
International	55	11%
National	185	36%
Regional	85	16%
State	150	29%
Local	41	8%
Unknown	2	0%

sonal job description; description of organization; education, training and performance; and follow-up, including a critique of the
questionnaire itself. Most respondents took from one to two hours
to complete the questionnaire.

In addition, we selected thirty professionals in seven states for
interviews. Again, these were chosen to represent a broad range of
organizations and geographical emphases. Most of the interviewees
had already completed and returned questionnaires, so project staff
had information about them and their organizations prior to the
interviews.

Of the thirty staff members we interviewed, eight represented
the central headquarters of national or international organizations;
eight were field staff of national or international organizations; six
led independent statewide groups, including, in some cases, coalitions of several groups; and seven represented regional or local
organizations. One interview was with the leader of a national
foundation.

With respect to the nature of the issues or problems addressed
by the organizations of the thirty interviewees, four of the organizations work primarily in the conservation of private lands; eight
focus on public-lands management, including national forests;
eight are state or regional policy advocates; four serve as training
or support centers for professional conservationists or natural resource students; and six act as advocates on a broad range of national or international issues.

The interviews were used to enrich the statistical findings of the questionnaire data, adding a new dimension that conversation and interchange can provide where rigid statistical analysis leaves off.

A Portrait of the NGO Professional and His Organization

The "average" conservation leader queried through the questionnaire is a forty-five-year-old white male who serves as the chief executive officer of his organization. He holds a bachelor's degree from a major American university, but probably not a graduate degree. He has served in his organization for seven and one-half years and in his current position of leadership for five. He says of his job that he has broad executive powers and is responsible for the overall direction, planning, management, and vitality of his organization. Yet he is apt to serve double or triple duty: Chances are he is also the principal fund-raiser and serves as well as a part-time writer, editor, and public relations officer. In exchange for carrying these responsibilities, he earns about $40,000 per year.

The CEO sees his work in conservation as a lifelong career, though he is less certain that he will remain with his current organization until retirement. He traces his interest in the environment back to the early years of his life. As a child, he loved the outdoors and had a parent or teacher who acquainted him with the beauties of nature and instilled in him a deep ethic about the principles of conservation, ecology, and environmental protection. It is this ethic—not careerism or the quest for power or the desire to use environmental issues as a means to effect broad political change— that lead him into his work and continues to refresh him. At one time he was—or he may still be—a conservation volunteer; he has worked professionally in a government agency, and perhaps in a for-profit business as well. But work in the NGO setting is what appeals to him most. Overall, he is quite satisfied with and rewarded by his position of leadership in the organization, though he readily confesses that his organization is beset with problems— mostly related to money, staff resources, outreach, and opportunities to develop new leadership (particularly on the board).

His organization is a membership-based advocacy group with around 3,500 members. The group bills itself as conservationist rather than environmentalist, preservationist, or educational. Yet he admits that the organization has come to use the term *conservation* loosely. As often as not, the group prefers *conservationist* to *environmentalist* for political reasons: The latter word connotes a radicalism that the organization would rather avoid.

The organization's primary geographical scope is the state in which it is located. The range of issues it addresses most likely pertain to fish and wildlife protection as well as the management of lands, both public and private. Its principal strategies involve educating the general public through the use of various media, and monitoring government agencies. It is also occasionally apt to lobby the legislature, organize coalitions with other groups, and train volunteers to act on behalf of the organization. It is extremely unlikely that the organization ever gets involved in the election of public officials, the use of ballot issues such as referenda and initiatives, conflict mediation, or the purchase of private land in order to preserve it.

The organization has an annual budget of about $360,000. It raises 24 percent of its funds from membership dues, 21 percent from private foundations, and 19 percent from a donor-patron program. Unlike private foundation grants, corporate gifts are a minor source of income (4 percent or less). The rest of the funds flow in from the sale of organization products (7 percent), government grants (6 percent), capital assets or user fees (3 percent each), and special fund-raising events such as concerts and raffles (up to 10 percent). Outside of membership dues, the funding that the staff leader considers to be most crucial to the future of the organization comes in the form of small contributions (less than $5,000 each) from its individual donors and patrons.

The organization supports five full-time staff (four of whom are professionals) and two part-time staff. Chances are, the CEO has hired at least one new professional staffer within the past two years. He gives his incoming staff high marks. It he were grading them overall, he'd give them a B+. He would rate them highest for their technical and interpersonal skills and lowest for their skill or knowledge in organization management, writing, conservation history, and environmental policy. Chances are great that he recruited the new staff from other NGOs, not from university programs or government agencies.

Although the organization is small, it has worked hard to install a variety of management tools and systems. It regularly conducts financial audits, but rarely or never has a management audit. It uses a written mission statement and a statement of its programmatic goals and objectives. It has written job descriptions for staff, but not for the board members (a serious omission in the eyes of the CEO). It offers paid vacations, regular wage increases, and a benefits package for both professional and nonprofessional staff. Chances are about even that the organization offers a retirement plan. Although the organization performs something it calls "strategic planning," it is more likely to have an annual operating plan than a long-range plan; thus its strategies and planning horizon tend to be very short-term. Interestingly, the CEO conducts formal evaluations of his staff, but his board does not evaluate him. Along with the absence of management audits, job descriptions for the board, and a written long-range plan, the CEO feels that the board's failure to evaluate him is a serious omission that should be corrected.

When asked what are the key obstacles impeding the greater effectiveness of his organization, the CEO's answer is unequivocal: money and time. His group needs more money to hire staff and consultants and more person-hours to attend to the many issues pressing upon it. When asked specific questions about the need for money, the leader reports that financial stability is as important as increased cash flow; if he could, he'd opt first for a financial endowment to ease the constant burden of fund-raising and second for an altogether larger budget to make the work of the organization more effective.

The CEO believes quite strongly that the administrative and fund-raising demands of his job distract him and his small staff from the substantive work of the organization—the very work they were hired to perform. One of his major complaints about the endless pursuit of money has to do with the grant policies of most private foundations: He feels very strongly that they ought to give more grants to general operating support and fewer grants that are restricted to specific projects and programs. The CEO and his staff are weary of the artifice that is frequently involved in raising funds for projects and programs.

He has other problems as well. Chances are he's having some difficulty with his board, a group of good-hearted volunteers whom he respects more than he appreciates. If he's moved to say anything about his board, he says he wishes the board would become more motivated or, more negatively, that the board should do some work—any work at all—for the organization. He might complain about a lack of motivational leadership on the board but doesn't feel that he has the time, or that it's necessarily his place, to foster that leadership. Thus, the board is a source of chronic anxiety. If he could be granted a few personal wishes to make his job more rewarding, the CEO would wish for a stronger, more involved board of directors. But that's not his only wish.

Nearly equal to it in importance is his desire for personal renewal and growth. In fact, if he were to choose between more opportunities for *personal* growth and more opportunities for *professional* growth, he'd take the personal growth hands down. He longs simply to have more time to himself outside of the workplace. He feels overworked, cramped by the demands of his job; he'd like somehow to re-create those moments in his life when his own learning and development were paramount, when he was living more for himself and less for the sake of solving the problems of the world.

His last wish brings him right back to the organization: He'd like to devise a way to activate the membership. In his eyes, their involvement is crucial; he sees too little of it and fears that despite the grass-roots origins of the organization, it has somehow grown apart from its own members. There is too little staff contact with them, and the board does not fully reflect their desires and needs. Moreover, his organization probably is not experiencing the explosive growth he sees among many of the large national and international groups. The renewed national interest in environmental issues is not trickling down very well to his level, perhaps because his organization has not become very sophisticated in the use of direct mail. He is also concerned with the composition of the membership, the staff, and the board—not only of his own organization but throughout the environmental movement. He sees that the issues so hotly pursued by the mainstream environmental groups seem to hold little appeal for minorities, the poor, and the disenfranchised. At the very least the mainstream movement is thus missing out on the benefits and increased power of these neglected constituencies.

All in all, the CEO seems fairly satisfied with his own position of leadership, and pleased with the conservation-environmental movement he's a part of. He does not want to leave his job for something else, nor does he yearn for greater recognition by his peers or anyone else. He is ambivalent about a raise in pay. Certainly he would accept one, but a higher salary does not appear at the top of his list. Contrary to what some critics say about the movement, the CEO does not feel that it has become too professional. He believes that the professionalism one now finds among conservation groups is a positive sign; if anything, he'd like to see them become even more professional. Interestingly, though he respects the commitment of conservation volunteers and the grassroots representation of the membership, he believes that the "real leadership" of the conservation-environmental movement does not come from the grass roots at all; it comes from the top down, from professionals like himself who staff the movement. Still, he remains dedicated to attempts to stimulate volunteer activism and grassroots involvement, and he is troubled by the gulf he perceives between national conservation organizations and the more local grass-roots groups. He tends to believe that this gulf is caused by the leaders of the large, national organizations, who seem at best to pay little attention to the needs and activities of local, regional, and state-based groups and at worst to erode their base of power and income by virtue of their expansive fund-raising efforts. Conversely, he feels that local groups are supportive of their national counterparts and hungry for the opportunity to work with them.

His overwhelming concerns about the health of the conservation movement do not, however, revolve around the relations among the different groups. They are about money and time: He feels there is far too little of both to meet the challenges faced at any level of environmental initiative, from the international to the local setting.

Aggregated Findings—the Key Issues

The foregoing paints a composite portrait of the average conservation CEO examined through the questionnaires and interviews. But, clearly, what the leaders did *not* say is often as significant as what they did say, and the differences among the various organizations and sectors of the movement are at least as telling as the similarities. In order to gain a richer understanding of the leadership demands and opportunities that exist throughout the conservation movement, it is necessary to examine the key findings of the study in greater detail. Then we will be prepared to investigate the imperatives of movement leadership according to the various sectors of the movement. The balance of this chapter will present the key findings from the staff questionnaire. A later chapter will interpret these data in the light of interviews and other sources of information beyond the questionnaire (see chapter 4).

Staff Leaders of the NGOs

Sixty-five percent of the respondents were either CEOs or the acting CEOs of their organizations; the remaining 35 percent occupy various other positions of staff leadership: vice president, program director, and so forth. Altogether, 93 percent occupy key positions of management and leadership. More than 10 percent of the respondents reported that they were actually unpaid volunteers who serve virtually as full-time CEOs of their organizations. We left these unstaffed organizations in the sample because in all other respects they so closely resembled the organizations that had paid staff at the time of the survey.

The overwhelming majority of these leaders—79 percent—are male. The average age is forty-five; a full 71 percent are between thirty and forty-nine years old. Only 3 percent are younger (twenty-five to twenty-nine years old).

The staff leaders are well educated: 99 percent of them have at least one college degree. One-fifth possess a doctorate or equivalent professional degree. Their educational backgrounds form no very coherent patterns. Forty-five percent of the leaders possess bachelor's degrees in the sciences. The rest have degrees in social sciences (25 percent), liberal arts (22 percent), and technical fields such as engineering (6 percent). Among the leaders with master's degrees, 60 percent are in the scientific fields, with forestry, biology, and environmental science being the most common. Among those with doctorates or professional degrees, law is the most common field, but only 8 percent of the leaders have a law degree. This finding parallels what may writers on leadership have observed: Leaders come from all backgrounds. Even in the fields of conservation and environmental protection, with their strong historic emphasis on the biological sciences, there is no preponderance of backgrounds in biology, though there are many leaders with degrees in the sciences.

The range of salaries paid to these leaders is also enormous. Of the 87 percent who accept compensation for full-time work, the majority earn between $20,000 and $60,000 per year, with the median income a respectable $40,000. A very small minority of conservation staff leaders (2 percent) earn above $100,000—a salary level that many associate with "executive-level income."

Tables 3 through 9 summarize the personal statistics of the NGO staff leaders surveyed.

Organizational Characteristics

About one-third of the groups surveyed said that their primary geographical scope of operations is the state in which they are located. Another one-fourth of the groups listed their focus as

TABLE 3   Staff Questionnaire—Sex of Respondents

	Number of Respondents	Percentage of Total
Male	197	79%
Female	51	21%

TABLE 4   Staff Questionnaire—Age of Respondents

	Number of Respondents	Percentage of Total
25–29	7	3%
30–39	80	33%
40–49	94	38%
50–59	48	20%
60 and older	16	7%
	Mean Age = 45	

TABLE 5   Staff Questionnaire—Highest Educational Level of Respondents

	Number of Respondents	Percentage of Total
No degree	2	1%
Bachelor's degree	115	50%
Master's degree	65	28%
Doctorate (or equivalent)	49	21%

TABLE 6   Staff Questionnaire—Job Title of Respondents

	Number of Respondents	Percentage of Total
CEO	147	60%
Program Director	31	13%
Executive Vice President	17	7%
Regional Director	13	5%
Acting CEO	12	5%
Administrative Assistant	6	2%
Chairperson	4	2%
Vice President	3	1%
Other	13	5%

TABLE 7   Staff Questionnaire—Respondent's Number of Years in Organization

	Number of Respondents	Percentage of Total
1 or fewer	31	13%
2–3	50	21%
4–6	53	22%
7–10	57	23%
11–15	26	11%
16–20	15	6%
21–37	12	5%
Mean Years in Organization = 7.5		

TABLE 8   Staff Questionnaire—Respondent's Number of Years in Current Job

	Number of Respondents	Percentage of Total
1 or fewer	62	26%
2–3	65	27%
4–6	48	20%
7–10	39	16%
11–15	16	7%
16–35	11	5%
	Mean Years in Current Job = 5	

TABLE 9   Staff Questionnaire—Respondent's Salary

	Number of Respondents	Percentage of Total
None	33	13%
$1 to $9,999	10	4%
$10,000 to $20,000	26	11%
$20,001 to $30,000	44	18%
$30,001 to $40,000	43	18%
$40,001 to $60,000	54	22%
$60,001 to $100,000	30	12%
Over $100,000	5	2%

national. The rest were international, local, or regional groups. As to their philosophical orientation, 38 percent of the groups bill themselves as conservationist, while 22 percent say they are environmentalist. Tables 10 and 11 summarize the philosophical orientation and the geographical scope of the organizations surveyed.

Three-quarters of the organizations surveyed are membership-based. The sizes of memberships and budgets vary greatly: About one-third of the groups have fewer than 1,000 members, while 9 percent report memberships above 100,000. The median membership is 3,500, while the median budget for all the organizations is $360,000 annually. If the organization is a division or field office of a parent group, its median budget is $200,000.

Staffing patterns also vary widely, but 72 percent of the organi-

TABLE 10 Staff Questionnaire—Philosophical Orientation of
Organization

	Number of Organizations	*Percentage of Total*
Conservationist	95	38%
Preservationist	24	10%
Environmentalist	55	22%
Educational	60	26%
Other	9	4%

TABLE 11 Staff Questionnaire—Geographical Scope of Organization

	Number of Organizations	*Percentage of Total*
International	34	15%
National	61	25%
Regional	46	19%
State	90	36%
Local	13	5%

zations have three or fewer full-time, paid staff. Fourteen percent reported having no full-time staff at the time of the survey. Many of those groups normally employ one staff person but were in the midst of hiring; others were involved in a transition to a full-time staff person or in the process of deciding whether to continue with paid staff at all. And, as noted earlier, there were a number of organizations in which unpaid volunteers serve as full-time CEOs with all the attendant responsibilities.

Tables 12 through 18 summarize the data that characterize the budgets, membership, and staffing patterns of the organizations surveyed.

Issues and Program Areas

We asked leaders to evaluate the percentage of resources—staff time, money, and volunteer activity—that their organizations commit to various issues and program areas. This was

TABLE 12 Staff Questionnaire—Annual Budget of Organization*

	Number of Organizations	Percentage of Total
Less than $10,000	13	6%
$10,000 to $50,000	15	6%
$50,001 to $100,000	28	12%
$100,001 to $200,000	40	17%
$200,001 to $500,000	46	20%
$500,001 to $1 million	28	12%
Over $1 million to $2 million	22	9%
Over $2 million to $5 million	17	7%
Over $5 million to $30 million	10	4%
Over $30 million	15	6%

Mean Annual Budget = $4,690,000
Median Annual Budget = $360,000

*Independent organization or headquarters of parent organization

TABLE 13 Staff Questionnaire—Annual Budget of Field Office or Affiliate of a Parent Organization

	Number of Organizations	Percentage of Total
Less than $10,000	3	6%
$10,000 to $50,000	6	13%
$50,001 to $100,000	4	8%
$100,001 to $200,000	13	27%
$200,001 to $500,000	9	19%
$500,001 to $1 million	7	15%
Over $1 million	5	11%

Mean Annual Budget = $508,000
Median Annual Budget = $200,000

TABLE 14 Staff Questionnaire—Does Organization Have Dues-Paying Membership?

	Number of Organizations	Percentage of Total
Yes	185	75%
No	63	25%

TABLE 15 Staff Questionnaire—Number of Dues-Paying Members in Organization

	Number of Organizations	Percentage of Total
Fewer than 1,000	65	36%
1,001 to 5,000	45	25%
5,001 to 10,000	22	12%
10,001 to 30,000	17	9%
30,001 to 100,000	16	9%
100,001 to 5 million	15	9%

Mean Number of Members = 95,730
Median Number of Members = 3,500

TABLE 16 Staff Questionnaire—Number of Full-time, Paid Staff in Organization, Field Office, or Affiliate*

	Number of Organizations	Percentage of Total
0	34	14%
1–3	72	58%
4–5	38	16%
6–10	36	15%
11–20	27	11%
21–50	27	11%
Over 50	14	6%

Mean Number of Full-time, Paid Staff = 30
Median Number of Full-time, Paid Staff = 4.5

*All staff, both professional and other

to get a sense of the nature of the organizations: What do their members or trustees want them to accomplish? Are they generally wedded to any particular areas of resource conservation or environmental protection? We offered a menu of seventeen areas of substantive activity and allowed for write-in responses in a category marked "Other."

The greatest percentages of organizational resources were reported to be in fish and wildlife management and protection (19 percent); national forest, parks, and public lands management (12

TABLE 17   Staff Questionnaire—Number of Part-Time, Paid Staff in Organization, Field Office or Affiliate*

	Number of Organizations	Percentage of Total
0	65	27%
1–3	112	46%
4–5	35	14%
6–10	14	6%
11–20	10	4%
Over 20	9	8%
Mean Number of Part-time, Paid Staff = 10		
Median Number of Part-time, Paid Staff = 2		

*All staff, both professional and other

TABLE 18   Staff Questionnaire—Number of Professional Staff in Organization, Field Office, or Affiliate

	Number of Organizations	Percentage of Total
0	13	6%
1–3	77	34%
4–6	59	51%
7–10	31	14%
11–20	25	11%
Over 20	25	11%
Mean Number of Professional Staff = 15		
Median Number of Professional Staff = 4		

percent); and private land preservation and stewardship (11 percent). The issues and programs receiving the fewest resources were population control (0.2 percent); nuclear power or weapons (1 percent); mining law and regulation (1 percent); and zoological or botanical gardens (1 percent). Significantly, the leaders reported spending 11 percent of their organizational resources on other issues and programs; these consisted of forty-nine different activities, including recycling, tropical resources, technical assistance, protection of native or tribal lands, and freshwater quantity (helping to maintain freshwater supplies or, in the American West, allocating water among various users). Table 19 summarizes the percentage of organizational resources spent on various programmatic areas.

Organizational Strategies

We asked the staff leaders to evaluate their use of various strategies to achieve their objectives. Leaders were offered a menu of sixteen broad kinds of strategies and asked to evaluate the importance of each on a scale from one to five. The kinds of strategies offered ranged from the "hard road" of direct-action politics and coalition building to various forms of public education and research, direct acquisition or management of lands and waterways, and conflict mediation. Our aim was to determine the general nature of conservation advocacy among the groups. Do they tend to be overtly political, or do most of their important strategies revolve around "softer" forms of activism? Are they more likely to rely on lawsuits or letter-writing campaigns, the dissemination of research or electioneering?

TABLE 19 Staff Questionnaire—Average Percentage of Resources Spent on Various Issues and Programs

Fish and wildlife management and protection	19%
National forest, parks, and public lands management	12%
Private land preservation and stewardship	11%
Toxic, hazardous, and solid waste management	8%
Protection of waterways (rivers, lakes, coasts)	7%
Water quality	6%
Urban and rural land-use planning	4%
Wilderness	4%
Agriculture	4%
Air quality	3%
Economic, sustainable development	3%
Marine conservation	3%
Energy conservation and facility regulation	2%
Zoological or botanical gardens	1%
Mining law and regulation	1%
Nuclear power or weapons	1%
Population control	0%
Other	11%

The aggregated data showed a strong preference for public education campaigns through the use of various media (print, electronic media, organizational self-publicity, conferencing, and public speaking). There is also a very strong reliance on monitoring government agencies. The two strategies used least both relate to direct electioneering: placing environmental initiatives or referenda on the ballot and influencing the election of public officials. These less-favored strategies, it must be said, might have less to do with true preferences among the organizations than with the legal and institutional framework in which most of them operate. A large portion of conservation and environmental groups are either tax-exempt, nonprofit corporations or have a tax-deductible "wing" or program area through which they may accept charitable contributions. As such, they are prohibited from directly influencing elections, and they are limited in the extent to which they can lobby or engage in other forms of direct political action. Moreover, many states do not have constitutional provisions for the use of initiatives and referenda. Some states that provide for them virtually never use them—the state of Wyoming is one example—often because the requirements for placing issues on the ballot are so strict that most citizens' organizations cannot afford to comply with them.

Table 20 presents the findings on the use of various strategies to achieve organizational goals.

How Conservation Staff Leaders Spend Their Time

Table 21 summarizes the leaders' use of time on the job. It is clear from these data that the majority of staff leaders are spending most of their time managing internal affairs. Fundraising, board and membership development, personnel management, and planning consume, on average, 57 percent of the staff leaders' time. Still, they manage to spend a little more than one-quarter of their time in program implementation and research—activities that might best be described as substantive rather than administrative. Of the remaining time, the leaders spend a mere 5 percent on public speaking, 4 percent dealing with the press and other media, and a minuscule 2 percent on their own professional development.

TABLE 20   Staff Questionnaire—Importance of Various Strategies Used to Achieve Goals and Objectives

	Irrelevant 1	Seldom 2	Sometimes 3	Very Important 4	Our Highest Priority 5	Mean
Educate through media	1%	5%	23%	54%	18%	3.8
Monitor government agencies	15%	8%	26%	41%	10%	3.2
Train volunteers to act	20%	13%	30%	32%	5%	2.9
Educate through nature encounters	18%	19%	29%	26%	8%	2.9
Organize coalitions	22%	13%	29%	30%	7%	2.9
Perform and disseminate scientific research	23%	19%	26%	23%	10%	2.8
Lobby lawmakers	25%	15%	25%	29%	7%	2.8
Perform and disseminate policy research	23%	20%	22%	28%	6%	2.7
Mobilize letter writing and political action	34%	20%	17%	23%	6%	2.5
Manage land and waterways	45%	17%	9%	19%	11%	2.3
Preserve land by purchase	54%	13%	8%	9%	16%	2.2
Litigate	45%	23%	20%	11%	1%	2.0
Mediate conflicts	42%	27%	23%	6%	3%	2.0
Perform and disseminate ethical research	48%	23%	18%	8%	3%	1.9
Influence elections	64%	16%	8%	7%	3%	1.7
Place initiatives and referenda on ballot	69%	19%	8%	4%	0%	1.5

TABLE 21   Staff Questionnaire—Average Percentage of Staff Leaders'
Time Spent on Various Tasks

Program or project implementation	25%
Fund-raising	16%
Planning	16%
Board development	8%
Staff recruitment or management	6%
Increasing number of members/volunteers	6%
Enhancing participation of members/volunteers	5%
Public speaking	5%
Press/media relations	4%
Performing programmatic research	4%
Personal or professional development/training	2%
Other activities	4%

It must be remembered that most of the organizations surveyed are relatively small; they carry the burden of enormous missions, and often multiple programs, on the backs of a mere half-dozen staff. Our sample of organizations was no aberration but an accurate reflection of the conservation movement as we find it today across the United States. In such organizations, the CEO usually cannot afford the luxury of a narrowly defined job. He or she serves in multiple capacities, often performing work that is left to specialized staff in larger organizations. When we asked the staff leaders to describe the duties and responsibilities that they routinely perform, the results were quite startling. Eighty-seven percent described themselves as the executive-level leader of their organization or field office. Forty-two percent said that they also served as the fund-raiser or development officer. Thirty-eight percent act, in addition, as a writer or editor. Many offered a list of other responsibilities they carry in performing their jobs as the executive of the organization. Some act as community organizers, researchers, and public relations officers. In many instances, the executive director thus serves as the sole administrator, the staff manager with authority to hire and fire, the sole fund-raiser, the writer-editor (or one of several writer-editors), the media spokesperson, and the membership development officer. In addition, the CEO is the only staffer who reports directly to the board, and whose job it often is to recruit new board members, develop leadership within the board, and serve as liaison between board and staff. These broad executive roles are certainly not unique to conservation organizations. Most sectors of the nonprofit community make the same requirements of executives in small organizations. But it must also be said that in practically no other sector of nonprofit enterprise do small organizations carry such enormous missions.

Funding

Conservation groups possess widely diversified streams of income, and they are quite sophisticated in their fund-raising strategies. They receive funds from at least a dozen different sources, ranging from membership dues, the sale of goods, and the acquisition of contracts to various kinds of grants and gifts. Given that most of the organizations are tax-exempt charities, they are eligible for private foundation funding and tax-deductible gifts from individuals; and, indeed, philanthropic grants and gifts provide, overall, the largest portion of revenues to the staffed organizations. Forty-four percent of the average annual income of the organizations comes from philanthropic sources. Of that amount, private foundation grants provide 21 percent of the total average income, while 19 percent comes from individual contributors who make gifts beyond dues and another 4 percent comes from corporate contributions.

Conversely, conservation groups do not depend much on public finance. Only 6 percent of their funds come from state and federal grants and contracts combined. They generally bring in more money from the sale of organization products (7 percent of their income) than they receive from government grants. The rest of their income is derived from sources including user fees, nongovernmental contracts, capital assets, and miscellaneous sources such as raffles and special fund-raising events. Table 22 summarizes the sources of revenues available to staffed conservation groups nationwide.

Their heavy reliance on philanthropic sources is especially interesting in light of the fact that three-quarters of those surveyed are membership organizations. Across the movement, including

TABLE 22   Staff Questionnaire—Funding Sources of Organizations

Percentage of Revenues from Membership Dues

	Number of Organizations	Percentage of Total
0%	59	25%
1%–10%	44	18%
11%–20%	35	15%
21%–30%	29	12%
31%–40%	23	10%
41%–50%	22	9%
Over 50%	29	12%

Mean Percentage of Revenue from
Membership Dues = 24%

Percentage of Revenues from Foundation Grants

	Number of Organizations	Percentage of Total
0%	70	29%
1%–10%	54	23%
11%–20%	30	13%
21%–30%	24	10%
31%–40%	11	5%
41%–50%	20	8%
Over 50%	31	13%

Mean Percentage of Revenue from
Foundation Grants = 21%

Percentage of Revenues from Individual Contributions

	Number of Organizations	Percentage of Total
0%	39	13%
1%–10%	91	38%
11%–20%	35	15%
21%–30%	35	15%
31%–40%	17	7%
41%–50%	13	5%
Over 50%	17	7%

Mean Percentage of Revenue from
Individual Contributions = 19%

TABLE 22   (*continued*)

Percentage of Revenues from Sales

	Number of Organizations	Percentage of Total
0%	120	50%
1%–10%	75	31%
11%–20%	22	9%
Over 20%	23	10%

Mean Percentage of Revenue from Sales = 7%

Percentage of Revenues from Corporate Gifts

	Number of Organizations	Percentage of Total
0%	118	49%
1%–10%	97	40%
11%–20%	18	8%
Over 20%	7	3%

Mean Percentage of Revenues from Corporate Gifts = 4%

Percentage of Revenues from Federal Grants and Contracts

	Number of Organizations	Percentage of Total
0%	184	77%
1%–10%	36	15%
11%–20%	5	2%
Over 20%	17	7%

Mean Percentage of Revenue from
Federal Grants and Contracts = 4%

Percentage of Revenues from Capital Assets

	Number of Organizations	Percentage of Total
0%	180	75%
1%–10%	41	17%
Over 10%	20	8%

Mean Percentage of Revenue from
Capital Assets = 3%

TABLE 22 (*continued*)

Percentage of Revenues from User Fees

	Number of Organizations	Percentage of Total
0%	198	83%
1%–10%	25	12%
Over 10%	13	5%

Mean Percentage of Revenue from
User Fees = 3%

Percentage of Revenues from Other (Nongovernmental) Contracts

	Number of Organizations	Percentage of Total
0%	208	87%
1%–10%	25	10%
Over 10%	13	5%

Mean Percentage of Revenue from
Other Contracts = 2%

Percentage of Revenues from State Grants and Contracts

	Number of Organizations	Percentage of Total
0%	198	83%
1%–10%	30	13%
Over 10%	12	5%

Mean Percentage of Revenue from
State Grants and Contracts = 2%

Percentage of Revenues from Other Sources

	Number of Organizations	Percentage of Total
0%	140	58%
1%–10%	49	20%
11%–20%	16	7%
Over 20%	36	15%

Mean Percentage of Revenue from Other Sources = 10%

both membership and nonmembership organizations, conservation groups depend on members' dues for 24 percent of their total funding. When the nonmembership groups are removed from the sample, the equation changes, but not substantially. Table 23 compares the income streams of membership organizations and all conservation groups combined.

The membership groups, on average, receive only 32 percent of their funding from members' dues; 40 percent comes from philanthropic gifts. But membership organizations rely on their members for the most important philanthropic contributions they receive—the "small" gifts (less than $5,000 each) from individuals. These donors are, across the board, the most important conservationist philanthropists. The staff leaders spend a great deal of time and effort grooming small donors. Significantly, their recruitment of members is often very strongly oriented toward capturing members who also have the means to act as philanthropists. Conservation leaders are keenly interested in recruiting members from the middle and upper middle class of American society, for these are the ones most able to provide the critical philanthropic support.

TABLE 23   Staff Questionnaire—Comparative Sources of Income for Membership Groups and All Groups Combined

	Membership Groups	All Groups
Membership dues	32%	24%
Individual contributions	19%	19%
Foundation grants	17%	21%
Sales	8%	7%
Corporate gifts	4%	4%
Capital assets	3%	3%
Federal grants and contracts	2%	4%
State grants and contracts	2%	2%
Other contracts	2%	2%
User fees	2%	3%
Other sources	9%	10%

Foundation Support

The foregoing is not to suggest, however, that foundations and other philanthropic sources are unimportant to conservation groups. Indeed, private foundations play a crucial role in the American conservation movement. Foundations take up most of the financial slack when members are absent (see Table 23). Many nonmembership organizations rely on them for most of their support. To membership and nonmembership groups alike, foundations provide capital for programs, projects, and, to a lesser degree, general operations. They often make seed money available to get new conservation initiatives moving. A few well-directed grants, even very small ones, often trigger matching grants and gifts from donors, thus helping conservation leaders initiate new programs that would otherwise not get off the ground.

When staff leaders were asked to evaluate the relative importance of various streams of philanthropic support to their organizations (see Table 24), foundation grants were second only to small individual contributions in importance. But as we learned through our interviews, the importance of foundations goes well beyond the giving of money. Leaders depend on foundations for programmatic ideas, information on productive networking with other groups, occasional technical support, and the sense of legitimacy and prestige

TABLE 24   Staff Questionnaire—Relative Importance of Various Philanthropic Sources of Income

	Unimportant 1	Somewhat Important 2	Very Important 3	Crucial 4	Mean
Small contributions from individuals (under $5,000)	5%	20%	33%	42%	3.12
Small foundation grants (less than $25,000)	7%	26%	39%	28%	2.87
Large foundation grants (more than $25,000)	20%	18%	24%	39%	2.81
Large contributions from individuals (above $5,000)	19%	26%	31%	23%	2.54
Corporate gifts	34%	36%	20%	10%	2.06

that comes with foundation grants. Well-funded organizations gain the attention of policymakers simply by virtue of the recognition they receive from national grant makers.

Grant seeking offers other indirect benefits as well. The planning required to write good proposals is often the only formal planning that the smaller organizations perform, and while the granting requirements of foundations are often time-consuming—some would say nettlesome—they force many staff leaders and their boards to engage in long-term thinking and to consider new ways to evaluate projects and programs. Foundations, too, have a stake in the efforts of conservationists. The Environmental Grantmakers Association, comprised of over 100 conservation philanthropists (mostly foundations), has been formed to provide an informal exchange of ideas and information to improve grant making in the environmental arena and to attract new conservation funders.

As the environmental crisis deepens worldwide, many believe that the list of foundations funding conservation and environmental protection will grow dramatically. That would be good news for conservation leaders nationwide but, as we shall see later, they do not believe that organizations of all types and in all regions of the country will necessarily benefit from increased foundation largess. Nor do all staff leaders believe that foundation grants are generally a good source of income.

Given conservationists' heavy reliance on foundations, we asked several questions concerning the leaders' attitudes toward them. The results, summarized in Table 25, were striking.

The leaders gave foundations mixed reviews. They agreed overwhelmingly that "foundations ought to give more funds to general support." They also agreed that too little foundation funding flows to "local and state-based conservation efforts," and that increased competition for funding has made foundations "less responsive and accessible." On the positive side, respondents generally felt that foundation officials are well-informed on issues, and they strongly disagreed that foundation officials are "blind to the power they wield over grantees."

These attitudes, along with others more fully expressed through the interviews, are symptomatic of several larger concerns expressed by staff leaders—concerns that transcend the search for

TABLE 25   Staff Questionnaire—Staff Leaders' Attitudes toward
Private Foundations

	Strongly Disagree 1	Disagree 2	Strongly Agree 3	Agree 4	Mean
Foundations should give more funds to "general support."	2%	11%	45%	43%	3.29
Foundations give too little money to local groups.	2%	35%	35%	25%	2.86
Foundation officers are unresponsive to grantees' needs.	3%	36%	43%	16%	2.83
Foundation officers are generally well-informed on environmental issues.	6%	31%	55%	8%	2.67
Foundations are blind to their power over grantees.	11%	62%	21%	5%	2.26

funding and reach to the core of environmental advocacy in the United States. We will explore these concerns in greater detail in chapter 5.

Management Tools

Conservation groups, regardless of size or scope, tend to use many sophisticated tools of organization and personnel management. Between 64 percent and 87 percent of the organizations surveyed report that they have and use the following tools: a written mission statement; organization goals and objectives; paid vacations, benefits packages, regular raises, and written job descriptions for staff; and regular financial audits.

Yet there are still many tools that conservation-group managers feel they need in order to lead their organizations more effectively. Among them are management audits, written job descriptions for board members, and formal evaluations of their CEOs. Other tools are viewed as unnecessary, such as written job descriptions or grievance policies for volunteers.

Table 26 presents a summary of the use of various management tools and benefits by conservation groups.

Needed Resources: Internal

As conservation and environmental groups have grown and matured, they have added and diversified resources of many kinds. Specialized staff positions and bifurcated management structures—separating business management from the management of substantive programs—have replaced the monolithic arrangements frequently found among nascent groups. Computers and specialized training programs for staff, board members, and volunteers are now in use throughout the movement. Numerous organizations have learned how to develop and maintain deferred-giving programs and other sophisticated forms of developmental fund-raising. An increasing number of conservation groups now possess endowments and cash reserve funds.

Still, many kinds of resources that would increase the stability and professionalism of conservation organizations are lacking. We asked the staff leaders to evaluate a list of "internal" resources with respect to usefulness in their organizations. The question allowed leaders to evaluate the internal resources they had already begun using, and to speculate on resources they might add if they had the wherewithal to do so. Their needs stand out in clear relief, as demonstrated in Table 27.

Ninety-five percent of them said that a financial endowment would be (or is) either useful or extremely useful (only 30 percent of the organizations surveyed currently have an endowment). Ninety-three percent called for a much larger budget, while 90 percent said that greater computer capabilities would be useful. Eighty-one percent said that the hiring of fund-raising staff would be useful (40 percent of the organizations already employ a fund-raising staff and report that they are indeed useful).

When leaders were asked to pick the highest priority from the list of internal resources, the results were both predictable and telling: 61 percent called for resources that would improve their organization's financial situation. A much larger budget, an endow-

TABLE 26 Staff Questionnaire—Organizations' Use of Various Management Tools and Benefits

	Don't Have but Need and Would Use	Have and Use	Have but Don't Use	Don't Have and Don't Need
Management audits	46%	29%	2%	20%
Written job descriptions for board members	45%	22%	9%	23%
Formal evaluation of CEO	42%	38%	3%	17%
Written long-range plan	40%	42%	9%	9%
Written job descriptions for volunteers	37%	16%	2%	44%
In-service professional training for staff	33%	43%	6%	19%
Retirement plan for staff	31%	48%	0%	21%
Grievance policy for volunteers	29%	11%	3%	55%
Formal evaluations of staff (other than CEO)	29%	52%	3%	16%
Written annual operating plan	28%	56%	3%	8%
Strategic planning	27%	59%	8%	5%
In-house orientation program for staff	26%	42%	2%	30%
Grievance policy for staff	23%	39%	6%	33%
Written policy for leaves and/or sabbaticals	23%	45%	2%	30%
Regular salary increases for staff	23%	64%	1%	12%
Written organization goals and objectives	17%	71%	7%	5%
Written job descriptions for staff	17%	64%	8%	12%
Benefits package for staff	12%	77%	0%	11%
Regular financial audits	9%	85%	1%	5%
Paid vacations for non-professional staff	7%	74%	0%	19%
Paid vacations for professional staff	4%	85%	0%	11%
Written mission statement	4%	87%	4%	2%

TABLE 27   Staff Questionnaire—Evaluation and Use of Various Internal Resources and Improvements

	Useless 1	Not Very Useful 2	Fairly Useful 3	Extremely Useful 4	Currently Used 5	Mean
Financial endowment	2%	2%	13%	82%	30%	3.74
Much larger budget	3%	5%	27%	66%	27%	3.56
Improved computer capability	3%	6%	34%	56%	68%	3.44
Hiring fund-raising staff	9%	10%	30%	51%	46%	3.22
Better access to information	4%	11%	47%	38%	32%	3.20
Assistance with strategic planning	4%	15%	42%	39%	44%	3.17
Hiring programmatic staff	11%	15%	26%	48%	42%	3.12
Training for board members	8%	16%	36%	40%	29%	3.08
Hiring administrative staff	10%	20%	29%	41%	45%	3.01
Staffed field program	19%	13%	22%	46%	36%	2.96
In-house staff training program	10%	25%	35%	30%	36%	2.84
Hiring professional researchers	11%	23%	38%	28%	33%	2.83
Improved workplace	15%	20%	36%	29%	41%	2.79
Training for volunteers	15%	25%	31%	29%	31%	2.74
Evaluation of organization by the membership	27%	19%	29%	24%	20%	2.52
Training in mediation	17%	39%	33%	10%	11%	2.36
Training in lobbying	28%	31%	20%	22%	17%	2.36
Training in resolution of interpersonal conflicts for staff	27%	39%	25%	10%	10%	2.17

ment, and the opportunity to hire fund-raising staff were by far the three top choices. Tables 27 and 28 summarize the leaders' choices among various internal resources.

Needed Resources: External

Conservation leaders frequently complain of isolation and the paucity of opportunities for midcareer training and refreshment. The staff questionnaire asked a series of questions regarding the usefulness of various resources, or opportunities, in these areas, especially with respect to how they might enhance a leader's ability

TABLE 28   Staff Questionnaire—Highest Priority Among Needed
Internal Resources

	Number of Respondents	Percentage of Total
Much larger budget	62	28%
Financial endowment	58	23%
Hiring fund-raising staff	22	10%
Assistance with strategic planning	11	5%
Training for board members	11	5%
Hiring programmatic staff	8	4%
Training for volunteers	7	3%
Hiring professional researchers	7	3%
Staffed field program	7	3%
Hiring administrative staff	6	3%
Improved computer capability	6	3%
In-house staff training program	5	2%
Training in mediation	4	2%
Evaluation of organization by the membership	4	2%
Better access to information	2	1%
Training in lobbying	2	1%
Training in resolution of the interpersonal conflicts for staff	1	0%
Improved workplace	0	0%

to perform more effectively. The questions were designed to offer
a range of "external" opportunities—new ways for staff leaders to
increase their own understanding of conservation history, science,
and law, as well as opportunities to share information with their
peers, develop joint strategies with policymakers and business leaders, or refresh themselves through the use of various kinds of sabbaticals or leaves of absence. Again, the results, summarized in
Table 29, are telling.

When staff leaders were asked this time to choose their highest
priority from among the external resources, the results were not
clear-cut. Table 30 summarizes them.

Interestingly, while 14 percent of the staff leaders listed a paid
sabbatical as their top priority, 15 percent characterized it as useless (see Table 29). The leaders are clearly split on the value of
sabbaticals; it would appear that those who desire them do so quite

TABLE 29 Staff Questionnaire—Evaluation and Use of Various External Resources

	Useless 1	Not Very Useful 2	Fairly Useful 3	Extremely Useful 4	Currently Used 5	Mean
Peer discussions on issues and programs	2%	4%	41%	53%	62%	3.45
Discussions with leading thinkers in resource policy	4%	10%	43%	42%	32%	3.24
Lawmakers' forum for legislators and conservation leaders	6%	16%	35%	43%	22%	3.16
Conservation planning forum with industry leaders and regulators	6%	16%	38%	39%	27%	3.11
Peer discussions on management	4%	14%	48%	34%	62%	3.11
An ongoing leadership development program	5%	17%	50%	29%	12%	3.02
A paid sabbatical	15%	18%	31%	36%	3%	2.88
Discussions with leading thinkers in environmental ethics	11%	24%	35%	30%	17%	2.85
International travel to compare environmental management	11%	25%	35%	29%	31%	2.82
Management discussions with leaders outside the conservation movement	7%	26%	49%	18%	37%	2.79
Field studies with leading ecologists	9%	29%	40%	22%	25%	2.76
Greater access to professional journals	9%	28%	44%	19%	30%	2.73
A teaching sabbatical to share knowledge with students	14%	30%	34%	22%	3%	2.65
Discussions with leading thinkers in conservation history	12%	30%	40%	18%	14%	2.64
A fellowship in natural resource management	16%	31%	29%	24%	3%	2.61
A loaned executive program with other nonprofit groups	19%	35%	31%	13%	6%	2.48
A program to study poverty in the U.S.	40%	37%	17%	6%	5%	1.90

TABLE 30   Staff Questionnaire—Highest Priority Among Needed
External Resources

	Number of Respondents	Percentage of Total
A paid sabbatical	30	14%
Conservation planning forum with industry leaders and regulators	27	12%
Peer discussions on issues and programs	24	11%
An ongoing leadership development program	22	10%
Peer discussions on management	21	10%
Lawmakers' forum for legislators and conservation leaders	20	9%
Discussions with leading thinkers in resource policy	16	7%
International travel to compare environmental management	11	5%
A fellowship in natural resource management	9	4%
A loaned executive program with other nonprofit groups	8	4%
A teaching sabbatical to share knowledge with students	8	4%
Field studies with leading ecologists	7	3%
Discussions with leading thinkers in environmental ethics	5	2%
Greater access to professional journals	3	1%
A program to study poverty in the U.S.	2	1%
Management discussions with leaders outside the conservation movement	2	1%
Discussions with leading thinkers in conservation history	0	0%

strongly—perhaps evidence that there are many weary leaders at the helms of conservation groups.

The staff leaders in general seem to favor new opportunities for discussions on both management and substantive issues with their peers. They are interested in programs to develop leadership, and in discussion and planning forums with lawmakers, regulators, and private business leaders. They are less inclined to favor opportunities to increase their own fund of knowledge through exposure to experts in ecology, ethics, and conservation history, and they have negligible interest in programs that would expose them to the roots of poverty or involve the discussion of management with nonprofit organization leaders outside the conservation field.

The Personal Needs of Conservation Leaders

Leaders were asked to evaluate a series of factors—both personal and organizational—that might make their work more rewarding and effective. Most of them chose the following as either very rewarding or their top priority: a better or more involved board of directors (62 percent); more time for themselves (60 percent); more opportunities for personal renewal or growth (57 percent); and greater participation by members or volunteers (55 percent). What they generally do not seem to desire as much are higher pay, greater amounts of personal recognition, or a more supportive staff. The leaders clearly do not desire to leave their jobs, transfer into some other organization, or receive a promotion (though this last option for most is moot in their current positions). Interestingly, they rate opportunities for greater personal growth and greater professional growth both quite high, but their preference would be for personal growth.

Table 31 summarizes the leaders' personal preferences among a list of possible rewards and opportunities.

Recruitment

Bringing new leadership into the conservation movement depends in part upon effective staff recruitment. According to the survey results, conservation groups all over the country were actively seeking professional staff within the past two years. Since most of the organizations surveyed are small (their median staff size, including part-time staff, is seven), one would expect fairly low numbers of new recruits entering the NGOs, and that is the case. Nevertheless, more than 70 percent of the organizations hired at least one staff person during the past two years, with 12 percent

TABLE 31   Staff Questionnaire—Evaluation of Factors That Could Make Work More Rewarding and Effective

	Irrelevant 1	Somewhat Rewarding 2	Very Rewarding 3	Top Priority 4	Needs No Improvement 5	Mean
Better or more in-volved board	8%	17%	39%	23%	13%	2.89
More time for my-self	14%	21%	46%	14%	6%	2.63
More opportunities for personal growth	17%	22%	42%	15%	5%	2.57
More membership or volunteer par-ticipation	17%	20%	43%	12%	8%	2.54
More opportunities for professional growth	19%	38%	28%	8%	7%	2.27
Greater organiza-tional security	30%	23%	20%	14%	14%	2.20
Higher pay	20%	44%	26%	3%	6%	2.13
More supportive staff	19%	25%	17%	4%	35%	2.10
More outside rec-ognition	28%	26%	32%	2%	11%	2.08
More peer recogni-tion	29%	36%	22%	2%	12%	1.96
Changing organiza-tions	57%	17%	9%	4%	12%	1.55
Promotion	48%	12%	7%	1%	32%	1.40
Different job, same organization	51%	10%	5%	1%	33%	1.36

hiring five or more. Table 32 summarizes the data on the hiring of new professional staff during a recent two-year period.

The NGOs recruited professional staff from a variety of settings (see Table 33). Of the organizations that hired new staff members, 57 percent recruited them from colleges and universities. Interestingly, only 34 percent found staff in university natural resource programs, while 23 percent found them in other university programs.

TABLE 32   Staff Questionnaire—Number of New Professionals Hired in Last Two Years

	Number of Respondents	Percentage of Total
0	67	29%
1	47	20%
2	40	17%
3	37	16%
4	13	6%
5	8	4%
6 or more	18	8%

TABLE 33   Staff Questionnaire—From Where Were Professional Staff Recruited?

	Number of Respondents	Percentage of Total
From other nonprofit organizations	109	61%
From university natural resource programs	61	34%
From government agencies	58	32%
From business	50	28%
From other university programs	41	23%

*Percentages in table do not equal 100 due to the fact that some organizations recruited multiple staff from multiple settings.

The largest percentage of NGOs (61 percent) hired staff away from other conservation NGOs. Significant numbers were also hired from government agencies (32 percent) and for-profit businesses (28 percent). (Multiple hirings from multiple sources cause the foregoing numbers not to equal 100 percent.)

As to the quality of new professional staff, the NGO leaders generally rated them high, with the highest marks given for communication and technical skills and the lowest for knowledge of science, environmental policy formation, and conservation history. Table 34 summarizes these ratings.

Attitudes

The staff questionnaire also attempted to measure, at least very roughly, the staff leaders' attitudes concerning various aspects of the conservation movement and the organizations that comprise it. Respondents were asked to register their degree of agreement or disagreement with a series of eighteen statements pertaining to conservation efforts among the NGOs. Eleven of the statements were couched in negative terms—as opinions critical of various aspects of the conservation movement. Seven of the statements were either normative opinions or statements of problems facing the conservation movement, but not ones placing blame or designating responsibility.

Tables 35 and 36 summarize the leaders' responses to these attitudinal questions.

Staff leaders expressed strong agreement with three of the critical statements: that poor and minority rural Americans see little of interest in the conservation message; that conservation staff are

TABLE 34 Staff Questionnaire—Evaluation of Newly Hired
Professional Staff

	Very Poor 1	Poor 2	Good 3	Excellent 4	Mean
Interpersonal communication	0%	3%	40%	57%	3.54
Technical skills	0%	4%	39%	50%	3.49
Oral communication skills	0%	4%	47%	49%	3.45
Writing skills	2%	8%	50%	39%	3.29
Organization management skills	1%	13%	49%	32%	3.17
Scientific knowledge	3%	20%	37%	22%	2.95
Training in environmental policy	1%	26%	38%	21%	2.92
Knowledge of conservation history	1%	23%	46%	13%	2.85
Overall evaluation	0%	2%	53%	44%	3.42

distracted from their substantive work by the burdens of organizational management and fund-raising; and that the conservation movement overall is "fragmented, territorial, and uncommunicative." They expressed strong disagreement with statements that local groups are unsupportive of national organizations, that national groups are actually detrimental to local conservation efforts, and that conservation NGOs tend to be poorly managed. Among the normative and noncritical statements, the only one receiving less than majority agreement is the opinion that the "real leadership in conservation lies at the grass roots, not among the professional organizations."

As we shall see later, many of these opinions touch on the themes of leadership and future direction of the movement that the CEOs and other leaders discussed at length during the interviews.

Summary

The foregoing presents a composite portrait of the staff leaders and organizations that comprise the American conservation movement. The general trends and needs, in many instances, are clearly outlined. According to what the staff leaders told us, their organizations are generally pressed by the scarcity of money and time (reflected most clearly by the absence of sufficient staff to perform the multiple duties of both business and substance). Conservation NGOs rely heavily on private philanthropy; even the membership groups, which comprise three-quarters of those surveyed, rely more upon charity than dues for their support, though both sources of income are critical. Their most important charitable gifts probably come from the members themselves. This heavy reliance on philanthropy means, among other things, that most NGOs will probably persist in their tendency to "educate" more than "activate." They must provide information and analysis, and not overtly deliver votes to conservationist candidates or ballot issues.

About one-third to one-half of the organizations report that they need many of the basic tools of management in order to make their organizations work better. By their own account, the leaders say their groups could use management audits, written job descriptions

TABLE 35   Staff Questionnaire—Staff Leaders' Attitudes on Negative and Critical Statements About the Conservation Movement

	Strongly Disagree 1	Disagree 2	Agree 3	Strongly Agree 4	Mean
Most minority and poor rural Americans see little in the conservation message that speaks to them.	2%	11%	46%	41%	3.35
The administrative, management, and fund-raising demands of conservation organizations distract their staff from what they ought to be doing—namely, the substantive work of the organization.	3%	25%	36%	37%	3.07
The conservation movement is fragmented, territorial, and uncommunicative.	5%	38%	46%	11%	2.63
National conservation organizations are generally unsupportive of unaffiliated local conservation groups.	8%	40%	39%	14%	2.57
U.S. conservation leaders are more reactive than farsighted; they lack real vision or originality.	6%	43%	41%	10%	2.54
The U.S. conservation movement is generally bereft of new ideas; it is mired in a sort of business-as-usual approach to environmental problems.	8%	48%	36%	8%	2.46

National conservation organizations have become altogether too "professional"; they have come to resemble the corporations they purport to fight.	12%	55%	26%	9%	2.31
There is no longer any such thing as "the conservation movement," since the word *movement* implies the unified effort of many people to achieve specific goals.	10%	58%	28%	5%	2.27
The contention that organizational demands distract conservationists from substantive effort is just another way of saying that the organizations are poorly managed.	15%	49%	32%	4%	2.26
National conservation groups are actually detrimental to local efforts, because they soak up funds that end up having little local effect.	20%	50%	21%	9%	2.20
Local conservation groups where I live are generally unsupportive of national conservation organizations.	12%	67%	21%	0%	2.09

TABLE 36 Staff Questionnaire—Staff Leaders' Attitudes on Normative and Noncritical Statements About the Conservation Movement

	Strongly Disagree 1	Disagree 2	Agree 3	Strongly Agree 4	Mean
Funding is insufficient to meet the enormous challenges faced by conservationists worldwide.	0%	5%	38%	57%	3.50
Funding is insufficient to meet the challenges faced by local conservationists in my area of the country.	0%	7%	37%	55%	3.47
The professional staffs of conservation organizations are overworked and undersupported.	1%	15%	41%	43%	3.26
National conservation groups should expand their field programs at the local level.	3%	19%	48%	22%	2.96
Leadership and the leading ideas of conservation have tended to emerge primarily from the nonacademic, nonprofit world.	3%	25%	48%	24%	2.94
The large number of conservation groups and their millions of supporters are proof that the cause of conservation has never been healthier than it is today.	3%	26%	54%	17%	2.85
The real leadership in conservation lies at the grass roots, not among the professional organizations.	6%	49%	29%	16%	2.54

for their board members and volunteers, a formal process to evaluate the chief executive officer, written long-range operating plans, in-service professional training programs for their staff, and retirement plans so that they and their staff can be thinking more seriously about their work as a lifelong career. These tools—with the exception of retirement plans—are all readily achievable at low cost by most NGOs. It merely requires the time, the effort, a little money, and sometimes the proper guidance in order to develop them.

But there are also plenty of internal resources that most staff leaders would find extremely useful, and these are not so easily achieved. The staff leaders' top choices would be for financial endowments to help ease the chronic burden of fund-raising, much larger budgets, improved computer capabilities, and new staff to help with fund-raising. But they also report that several other kinds of resources would be useful as well: greater access to information; help with strategic planning; new staff to manage projects and programs, run field offices, assist with administration, and perform research; training for board members and volunteers; in-house training for staff; a better office environment; and an organizational evaluation performed by the members. Most of these require the marshaling of new sources of funds and a degree of professional execution that seems to lie beyond the capabilities of many organizations. Yet small conservation NGOs all around the country have sometimes managed to acquire most of these resources, primarily because their leaders at some point insisted on them. They are *not* beyond the grasp of most conservation groups, but developing them takes a very concerted effort—in many cases tantamount to the efforts made on behalf of the substantive issues. Many leaders we encountered agree that such efforts at building their organizations need not distract them from their main purpose but, indeed, if pursued strategically, can greatly enhance their overall effectiveness.

The data presented so far also demonstrate that leaders wish to reach much more outside of their own organizations. Three-quarters or more of them would find usefulness in a variety of new, external opportunities. They would seize the opportunity to discuss issues, programs, and management with other NGO leaders, as well as recognized experts in natural resource policy. They would participate in structured forums with lawmakers, industry leaders, and regulators, and they would use an ongoing leadership development program designed specifically for conservationists. But, again, these opportunities for more external resources come at a cost; most of them would work (or work much better) if they came with the money to establish and maintain them. And at the very least, they would require some reallocation of the leaders' time—a resource at least as scarce as dollars for most of the movement's organizations.

NGO staff leaders report that among the factors that would make their work more rewarding, greater board and membership involvement would be at the top of their list. But they also long for opportunities that would enhance their own sense of personal growth. Simply having more time to themselves, away from the pressure of issues and administrative demands, would help. Some of the leaders apparently long for the opportunity to take sabbaticals or other forms of leave, yet these are practically unheard of among the conservation NGOs.

The organizations surveyed tend to be fairly small nonprofit enterprises, though there are a few giants among them. Most run on less than half a million dollars per year and have fewer than a dozen staff members. Three-quarters of them are membership-based but still rely very heavily on charitable contributions—from members and foundations, primarily—for a large portion of their support. Little wonder, given that the median size of their memberships is only 3,500—hardly a sufficient number to support more than the barest minimum of professional activity.

Overall, NGOs cover a very broad range of issues. They are most likely to be involved with fish and wildlife, public lands and parks management, private land stewardship, or waste management. They tend to be more educational than overtly political in their approach. Their leaders are very much consumed by the managerial, administrative, and fund-raising aspects of the organization, with far less time and attention paid to substantive and outreach activities.

Many of these organizations, though substantial institutions in their region of operation and perhaps highly effective, nonetheless appear to be very precariously perched. They are not likely to have endowments large enough to sustain them on an ongoing basis; their efforts to acquire large numbers of new members are likely to be undercapitalized. Thus, they depend on annual (in actuality, perpetual) fund-raising campaigns to see them through each year. Given the problems they set out to solve, most are grossly under-supported. They have not yet achieved the institutional status that would give them greater security and financial resiliency.

Yet many conservation and environmental organizations have achieved greater security and resiliency. The differences between the haves and the have-nots are quite telling. We shall now turn to an examination of those differences to find clues to the needs of leaders and their organizations throughout the movement.

Significant Differences Among Staffed Conservation Groups

The size and geographical scope of conservation groups are the variables that reveal the most important differences in the needs and attitudes of the leaders surveyed and the demands that their organizations place on them. These variables are much more important to most aspects of leadership and management than the philosophical orientation of the groups (conservationist, environ-mentalist, preservationist, or educational), the issues they address, or the strategies and tactics they use to pursue their goals.

SIZE—THE MOST IMPORTANT PARAMETER. Thirty-two per-cent of the organizations surveyed are large nonprofit organizations according to the parameters devised by management consultant Jonathan Cook.[1] Cook suggests that a nonprofit organization is large if it possesses one or more of the following:

- An annual budget of $1 million or higher.
- A staff of thirty or more full-time professionals.
- An endowment sufficient to sustain the organization at its cur-rent level of activity on an ongoing basis.

Cook maintains that for nonprofit organizations in the United States, some of the most crucial differences in organization lead-ership and management revolve primarily around the size of the organization. Large groups achieve the stability and permanence of standing institutions in which most tasks of management are delegated. Large organizations generally require managers with greater skills and experience, though on balance Cook concludes that they are easier to manage simply because they make fewer demands on their leaders.[2] They enjoy the benefits—and suffer the pitfalls—of an increased division of responsibility. They are sheltered from the chronic financial crises that afflict most small organizations, and their size allows them to pursue levels and kinds of outreach that are unavailable to small groups. Still, they suffer from what Peter Drucker has called "tendencies toward ineffectiveness":[3] They are often unable to act quickly in response to opportunities and problems; they become "fossilized" as a result of the special hold of some internal constituency; they grow to exist for the sake of their own prosperity instead of the needs of their members or clients; they spend money inefficiently due to the absence of market pressure; and they try to "grab all of the turf and do everything," instead of concentrating on what they can actually accomplish.[4]

Conversely, most small organizations remain in a perpetual state of instability. They struggle continually with finances, high levels of staff and volunteer turnover, and often the inability to achieve a consistent organizational focus. They tend to perform technical management functions poorly due to their leaders' lack of skill and experience.[5] They have special—and usually fatal—difficulties with strategic planning; their leaders often scoff at the very notion of "good management," associating it with many of the world's evils. Nevertheless, they can be highly effective organizations, responding quickly to opportunities and problems, concentrating their resources on substantive activities, and spending little on maintenance, management, and administration. Yet over time, Cook insists, size for most organizations becomes the key factor in their survival: Small groups either grow and "graduate" (or merge) into institutions or they collapse. In any sector of nonprofit enterprise, there are dozens, sometimes hundreds, of defunct or nearly defunct organizations for each surviving institution.

Most organizations in our sample do not qualify as large organizations according to any of Cook's parameters. Sixty-nine percent of them have budgets under $1 million, but several are affiliates of larger, national groups and are thus more securely supported by a parent organization and more closely resemble large organizations. A few others with budgets of less than $1 million probably possess sustaining endowments, but the questionnaire did not try to determine which groups are sustained by endowments and which are not. We thus did not use this parameter as a measure of organizations in the sample. Staff size among the organizations also proved to be a troublesome measure. Several groups included full-time contractors as professional staff; others had trouble differentiating between professional and nonprofessional staff, since so many conservation staffers perform such a wide range of roles (for example, the CEO is sometimes also the office manager). Still others are able to use volunteers in ways that are tantamount to the use of paid, professional staff. We also found that given the use of funds among some conservation organizations—especially those involved in the acquisition or management of private lands—several groups in our sample use very few professional staff yet possess multimillion-dollar annual budgets. As we looked for correlations between staff size and budget among conservation groups, we found that a staff of around twelve professionals correlated best with the $1 million cutoff: 32 percent of the groups had budgets of $1 million or more, irrespective of staff size; 35 percent had budgets in the millions as well as twelve or more staff members. Since annual budgets provided less ambiguous data than staff size, we accepted the $1 million cutoff as our principal measurement of size.

We hypothesized that the large organizations in the sample were most likely to have an international-national scope of operations, while the small groups would tend to be regional, state, or local. In fact, size and geographical scope correlated as we expected for the more locally focused groups, but not for the international-national groups. Exactly half of the international-national organizations are large, while over 80 percent of the state-regional-local groups are small. With respect to the philosophical orientation of the organizations, we found that organizations describing themselves as conservationist tended to be large, while the majority of environmentalist-preservationist and educational groups were small. (Since so few organizations billed themselves as preservationist, and those so closely resembled environmentalist groups in most every respect, we combined the two under the single label of environmentalist). The advanced age of many conservationist organizations might be the answer to why the majority of them are large: The conservation movement per se has been in existence much longer than the environmental movement. If Cook's theory on age and size is correct, most true conservation groups should by now be either large or defunct.

Table 37 summarizes the findings on organizational size as a function of both geographical scope and philosophical orientation.

Analysis of the professionals' data revealed many statistically significant differences between large and small conservation NGOs, and some significant differences between the international-national groups (INs) and the state-regional-local groups (SLs). In a few instances, significant differences also arose according to the philosophical orientation of the groups.

SOURCES OF FUNDS. In their acquisition of funds, the small organizations are significantly more reliant on membership dues and foundation grants for their support. Conversely, the large organizations receive significantly greater percentages of their funding from federal grants and contracts, the sale of goods, and corporate gifts (though corporate funding remains very low for all). Table 38 summarizes these findings.

When the membership-based organizations are isolated from the sample, significant differences in funding, though fewer in number, become even more apparent. The small membership-

TABLE 37   Size of Group According to Geographic Scope and Philosophical Orientation

	Large (annual budget over $1 million)	Small (annual budget under $1 million)	Percentage of Sample
Geographical Scope			
International-national	50%	50%	40%
State-regional-local	19%	81%	60%
Philosophical Orientation			
Conservationist	55%	45%	40%
Environmentalist (includes Preservationist)	38%	62%	34%
Educational	26%	18%	82%

TABLE 38   Significant Differences in Funding Sources According to
Size of Organization (All Organizations)

	Large ($1 million and over)	Small (under $1 million)	Significant Difference
Membership dues	21%	27%	yes
Individual contributions	19%	18%	no
Foundation grants	18%	24%	yes
Sale of goods	11%	6%	yes
Federal grants and contracts	7%	2%	yes
Corporate gifts	5%	2%	yes
User fees	3%	2%	no
Capital assets	3%	3%	no
Other, nongovernment contracts	3%	2%	no
State grants and contracts	2%	2%	no
Other sources	9%	11%	no

based groups are far more reliant on membership dues than their larger counterparts. Given that many of these groups operate from year to year on an extremely narrow financial margin, it is easy to see how critical membership support must be; yet few of the small groups possess well-developed programs for membership recruitment. A very large number of these groups report that their membership base has remained nearly stagnant for a decade or more. While their larger counterparts in the movement have learned how to capitalize on the burgeoning national interest in environmental issues and are gaining members, in some cases at an unprecedented pace, the small groups continue to stagnate. Their heavy reliance on a financial base that does not grow, or grows only very slightly, has enormous implications for their future. A large percentage of these groups make up for their lack of membership income by resorting to foundation grants, which, unlike the "hard money" that comes from individual supporters, are usually restricted to programs and projects of interest to the donors. The groups thus reduce their own capacity to pursue some issues that might be extremely significant to both their members and their arena of activity. We will return to this problem in chapter 5.

The large groups in general prove themselves to be more evenly diversified in their streams of income. They rely less on foundation grants and more on individual contributions than their smaller counterparts, though these differences are not statistically significant. Table 39 summarizes these data.

When the funding of INs and SLs is compared, a few interesting findings emerge. Although the small *membership* groups rely more heavily than the large groups on members' dues (see Table 39), the international-national membership organizations, which tend to be larger than the SLs, are significantly more reliant on membership dues than their state-regional-local counterparts (see Table 40). This finding alone is quite ambiguous, but a closer examination of the questionnaires reveals two likely reasons. First, the membership-based INs recruit members much more successfully than their state-regional-local counterparts, perhaps because they have greater appeal to potential members, who are contacted through the now-ubiquitous device of direct mail. Many state-regional-local groups are not located in areas where direct mail works so successfully and, in any event, fewer of them use it. Moreover, there are several very successful INs that are run almost entirely on membership support. For one reason or another, they do

TABLE 39   Significant Differences in Funding Sources According to Size of Organization (Membership Organizations Only)

	Large ($1 million and over)	Small (under $1 million)	Significant Difference
Membership dues	27%	35%	yes
Individual contributions	21%	17%	no
Foundation grants	16%	17%	no
Sale of goods	11%	7%	yes
Federal grants and contracts	4%	2%	no
Corporate gifts	5%	3%	yes
User fees	2%	2%	no
Capital assets	4%	3%	no
Other, nongovernment contracts	1%	2%	no
State grants and contracts	1%	2%	no
Other sources	8%	10%	no

TABLE 40 Significant Differences in Funding Sources According to
Scope of Organization (Membership Organizations Only)

	International-National	State-Regional-Local	Significant Difference
Membership dues	37%	29%	yes
Individual contributions	17%	20%	no
Foundation grants	16%	17%	no
Sale of goods	9%	8%	no
Federal grants and contracts	4%	1%	yes
Corporate gifts	4%	4%	no
User fees	2%	2%	no
Capital assets	3%	3%	no
Other, nongovernment contracts	3%	1%	no
State grants and contracts	1%	2%	no
Other sources	4%	12%	yes

not or cannot accept charitable contributions. There are far fewer SLs that operate entirely on membership support. Second, among the *nonmembership* INs are many organizations that rely almost completely on private philanthropy and are highly successful grant seekers. The presence of these groups significantly reduces the degree of reliance on membership income when the nonmembership groups are not removed from the IN sample. These groups mask the great importance of membership income among the membership-based INs. Some organizations that claim an international-national focus can afford to be so reliant on membership income—or private philanthropy—because they are so good at acquiring it.

There were also significant differences in attitudes toward private foundations. Some of the interesting differences that arose depended on the philosophical orientation of the respondents. The environmentalists were apt to be significantly more critical of foundation officials' knowledge of the issues. While environmentalists, conservationists, and educators all agreed that foundation officials are "generally well informed," the environmentalists' agreement was weak. In the privacy of the interviews, many staff leaders were critical of foundations and of the restriction on activities that comes with heavy reliance on "soft" funding. Some conservation leaders would reject foundation philanthropy entirely if they could figure out a way for their organizations to live without it.

Other significant differences arose according to the size and scope of the responding organizations. Not surprisingly, the state-regional-local groups feel very strongly that foundations give too little money to local and state-based organizations. The international-national leaders tend to agree, but their agreement is comparatively weak. The same significant difference in opinion on the same question occurred between small and large organizations: Small groups tend to be far more critical of foundations' parsimony in the state-local arena. Interestingly, the small group leaders agreed much more strongly that foundations ought to give more funds for general support (though leaders of large organizations also agreed). As we shall see later, this finding is a clear reflection of the nature of the financial stresses that come with managing a small organization.

MANAGEMENT TOOLS AND STRATEGIES. As might be expected, the greatest differences between the large and small NGOs are found in their use of formal management tools. In nearly every area of organization management we found significant differences in the use of—or the claim that they lack but need—various management tools. When these differences are measured according to geographical scope, the significance is not nearly as pronounced, because half of the INs are themselves small organizations. Table 41 summarizes the significant differences in the use of management resources according to the size of the organization; Table 42 summarizes them according to the geographical scope of operations.

When we analyzed the organizations' use of various internal resources intended to increase their effectiveness, we found differences of similar significance. The large groups are roughly twice as likely to use the following: training programs for volunteers and staff; strategic planning; administrative, fund-raising, and programmatic staff as well as professional researchers; more and better information sources; staffed field programs and financial endowments. Table 43 summarizes these findings.

With respect to the use of various external resources, far fewer differences appear. As would be expected, the international-

TABLE 41 Significant Differences in the Use of Various Management Tools and Benefits According to Size of Organization (All Organizations)

	Large ($1 million and over)	Small (under $1 million)	Significant Difference
Staff retirement plan	83%	24%	yes
Evaluations of staff performance	80%	33%	yes
Written annual operating plan	75%	43%	yes
Written long-range operating plan	68%	26%	yes
Written policy for leaves and/or sabbaticals	62%	35%	yes
Evaluation of CEO	58%	23%	yes
Orientation program for new staff	57%	32%	yes
Grievance policy for staff	56%	28%	yes
Evaluations of programs	55%	23%	yes
Policy promoting in-service training	54%	36%	yes
Management audits	43%	21%	yes

TABLE 42 Significant Differences in the Use of Various Management Tools and Benefits According to Scope of Organization (All Organizations)

	International-National	State-Regional-Local	Significant Difference
Written annual operating plan	63%	51%	yes
Evaluations of staff performance	60%	47%	yes
Staff retirement plan	59%	40%	yes
Written long-range operating plan	53%	35%	yes
Evaluation of CEO	42%	30%	yes
Evaluations of programs	40%	34%	yes
Management audits	39%	23%	yes

TABLE 43   Significant Differences in the Use of Internal Management Resources According to Size of Organization (All Organizations)

	Large ($1 million and over)	Small (under $1 million)	Significant Difference
Fund-raising staff	65%	32%	yes
Strategic planning	61%	34%	yes
Administrative staff	59%	35%	yes
Programmatic staff	53%	34%	yes
In-house staff training program	53%	25%	yes
Staffed field program	53%	24%	yes
Training program for volunteers	49%	20%	yes
Financial endowment	44%	21%	yes
Professional researchers	42%	26%	yes
Improved access to information	39%	26%	yes

national organizations report that travel to other countries to compare environmental management programs is of far greater importance to them than it is to the state-regional-local groups. The INs are also nearly twice as likely to be engaged in ongoing discussions with natural resource policy experts. But the leaders of the SLs are far more likely to be involved in some form of ongoing leadership development program. That finding is somewhat surprising, given the scarcity of such programs in many parts of the country.

When asked to evaluate the usefulness of various external resources irrespective of whether each is currently being used, a few interesting differences arose. The SL leaders, as well as the leaders of the small groups, are significantly more interested in exchanging information on issues and programs with their peers than are the leaders of the INs and the large organizations. They are also significantly more interested in studying conservation history. The INs chief departure from their SL counterparts came, again, in their interest in international travel.

There are also many significant differences with respect to the importance of various strategies used to achieve organizational goals. The scope of operations provides the most telling differences here. The state-regional-local groups are significantly more involved in monitoring government agencies, training volunteers to represent their organizations, lobbying, and engaging in direct political action. The INs are significantly more likely to perform scientific research. This finding buttresses a contention made by several state and local leaders we interviewed but contested by others: namely, that the SLs are more involved in political work. We also found significant differences in strategies according to the philosophical orientation of the groups: The environmentalists were much more likely to organize coalitions, engage in direct political action, litigate, and lobby than their conservationist counterparts. Educational groups, as one might expect, reported being far less political than either the environmentalists or the conservationists. Table 44 presents these findings.

TABLE 44   Significant Differences in the Importance of Various Strategies Used to Achieve Organizational Goals, According to Scope and Orientation

	International-National	State-Regional-Local
Monitoring government agencies	likely	highest priority
Training volunteers to act	likely	very likely
Performing scientific research	very likely	unlikely
Lobbying	unlikely	very likely
Direct political action	very unlikely	likely
Direct litigation	lowest priority	unlikely
Influencing elections	lowest priority	very unlikely

	Conservationist	Environmentalist	Educational
Organizing coalitions	likely	very likely	likely
Performing scientific research	likely	unlikely	very likely
Lobbying	likely	very likely	very unlikely
Direct political action	unlikely	likely	very unlikely
Land-waterway management	likely	unlikely	very unlikely
Direct litigation	very unlikely	likely	lowest priority
Influencing elections	lowest priority	very unlikely	lowest priority

ATTITUDES. The staff leaders' attitudes toward the conservation movement varied somewhat according to the size of their organization. The significant differences tended to be merely in the strength of agreement or disagreement with various statements about the environmental movement. All in all, the staff leaders generally felt the same about most of the statements, with two exceptions: The leaders of the small organizations feel that their national counterparts have become too professional and corporate, and they believe that national organizations are detrimental to local conservation efforts because they capture funds that are never spent on local issues. These disagreements, as roughly measured as they were in the questionnaire data, go to the heart of a major problem facing American conservation leaders. As we shall see later, the leaders of various sectors and levels of the environmental movement have a very long way to go to stop the erosion that has begun to tear away at the foundations of the movement. Ironically, at a moment when conservation groups have gained unprecedented numbers of members and supporters, they have never been so distant from their own constituencies, or so confused about how to harness in effective new ways the mass of support that now exists. Conservation leaders are clearly unprepared for their own great success.

Chapter 3

Volunteer
Leadership

*The most effective leadership is community leadership—people
living among the problems and making time to correct them. The
future of the environmental movement must be in a symbiosis: local involvement and national leadership in identifying issues.
There is no substitute for a well-informed volunteer who is con-
vinced that he or she can have an effect on "the system."*

—*Utah volunteer*

*There is a critical lack of effective mentors. . . . One area your
study has missed the mark on is the whole area of burnout, nurturing and recognition of volunteers. Often, rescuing a trained, experienced volunteer is worth more than training twenty green
zealots to be just barely effective. Few staff professionals can grasp
the sense of isolation that the volunteer experiences in many regions
of this country.*

—*Oklahoma volunteer*

As we performed our research, it became clear that
long-term volunteers are often in the best position to report on the
health and effectiveness of leadership in all levels of the conservation-environmental movement. Like the paid professionals, volunteers also have needs that must be met in order to keep them active,
productive, and effective. But to what extent are the needs of

proven volunteers known or discussed throughout the conservation-environmental movement? How often do they receive specialized training, and how are they recognized for the countless hours they give? Where is volunteer recruitment and development working best and why? In order to begin to answer these and other questions, we turned our attention to the best volunteers we could find. Here is how we performed this portion of the investigation.

Method

Following the receipt and analysis of the staff questionnaires, the Leadership Project sought to identify distinguished volunteer leaders in all fifty states. While the emphasis of the project was on professional leadership among conservation NGOs, we also wanted to assess training and leadership development needs as they are perceived by effective, seasoned volunteers in all states. We were not looking for the views of the "average" volunteer, but of those who possess distinguished records of leadership. We wanted to assess the needs of volunteers who have been around for many years—who have found their way through a great many struggles, have seen the ebb and flow of numerous organizations, and now probably possess the knowledge and experience that come with greater commitment and longer service. As with the data on conservation professionals and their organizations, we wanted to see if the opinions and needs expressed by these outstanding volunteers could be communicated to funders and other support providers in such a way as to lead to the enhancement of volunteer effectiveness through strategic grant making, new training programs, or other resources tailored to the volunteer corps of the American conservation movement.

There were other questions we wanted to cover as well: To what extent do professionals and volunteers agree (or disagree) about the attributes of leadership? Are they in agreement on key opportunities for making the environmental movement more effective through conscious forms of leadership and organizational development? Do their views differ on the relationship between international-national organizations and those working at regional, state, and local levels? Are the professionals and volunteers gener-

ally unified in their views on their own movement? Do any perspectives peculiar to volunteers leap out, and might those be useful
to the increasingly influential corps of professional staffers? Do the
great volunteers found throughout the country tend to cluster
around any particular organizations, or are they diffuse? Do they
tend to operate through well-known, well-established organizations, or do most of them emerge from smaller, less prominent
groups of their own making? What is the magnitude of the all-
volunteer association compared with its professional-volunteer
counterparts?

To draw our sample of outstanding volunteer leaders, we consulted respondents to the staff questionnaires. Believing that paid
staffers were well equipped to help us identify key conservation
volunteers, we asked staff leaders across the country for the names
and addresses of the most effective conservation volunteers currently at work in their states (or regions of operations). We did not
ask staff to identify the great volunteers only within their own organizations, but to think as broadly as possible: Whose names or
faces come to mind, we asked, when you think of the truly outstanding conservation volunteers in your state or locale? Who are
the finest and most effective volunteers you have encountered, regardless of organizational affiliation? We hypothesized that in many
states, certain volunteers would probably crop up on everyone's list;
many of these leaders would be involved with several conservation
groups, serving on one or more boards of directors and in some
cases managing their own all-volunteer association.

Our hypothesis proved correct: In many states, a small handful
of individuals effectively define conservation volunteerism, and
they are known throughout the tightly knit environmental community. In other states, especially the more heavily populated ones, the
professionals' knowledge of great volunteers proved more diffuse;
still, staff leaders had no difficulty in providing us with candidates.
In addition to the prominent and well-known volunteers, we also
uncovered a number of quiet success stories—volunteers who stay
far from the limelight and whose great efforts on behalf of conservation (or some particular organization) are known only to a few. In
virtually no instance did a staff person's nomination list include only
volunteers from his or her own organization; indeed, most staffers

gave us at least three names, of which one or none came from the staffer's own group. We were confident that we had obtained a list of widely respected, highly effective conservation volunteers throughout the United States.

The list of volunteers grew to 305. Forty-eight states, as well as the District of Columbia, were represented. Table 45 presents the number of volunteers per state in the sample and the number who responded.

The surveying instrument used to query the volunteer leaders was a twelve-page mailed questionnaire (see appendix B). Completed questionnaires were returned by 180 respondents (59 percent of the sample). One hundred and sixty-one questionnaires were tabulated; the rest were unusable due either to the lateness of their arrival or their illegibility.

Questions fell into five categories: personal identification; description of organization; evaluation, needs, and attitudes; occupation, education, and training; and evaluation of the questionnaire itself. In recognition of the fact that, unlike paid professional staff, volunteers frequently serve numerous conservation groups simultaneously, we gave respondents the opportunity to identify a *primary* organization and to answer the questionnaire with respect to it. In the case of volunteers who do not act through any organization, we allowed for all organizational questions to be bypassed. Less than 5 percent of the respondents answered the questionnaire without reference to an organization—a fact that bears important evidence about the environmental movement: Contrary to some opinion, most volunteer conservationists, like the paid, professional staff of the movement, act through the offices of organizations.

Before we turn to the analysis of information from our volunteer leaders, it must be said that our sampling technique deliberately led to the identification of the very finest and most distinguished volunteer leaders, as perceived by professional staff among the NGOs. The data we are about to reveal therefore are not meant to represent the average or normal conservation volunteer, but rather the distinguished volunteer leaders who are working across the United States. We designed the questionnaire so that respondents were able to identify their primary organization as accurately as possible. Thus, for example, if a given volunteer in Florida works

TABLE 45 Volunteers' Questionnaire Sample—Number of Volunteers
Sampled in Each State and Number Responding to
Questionnaire

	Number in Sample	Number Responding
Alabama	6	2
Alaska	7	2
Arizona	8	5
Arkansas	9	5
California	8	3
Colorado	9	6
Connecticut	6	3
Delaware	1	1
District of Columbia	5	3
Florida	3	1
Georgia	4	2
Hawaii	6	1
Idaho	6	6
Illinois	7	3
Indiana	7	4
Iowa	5	3
Kansas	3	2
Kentucky	9	4
Louisiana	11	6
Maine	5	4
Maryland	10	7
Massachusetts	8	5
Michigan	7	4
Minnesota	6	5
Mississippi	0	0
Missouri	7	3
Montana	10	6
Nebraska	9	4
Nevada	5	2
New Hampshire	2	2
New Jersey	6	3
New Mexico	8	4
New York	3	1
North Carolina	5	2
North Dakota	4	3
Ohio	7	6
Oklahoma	11	6
Oregon	4	3

TABLE 45 *(continued)*

	Number in Sample	Number Responding
Pennsylvania	6	6
Rhode Island	5	4
South Carolina	6	4
South Dakota	0	0
Tennessee	8	3
Texas	5	3
Utah	5	4
Vermont	4	3
Virginia	7	5
Washington	10	7
West Virginia	3	1
Wisconsin	4	4
Wyoming	5	4
Totals	305	180

on behalf of a local Sierra Club chapter and has little or no role in the affairs of the national organization, the questionnaire allowed him or her to respond relative to the local chapter. We found great variation in chapters and affiliates of national organizations according to data recovered from the questionnaires and interviews. For example, state affiliates of the National Wildlife Federation are virtually independent organizations with their own memberships and structures of governance; state chapters of The Nature Conservancy, on the other hand, are much more closely tied to both the mission and operating structure of the national headquarters. Although The Nature Conservancy chapters have their own boards, they are much more tightly allied to the mission, goals, and implementation methods of The Nature Conservancy's headquarters. Some affiliates of national groups seem to work almost exclusively on local or statewide issues with little reference to the federal agenda of the parent organization. Others carry the parent's slate of national—or even international—issues into the local arena.

A Portrait of the Distinguished NGO Volunteer Leader

The "typical" volunteer queried through the questionnaire is a forty-five-year-old white male who serves on the board of at least one NGO conservation group. He is very highly educated, possessing at least one graduate degree as well as a bachelor's degree. Conservation is a passion and an avocation but not directly related to his career, which is in a professional or managerial occupation. He has never worked professionally for a conservation agency or organization, and does not want to.

His interest in conservation is lifelong, probably going back to childhood. He inherited a love of nature from his family, or perhaps a teacher (or mentor) early in his life introduced him to the natural world, and he has been devoted to its protection ever since. Like his professional counterparts in the NGOs, he did not get involved in conservation groups because of political motives or the desire for power, but rather from a deeply felt commitment to ensuring that future generations will be able to enjoy the natural world and live without fear of environmental harm. His work in conservation is driven primarily by a personal ethic; his activism and advocacy are means, not ends.

Indeed, to the extent that his advocacy has taken a political course, he reports on having been, at least initially, a reluctant participant. He is sometimes astonished that a simple love of nature has carried his voice into the halls of Congress or the state legislature. But there is nothing reluctant about him now: He is a fighter, committed to environmental reform and willing to take the issues into any arena. Nevertheless, he is not an ideologue; his voice is reasoned, his approach respectful of others and their opinions, even when they are radically at odds with his own. Increasingly, he is drawn to "cooperative" approaches; he sees merit in building relationships with both policymakers and resource developers.

The organization (or field office) that he lists as his primary affiliate is a membership-based entity with around 2,000 members and an annual budget of $80,000. It is not an affiliate of a larger organization, but an independent, home-grown entity. It is most likely environmentalist in outlook (as distinguished from conservationist, preservationist, or educational), and its primary geographic scope of operations is the state or region in which it is located. Because this small organization has so few staff (one full-time and one part-time) and so little money, the volunteers who support it serve in many positions that are occupied by staff in larger organizations. Volunteers act not only as board members and advisors to the staff, but also as fund-raisers, community organizers, lobbyists, office assistants, and assistants in substantive programs. These volunteers clearly are part of the "human capital" that must be employed in order for an environmental agenda to advance throughout the states.

The range of issues addressed by this small organization most likely include water quality and the protection of waterways, fish and wildlife, and perhaps public lands management (including parks and other natural areas). It is very unlikely that the organization addresses overpopulation, marine conservation, mining law, or agriculture. Like its NGO counterparts with more staff and larger budgets, this little group relies most heavily on a strategy of public education in order to accomplish its objectives: It uses various media, including its own publications, to gain support for the issues it addresses. Other very important strategies include lobbying, monitoring government agencies, and training volunteers to act on behalf of the organization. It is very unlikely to be involved in ballot initiatives and referenda, research in environmental ethics, mediation, or directly influencing the election of public officials.

Money and time are the key obstacles facing the group, according to its volunteer leader. His first choices among a list of needed internal resources include a financial endowment and a larger budget. These vastly exceed all other needs he expresses. But his other selections from the wish list of new resources form an interesting pattern: After money, he tends to want assistance with strategic planning, better access to information, and greater data processing capabilities. The lower-priority needs of the organization, according to the leader, relate to training and staffing. He would choose various forms of training (leadership training for board and volunteers, for example) ahead of hiring staff.

The volunteer leader reports that the greatest strengths of his organization lie in the relations among people. He gives his group very high marks for board-staff relations, staff-volunteer relations, and relations among or between the members of the staff (not surprising, given the average staff size of two). The low marks he gives his organization are related to money, planning, and evaluation. The leader says that his group has poorly diversified income (a threat to organizational stability) and a weak apparatus both for raising funds and for evaluating effectiveness. He also reports that planning, while fairly effective, could be much improved.

Our composite volunteer is keen on in-service training to enhance his own effectiveness. Over the past two years, his organization has obtained specialized training for him, most likely in communications, fund-raising, and board member effectiveness. He reports that training was a very positive experience, with good results for himself and his organization. And there are other training and enhancement opportunities he would enjoy if they were available and affordable. Among a list of new opportunities, he favors those that would enhance his relations with lawmakers, increase understanding between environmentalists and developers, and sharpen his own knowledge of natural resource policy-making. It is clear that he desires greater levels and more kinds of cooperation among the various people who make decisions affecting environmental quality. He tends not to favor sabbaticals or fellowships to refresh himself and put new arrows into his own quiver, but clearly prefers more activist, "kinetic" programs where he can learn and have an impact simultaneously.

His broad attitudes about the conservation-environmental movement are very positive, yet he sees problems within the movement that need to be addressed by the greater body of activist organizations. While he definitely perceives a "gulf" between national and local groups, he feels very strongly that the two camps support one another. The gulf he reports seeing seems to him to be inevitable—a natural occurrence related to the differing motives and constituencies of national and local (or state-based) organizations. Among his other strong opinions are the following: funding is insufficient at all levels of conservation activity, from local to international; minorities and the poor in the United States see little of interest in the conservation message; NGO staff are overworked and undersupported; and national organizations ought to expand their programs at the local level.

Like the NGO staffers with whom he works, our experienced

volunteer leader feels that conservation and environmental groups are woefully undersupported; that the ideals and strategies promoting good conservation have not reached deeply enough into society; and that advocacy and activism must now be taken to new fronts—into the corporate boardroom, the local halls of policy, and the schools and churches. He remains optimistic that movement leaders will be able to instill a deeper commitment to conservation and environmental protection in all levels of society.

The Key Issues of Management and Leadership—Organizations Represented in the Sample

The foregoing portrays the mean and median responses from our corps of volunteers, expressed through a composite portrait created from the data. But, again, the range of responses was, in many instances, much more telling than the averages. The volunteers we surveyed, and the organizations they represent, are in some ways even more diverse than the professionals and their groups. Nearly half of our sample represents organizations with no paid staff and fewer than 1,000 members; nearly 30 percent of them possess budgets of under $10,000 per year; and nearly 50 percent have budgets below $50,000. For the most part, these very small groups serve as vehicles of expression for a single outstanding leader or a small cadre of volunteers who operate locally. Nearly one-fourth of our respondents described their job within the organization as chief executive officer (a title normally reserved for staff) rather than chairperson, board member, or some other role implying a clear division of management between a governing body and a staff. If a volunteer is the chief executive, and there are no paid staff, then the organization most likely exhibits a very simple structure. Indeed, many of these outstanding volunteer leaders *are* the staff of their organizations, and probably also the founders. It is their personal energy that makes these organizations run—and for all the work that this entails, these great spirits accept no compensation.

At the other end of the spectrum, about one-fifth of the organizations represented by these volunteer leaders have budgets of over $500,000, memberships exceeding 10,000, and ten or more full-time staff members. In these settings, the volunteers we surveyed are almost certainly board members and serve (or have served) as the chairperson. The needs of these moderate-sized nonprofit corporations are, of course, quite different from the needs of an all-volunteer group with no office and a shoestring budget. In the larger, more institutionalized organization, the volunteer does not act in lieu of a staff, but rather manages the staff; he is probably involved in decisions to hire and fire professional-level executive officers. He helps evaluate the staff's performance as a function of the executive's performance and attends to a much higher degree of fiduciary responsibility. Chances are that the management roles and lines of authority within the organization are far more structured and complex than they are in an all-volunteer group managed by an unpaid CEO. There are payrolls to be met, programs to manage, staff to oversee, audits to perform. It is a boardroom organization, not a kitchen-table group. Board leaders are probably further from the daily work of running the group, but they are no less liable if things go awry. If these organizations are managed well, volunteer leaders can resign without fear of having them collapse; for many of the founder-leaders of the all-volunteer associations, this does not hold true.

Between these two poles lie the remainder of the volunteer leaders and their organizations—about one-third of the groups. They have memberships ranging from 1,000 to 10,000, one to ten full-time staff members, and budgets between $50,000 and $500,000.

Despite these many important differences, however, our analyses of significant differences according to the organization's size, philosophical orientation, and geographical focus revealed far fewer differences than we found among the professionals. The volunteers we surveyed, regardless of where they labor, generally agree on most attributes of leadership and management that could improve their own and their organization's effectiveness.

Tables 46 through 50 summarize the data on the budget, membership, and staff size of the organizations or field offices represented in the volunteers' data base.

TABLE 46 Volunteers' Questionnaire—Annual Budget of
Organizations or Field Offices

	Number of Organizations	Percentage of Total
Under $1,000	8	7%
$1,001 to $10,000	26	22%
$10,001 to $50,000	23	19%
$50,001 to $100,000	9	8%
$100,001 to $300,000	14	12%
$300,001 to $500,000	14	12%
$500,001 to $1 million	7	6%
Over $1 million	18	15%
Median Annual Budget = $80,000		

TABLE 47 Volunteers' Questionnaire—Does Organization or Field
Office Have Dues-Paying Membership?

	Number of Organizations	Percentage of Total
Yes	134	86%
No	22	14%

TABLE 48 Volunteers' Questionnaire—Number of Dues-Paying
Members in Organization or Field Offices

	Number of Organizations	Percentage of Total
1,000 or fewer	55	46%
1,001 to 5,000	28	23%
5,001 to 10,000	13	11%
10,001 to 20,000	9	8%
20,001 to 100,000	6	5%
Over 100,000	9	8%
Median Number of Members = 2,000		

TABLE 49 Volunteers' Questionnaire—Number of Full-time, Paid Staff
in Organization or Field Offices

	Number of Organizations	Percentage of Total
0	68	47%
1–5	41	28%
6–10	13	9%
11–20	14	10%
21–100	5	3%
Over 100	4	3%
Median Number of Full-time, Paid Staff = 1		

TABLE 50 Volunteers' Questionnaire—Number of Part-time, Paid Staff
in Organization or Field Office

	Number of Organizations	Percentage of Total
	61	45%
1–5	64	48%
6–10	2	2%
11–20	6	4%
21–60	3	2%
Median Number of Part-time, Paid Staff = 1		

The types of organizations (Table 51) also vary widely. A slight majority (51 percent) are independent local, state, or regional groups and coalitions that are not affiliated with larger national or international organizations. Also strongly represented are international-national groups (38 percent), the great majority of which have local chapters or field offices. The remaining 11 percent of the organizations describe themselves as trade associations.

As to their geographical focus, most of the organizations (58 percent) are regional, state, or local; 38 percent are national or international; and 4 percent answered the question in a manner that did not permit classification. Table 52 summarizes these data.

Among the international-national groups represented, four or-

TABLE 51   Volunteers' Questionnaire—Type of Organization

	Number of Organizations	Percentage of Total
International-national with chapters or field offices	55	35%
International-national without chapters or field offices	5	3%
Independent regional or state-based	42	27%
Coalition	19	12%
Local	19	12%
Trade association	17	11%

TABLE 52   Volunteers' Questionnaire—Geographical Scope of Organization

	Number of Organizations	Percentage of Total
International	27	17%
National	33	21%
Regional	19	12%
State	57	36%
Local	15	10%
Other	6	4%

ganizations dominate the sample: the Sierra Club (13 percent of all respondents), the Audubon Society (11 percent), The Nature Conservancy (6 percent), and affiliates of the National Wildlife Federation (4 percent). Given that knowledgeable staff leaders from the greatest possible variety of organizations in all fifty states provided us with our sample, these are telling statistics. It would appear that these four groups are predominant among the national organizations in their ability to attract (or develop) outstanding local volunteer leaders across the country—at least from the point of view of the paid, professional staff at work in all fifty states. It must be noted that the staff leaders providing us with names of volunteers did not similarly represent these four organizations; indeed, no organizations or particular kinds of organizations were overrepresented among the staff we consulted for our list of volunteers.

The scarcity of volunteer leaders from international-national organizations without vigorous, nationwide field programs bears no reflection on the quality of volunteers among those organizations, but is a direct result of the sampling method. In our zeal to find volunteers in each state, we neglected to populate the sample with the able and dedicated volunteers who work on behalf of international-national groups without an enormous field presence. Indeed, a number of large, prominent national groups have no field offices at all; some have no memberships. This omission biases the data.

Most of the organizations were described as either environmentalist (38 percent) or conservationist (36 percent) in orientation (see Table 53). As to their substantive focus—the issues or problems they address—the organizations were reported to be most strongly involved with water quality and waterway protection, fish and wildlife, public lands management, and the preservation of wilderness. The organizations in the sample were least likely to focus on zoological or botanical gardens, population control, or nuclear issues (see Table 54).

The emphasis on public lands management (including wilderness areas) is an especially telling feature of the sample. The older conservationist organizations, it must be remembered, have very deep roots in the issue of public lands management—and not just the massive federal lands (one-third of the U.S. landmass) but also state lands and parklands managed by various levels of government. One could argue that the U.S. conservation-environmental movement virtually owes its origins to public lands issues. Moreover, the dominance of the federal lands presence among the western states

TABLE 53   Volunteers' Questionnaire—Philosophical Orientation of Organization

	Number of Organizations	Percentage of Total
Conservationist	54	36%
Preservationist	15	10%
Environmentalist	58	38%
Educational	25	16%

TABLE 54   Volunteers' Questionnaire—Focus of Organization (Issues and Programs)

	Unimportant 1	Somewhat Important 2	Very Important 3	Highest Priority 4	Mean
Water quality	4%	14%	41%	32%	3.10
Waterway protection	5%	17%	45%	32%	3.03
Fish and wildlife	8%	19%	39%	34%	2.99
Public lands management	10%	21%	32%	37%	2.95
Wilderness	15%	22%	37%	27%	2.76
Environmental education	11%	30%	36%	24%	2.72
Air quality	13%	32%	37%	18%	2.60
Private land preservation	25%	26%	22%	28%	2.52
Toxic waste management	20%	29%	29%	21%	2.51
Land-use planning	16%	39%	27%	18%	2.47
Energy conservation	30%	46%	19%	6%	2.00
Agriculture	29%	48%	20%	4%	1.99
Mining law and regulation	38%	31%	26%	5%	1.99
Marine conservation	55%	22%	14%	9%	1.77
Nuclear power or weapons	66%	26%	6%	2%	1.45
Population control	66%	26%	7%	2%	1.45
Zoological or botanical gardens	77%	18%	4%	1%	1.28

translates into an overwhelming tendency for conservationists in that region to be almost uniformly involved in public lands issues. Indeed, it's hard to find a group in the West that is not involved to some degree in those issues. The heavy emphasis on public lands management therefore does not express a bias in the sample toward western organizations; rather, it is a historical and geographical reality of the American conservation movement, no matter how strange it may seem to many urban environmentalists.

The strategies used by the volunteers' organizations tend to concentrate on broad public education campaigns and efforts aimed at influencing environmental policy. Educating the public through the use of various media is by far the most important strategy reported, with three-quarters of the leaders listing it as either very important or their highest priority. Next in importance come a variety of political tactics. Over 50 percent of the volunteers said that their organizations consider lobbying, monitoring government agencies, and engaging in direct political action to be either very important or of the highest priority. Also high on the list are environmental education (through encounters with nature), at 51 percent, and training other volunteers to represent the organization, at 58 percent. Table 55 summarizes the data on the importance of various strategies used to achieve goals and objectives.

In general, the organizations reported on by the volunteers tend to be more politically oriented than those reported on by the professional staff. We will return to this important difference later.

Volunteer Leaders and Their Needs

Sixty-two percent of the volunteer leaders surveyed are male (see Table 56). Well over half are between thirty-six and fifty-five years old, while a full 18 percent are over sixty-five (see Table 57). They tend to be older than the leaders in our staff survey and, indeed, there was a distinct shortage of young people among the volunteers' sample. The paucity of young volunteer leaders—only 7 percent are under thirty-five—might be more a result of the sampling method than a true reflection of conservation volunteers across the United States. Since our sampling was geared to identifying well-established volunteers with demonstrated records of accomplishment, we perhaps omitted numerous youthful volunteer leaders who simply have not been around long enough to have landed on the all-star list. It might also be the case that successful volunteers are such by virtue of having already established themselves in their vocations; these might be the ones with more time to commit to volunteer activities.

Still, some of the leaders we surveyed expressed dismay at the scarcity of younger volunteers and the difficulty of retaining staff who are often burdened by the lack of compensation. As one New Mexico volunteer put it:

TABLE 55 Volunteers' Questionnaire—Importance of Various
Strategies Used to Achieve Goals and Objectives

	Irrelevant to Us 1	Very Seldom Used 2	Sometimes Used 3	Very Important 4	Our Highest Priority 5	Mean
Educate through media	1%	3%	21%	53%	22%	3.91
Lobby lawmakers	7%	7%	23%	41%	22%	3.64
Monitor government agencies	5%	10%	19%	48%	18%	3.62
Train volunteers to act	5%	14%	24%	45%	13%	3.47
Educate through nature encounters	8%	11%	30%	34%	17%	3.41
Mobilize letter writing and political action	9%	16%	21%	38%	16%	3.37
Organize coalitions	11%	12%	37%	31%	9%	3.16
Perform and disseminate scientific research	25%	22%	25%	18%	10%	2.64
Litigate	22%	22%	28%	24%	3%	2.64
Manage land and waterways	41%	15%	12%	15%	18%	2.54
Perform and disseminate policy research	24%	28%	28%	13%	8%	2.52
Preserve land by purchase	47%	17%	11%	7%	18%	2.32
Influence elections	40%	22%	12%	21%	6%	2.30
Mediate conflicts	29%	29%	33%	8%	2%	2.27
Perform and disseminate ethical research	51%	29%	13%	5%	2%	1.78
Place initiatives and referenda on ballot	54%	23%	16%	6%	1%	1.76

We are getting older, and there are too few new and young folks getting involved. We (the experienced ones) need to impart our knowledge to the new generation. We also need to bridge the gap between environmental groups and minorities and just plain community folks. And we need to figure out how to keep "aging activists" in the movement by

TABLE 56 Volunteers' Questionnaire—Sex of Respondents

	Number	Percentage of Total
Male	99	61%
Female	62	39%

TABLE 57 Volunteers' Questionnaire—Age of Respondents

	Number	Percentage of Total
Under 35	11	7%
36–45	52	32%
46–55	41	26%
56–65	28	17%
Over 65	29	18%

paying them so they can be professional full-time and still have a family, a decent car and housing. We're starting to lose the older professionals who are going back to school or who leave for more lucrative positions (i.e., ones that provide decent pay, health insurance, maybe even a pension).

Such sentiments are widespread. Both the professional staff and the volunteers we surveyed expressed concern that the recruitment and conscious development of new leaders is haphazard. Moreover, there is concern that recruitment, to the extent that it occurs at all, increasingly focuses on staff positions for aspiring environmental professionals. While environmental job directories now exist both nationally and within various regions, some leaders complain that there is far less attention paid to advising would-be volunteers on the choices available to them.

Indeed, a strikingly large number of the volunteers (27 percent) expressed an interest in becoming paid, professional staff. Many commented that if they could find a way to make a smooth transition into paid employment in the environmental movement—without enormous sacrifice—they would do so. Several suggested that one way to resolve the recruitment dilemma is precisely by having volunteers "graduate" into professional work within their organizations: With their knowledge of and sensitivity to the needs of aspiring volunteers, these leaders felt that they themselves would make ideal staffers for membership organizations. Several of the volunteers who aspire to become paid staff report that their educational backgrounds are deficient for the job, but for the great majority of the volunteers surveyed, educational attainment is far from lacking (see Table 58). Indeed, 71 percent of volunteers now work in professional or managerial occupations (see Table 59). Presumably, these highly skilled people would make excellent professional environmentalists if they were willing to change occupations.

Thirty-one percent said that at one time or another they had worked professionally in conversation. Of those, half had worked for NGOs, the rest in conservation or environmental agencies of federal, state, or local governments. By and large, however, the majority of these distinguished volunteers seem satisfied with their current roles and status and would not change them. Indeed, many wrote in comments expressing their belief that they are more effec-

TABLE 58 Volunteers' Questionnaire—Highest Educational Level of Respondents

	Number of Respondents	Percentage of Total
Bachelor's degree	127	79%
Master's degree	57	35%
Doctorate (or professional) degree	29	18%

TABLE 59 Volunteers' Questionnaire—Occupation of Respondents

	Number of Respondents	Percentage of Total
Professional	92	57%
Managerial	23	14%
Retired	22	14%
Technical	10	6%
Unemployed	6	4%
Skilled Labor	4	3%
Other	4	3%

tive as volunteers than they could ever be as paid, professional staff. As volunteers, they can attend less to the daily demands of running an organization and more to the substantive tasks at hand. Most of them are clearly unwilling to trade places with the professionals in their movement.

Organizational Evaluations

As is the case with the professionals, it is difficult to separate the volunteers' needs from the needs of their organizations: They are strongly identified with the groups to which they belong. For many, the organization seems like a personal appendage; it is not something they objectify or abstract, but rather a very personal passion. When these volunteers took time to analyze their organizations, their comments often indicated that they were analyzing themselves about as much as the organization.

It is most interesting to compare their organizational evaluations with those of the professionals. While the professionals told us repeatedly that they were troubled with board-staff relations—with the lack of board member motivation, the board's failure (or refusal) to evaluate its CEOs, and the lack of clarity in the board's expectations of staff—the volunteers from staffed organizations (about 60 percent of whom are board members) reported that their relations with the staff were their organization's strongest attribute. Three-fourths of them said that staff-volunteer, staff-board, and interstaff relations are either very good or excellent. Seventy percent credited the board with its ability to stay within its boundaries of authority and not meddle with staff and other vital parts of the organization (a frequent complaint of staff members).

Indeed, among a list of organizational attributes ranging from these personnel matters to planning and evaluation to fund-raising and diversity of income, the volunteers were collectively positive in their overall evaluations. They do, however, report fairly serious problems in the following areas: the diversification of organizational income (36 percent said it was a serious or severe problem), the use of tools of evaluation, the organization's fund-raising ability, and the effectiveness of planning. In all of these areas, 70 percent or more of the volunteers reported problems ranging from the need for improvement to serious or severe problems. Table 60 summarizes the volunteers' organizational evaluations.

Needed Resources: Internal

Like their professional counterparts, the volunteer leaders are overwhelmingly concerned with funding. Among various internal resources that might enhance their effectiveness, the volunteers were strongly inclined to choose the same resources that staff leaders chose: larger budgets and financial endowments. Certainly, this pronounced concern with financial health is not unique to conservation but is ubiquitous throughout the nonprofit sector, and especially the social-change sector. It does, however, underscore the magnitude of concern among seasoned conservationists who have witnessed the disabilities caused by the lack of money. This concern should not be dismissed or diminished merely because it is the ubiquitous lament of the not-for-profit (and indeed much of the for-profit) sector. Conservationists at all levels can do a much better job of fund-raising and making their organizations more secure financially. The volunteers we surveyed were very aware of how small their organizations are; many complain that the issues they face simply demand a greater magnitude of effort, which they are unable to provide. Money is thus their foremost concern. We will return to this theme in chapter 4.

Other internal resources ranking high on the volunteers' lists include better access to information, assistance with strategic planning, training for board members, hiring professional research staff, and improved computer capability. Table 61 summarizes the volunteers' selections among a list of internal resources. Table 62 summarizes their choices for the highest priority on the same list.

Needed Resources: External

Just as we did with the professional staff, we gave the volunteers a list of possible options for external resources that enhance their effectiveness and that of their organizations. The list ranged from personal options (sabbaticals and specialized training in such areas as natural resource policy, ecology, and environmental

TABLE 60 Volunteers' Questionnaire—Evaluation of Organizational Attributes

	Severe Problem 1	Serious Problem 2	Good but Needs Improvement 3	Very Good 4	Excellent 5	Mean
Board-staff relations	0%	4%	24%	33%	40%	4.08
Staff-volunteer relations	1%	3%	19%	43%	34%	4.06
Relations among staff	2%	3%	18%	44%	33%	4.02
Clarity of mission and goals	1%	4%	30%	37%	28%	3.88
Board's ability to stay within its boundaries	1%	6%	22%	47%	23%	3.85
Overall effectiveness of organization	0%	1%	45%	30%	23%	3.75
Effectiveness of management	0%	7%	49%	29%	15%	3.52
Effectiveness of strategies	0%	6%	59%	21%	14%	3.43
Board's ability to establish organizational policy	1%	10%	52%	27%	10%	3.36
Effectiveness of public communication	1%	10%	56%	27%	7%	3.30
Effectiveness of planning	0%	12%	59%	23%	6%	3.23
Organization's fund-raising ability	5%	21%	54%	12%	9%	2.99
Use of evaluation tools for programs and projects	1%	25%	58%	13%	3%	2.92
Diversification of income to enhance security	2%	34%	41%	14%	9%	2.92

TABLE 61 Volunteers' Questionnaire—Evaluation and Use of Various Internal Resources and Improvements

	Useless 1	Not Very Useful 2	Fairly Useful 3	Extremely Useful 4	Currently Used 5	Mean
Financial endowment	4%	4%	10%	64%	17%	3.67
Much larger budget	1%	4%	31%	71%	2%	3.65
Better access to information	1%	14%	31%	40%	14%	3.27
Assistance with strategic planning	4%	16%	27%	35%	19%	3.15
Improved computer capability	4%	12%	25%	29%	30%	3.11
Hiring professional researchers	9%	15%	25%	40%	12%	3.09
Training for board members	6%	17%	33%	31%	13%	3.03
In-house staff training program	21%	21%	23%	13%	22%	2.95
Training for volunteers	4%	18%	25%	26%	26%	2.94
Training in lobbying	11%	10%	25%	26%	28%	2.92
Evaluation of organization by the membership	16%	24%	29%	19%	13%	2.89
Hiring fund-raising staff	13%	15%	16%	31%	26%	2.87
Staffed field program	13%	17%	18%	19%	33%	2.64
Hiring programmatic staff	18%	21%	16%	25%	21%	2.61
Training in mediation	18%	25%	27%	24%	7%	2.60
Hiring administrative staff	17%	19%	8%	25%	32%	2.58
Improved workplace	17%	16%	23%	13%	32%	2.45
Training in resolution of inter-personal conflicts for staff	19%	42%	24%	10%	4%	2.27

ethics) to opportunities for collaboration and cooperation (lawmakers' forums, planning sessions with industry leaders and regulators, and so on). The purpose of this menu of prospective activities was not to tie leaders' perceived needs to any specific solutions, but rather to assess in broad terms the kinds of resources that organizations might not be using and might find beneficial if they were available. We constructed this menu partly from oft-heard complaints of the isolation these leaders experience—the sense that they perform their work somehow divorced from enriching contact with other conservation leaders and decision makers, and far from opportunities for in-service training and refreshment. The numerous comments we received in addition to the quantifiable data suggested that we had asked a series of very meaningful questions for many volunteers and professional staff throughout the movement.

The volunteers appear to be most interested in opportunities for collaboration with lawmakers and industry leaders and regulators (though very few report on experiencing such collaborations to date). They seem less interested in designing and implementing collaborative strategies, not merely with other conservationists but with other key actors in the debate: agents of government and business. These opportunities take precedence over personal training, leaves and sabbaticals, and other forms of personal enhancement, however.

In the same menu of options, we also gave volunteers the opportunity to report on which of the activities they are already engaged in. Interestingly, the great majority of them do not take advantage of any of the external resources offered on the list. Unlike the paid professionals of the environmental movement, the volunteers tend not to involve themselves even in such efforts as "open discussions about issues, programs, and other matters of substance with staff and volunteers in other conservation organizations." The often-voiced complaint of isolation is no hollow complaint: There are apparently few opportunities even for the simplest forms of shoptalk with other environmental advocates. Some of the more structured opportunities listed in the menu are quite simply out of the question.

Tables 63 and 64 summarize the volunteers' selections of external resources, including their choices for the highest priority among them.

TABLE 62   Volunteers' Questionnaire—Highest Priority Among
Needed Internal Resources

	Number of Respondents	Percentage of Total
Financial endowment	33	23%
Much larger budget	32	22%
Assistance with strategic planning	11	8%
Training for board members	9	6%
Hiring administrative staff	8	6%
Hiring programmatic staff	7	5%
Training in mediation	7	5%
Hiring professional researchers	6	4%
Training for volunteers	5	4%
Better access to information	4	3%
Improved workplace	3	2%
Staffed field program	3	2%
Training in lobbying	2	1%
Evaluation of organization by the membership	2	1%
Hiring fund-raising staff	2	1%
In-house staff training program	1	1%
Improved computer capability	1	1%
Training in resolution of interpersonal conflicts for staff	0	0%

Attitudes

Volunteers are overwhelmingly positive in their attitudes toward the conservation-environmental movement; indeed, they are generally more positive and less self-critical than the professionals. Once again, their strongest opinions relate to funding: About 90 percent of them agree that too little money is available to meet the enormous challenges faced by conservationists working on global, as well as local, issues.

For the most part, their attitudes line up closely with those of their professional counterparts. Tables 65 and 66 summarize them.

Comparisons According to Size, Scope, and Geographic Orientation

With one outstanding exception, the volunteers' responses and attitudes showed few significant differences according to the size, geographical scope, or philosophical orientation of the organization. The exception was this: When we compared the volunteers' organizations according to size ("large" groups being those with budgets exceeding $1 million annually), we found numerous significant differences in their organizational evaluations. Volunteers from the "small" groups rated their organizations significantly lower in eight of fourteen attributes. Clearly, the volunteers from the small organizations see the need for much improvement in these eight areas. They are summarized in Table 67.

Comparisons with Responses from Professional Staff

Interesting and useful patterns emerge when we compare some of the volunteers' responses with the staff responses; indeed, in some areas we see a strong convergence of opinion, especially with respect to future opportunities for strengthening the leaders of the movement and their organizations.

Volunteers and professionals tend to agree on the usefulness of various internal resources that might be made available to them. Among their top six choices from a menu of eighteen, volunteers and professionals agreed on five, though their rankings varied slightly. Table 68 summarizes these overlapping priorities.

TABLE 63 Volunteers' Questionnaire—Evaluation and Use of Various External Resources

	Useless 1	Not Very Useful 2	Fairly Useful 3	Extremely Useful 4	Currently Used 5	Mean
Lawmakers' forum for legislators and conservation leaders	3%	9%	26%	54%	8%	3.42
Conservation planning forum with industry leaders and regulators	4%	13%	24%	49%	10%	3.32
Discussions with leading thinkers in resource policy	3%	10%	41%	42%	5%	3.28
Peer discussions on issues and programs	2%	4%	37%	28%	28%	3.28
Field studies with leading ecologists	3%	18%	35%	37%	7%	3.14
An ongoing leadership development program	6%	14%	35%	39%	5%	3.11
Discussions with leading thinkers in environmental ethics	7%	17%	34%	36%	5%	3.07

Peer discussions on management	4%	20%	34%	19%	23%	2.87
Greater access to professional journals	4%	21%	32%	18%	25%	2.84
Discussions with leading thinkers in conservation history	6%	32%	41%	19%	2%	2.75
Management discussions with leaders outside the conservation movement	7%	35%	37%	13%	9%	2.61
A fellowship in natural resource management	23%	27%	25%	25%	1%	2.52
A paid sabbatical	23%	29%	16%	30%	1%	2.52
A teaching sabbatical to share knowledge with students	25%	22%	32%	20%	2%	2.47
International travel to compare environmental management	15%	33%	25%	14%	13%	2.44
A program to study poverty in the U.S.	38%	46%	12%	4%	1%	1.82

TABLE 64 Volunteers' Questionnaire—Highest Priorities Among
Needed External Resources

	Number of Respondents	Percentage of Total
Conservation planning forum with indsutry leaders and regulators	25	16%
Lawmakers' forum for legislators and conservation leaders	25	16%
A paid sabbatical	16	10%
An ongoing leadership development program	14	9%
Peer discussions on issues and programs	11	7%
Field studies with leading ecologists	10	6%
Peer discussions on management	7	4%
Discussions with leading thinkers in environmental ethics	7	4%
Discussions with leading thinkers in resource policy	6	4%
International travel to compare environmental management	4	3%
A teaching sabbatical to share knowledge with students	3	2%
A fellowship in natural resource management	2	1%
Greater access to professional journals	0	0%
A program to study poverty in the U.S.	0	0%
Management discussions with leaders outside the conservation movement	0	0%
Discussions with leading thinkers in conservation history	0	0%

Those who provide management or leadership training support to the U.S. conservation movement should pay special attention to these remarkably similar responses: The professionals and the volunteers agree that they need the most assistance in the pursuit of funding, the establishment of endowments, the improvement of access to information, strategic planning, and better computer equipment. They perceive that they need these improvements ahead of hiring new staff or enhanced forms of training for staff, board, or volunteers. Clearly, their demands for more money, capital improvements, and greater financial stability cannot be met without enhanced training, especially in strategic planning; but efforts at in-service training which do not speak to the dire financial condition of most U.S. conservation groups will likely fall on deaf ears.

This is not to say that support providers should redouble offerings such as "fund-raising workshops" and other simpleminded, linear programs offering a financial panacea. Most of the leaders we surveyed and interviewed clearly do not need fund-raising tune-ups nearly as much as they need to rethink their organizations and the relationships within them. Few U.S. conservation groups are poised to raise much more money than they are currently raising, no matter how many fund-raising workshops they attend; practically none stands ready to achieve the financial goal that is clearly needed, no matter how out of reach it appears to their adherents: a tripling or quadrupling of their current budgets. Their problem is not a lack of knowledge about raising money; rather, it is a problem of organizational design. Most of the groups and their leaders can plan fairly effective strategies to "educate the public" or lobby the legislature or monitor the regulatory agencies, but they are woefully inept at planning for their own organizations to become successful businesses. They simply lack the kinds of people who can help them with this problem. Given their overwhelmingly negative attitudes about both business and money, they are not likely to rush out and recruit such assistance. This would take an act of courageous leadership. We will return to this theme in chapter 4.

With respect to their selections from the menu of external resources, the volunteers' choices again very closely paralleled those of their professional counterparts, as summarized in Table 69. These choices may suggest to support providers, especially funders, the kinds of activities that would be of greatest assistance to the future training of both professional and volunteer conservationists.

One area of stark disagreement between the volunteers and the professionals occurs over attitudes toward hiring staff. While professional staff leaders tend to want to increase and diversify staff

TABLE 65 Volunteers' Questionnaire—Volunteer Leaders' Attitudes on Negative and Critical Statements About the Conservation Movement

	Strongly Disagree 1	Disagree 2	Agree 3	Strongly Agree 4	Mean
Most minority and poor rural Americans see little in the conservation message that speaks to them.	1%	11%	54%	34%	3.21
The administrative, management, and fund-raising demands of conservation organizations distract their staff from what they ought to be doing— namely, the substantive work of the organization.	1%	29%	46%	24%	2.92
National conservation organizations have become altogether too "professional"; they have come to resemble the corporations they purport to fight.	5%	54%	32%	9%	2.43
The conservation movement is fragmented, territorial, and uncommunicative.	6%	52%	35%	7%	2.43
National conservation organizations are generally unsupportive of unaffiliated local conservation groups.	11%	50%	33%	7%	2.35

The U.S. conservation movement is generally bereft of new ideas; it is mired in a sort of business-as-usual approach to environmental problems.	8%	59%	27%	6%	2.31
U.S. conservation leaders are more reactive than farsighted; they lack real vision or originality.	11%	57%	25%	7%	2.29
The contention that organizational demands distract conservationists from substantive effort is just another way of saying that the organizations are poorly managed.	7%	67%	24%	2%	2.21
There is no longer any such thing as "the conservation movement," since the word *movement* implies the unified effort of many people to achieve specific goals.	15%	58%	26%	3%	2.15
Local conservation groups where I live are generally unsupportive of national conservation organizations.	16%	70%	13%	2%	2.01
National conservation groups are actually detrimental to local efforts, because they soak up funds that end up having little local effect.	20%	65%	14%	1%	1.95

TABLE 66 Volunteers' Questionnaire—Volunteer Leaders' Attitudes on Normative and Noncritical Statements About the Conservation Movement

	Strongly Disagree 1	Disagree 2	Agree 3	Strongly Agree 4	Mean
Funding is insufficient to meet the enormous challenges faced by conservationists worldwide.	1%	8%	36%	56%	3.46
Funding is insufficient to meet the challenges faced by local conservationists in my area of the country.	1%	11%	43%	46%	3.33
The professional staffs of conservation organizations are overworked and undersupported.	1%	11%	54%	34%	3.21
National conservation groups should expand their field programs at the local level.	0%	19%	58%	23%	3.05
The large number of conservation groups and their millions of supporters are proof that the cause of conservation has never been healthier than it is today.	2%	19%	60%	20%	2.97
Leadership and the leading ideas of conservation have tended to emerge primarily from the nonacademic, nonprofit world.	4%	25%	53%	18%	2.85
The real leadership in conservation lies at the grass roots, not among the professional organizations.	3%	43%	32%	23%	2.74

TABLE 67 Significant Differences in Organizational Evaluations
According to Size of Organization

Organizational Attribute	Mean Rating of Small Groups (annual budgets below $1 million)	Mean Rating of Large Groups (annual budgets above $1 million)
Effectiveness of strategies	3.30	3.92
Diversification of income to enhance security	2.71	3.64
Organization's fund-raising ability	2.87	3.59
Effectiveness of management	3.33	3.96
Overall effectiveness of organization	3.63	4.15
Board's ability to establish organizational policy	3.30	3.77
Use of evaluation tools for programs and projects	2.86	3.23
Effectiveness of planning	3.15	3.48

TABLE 68 Comparison of Volunteers' and Professionals' Leading
Choices Among Internal Resources

	Ranking by Volunteers	Ranking by Professionals
Financial endowment	1	1
Much larger budget	2	2
Better access to information	3	5
Assistance with strategic planning	4	4
Improved computer capability	5	3
Hiring professional researchers	6	12

with the addition of fund-raisers and programmatic specialists, the volunteers rate the hiring of all staff quite low, regardless of emphasis in prospective staff positions. Comments included with the questionnaires revealed that many volunteers clearly see the hiring of staff as either financially unattainable or undesirable. Many leaders in the all-volunteer groups indicated a preference for continuing without professional staff; they are not prepared to commit to the additional resources and restructuring that inevitably come with the hiring of staff. Moreover, some reported disastrous past experiences with staff and expressed the firm desire to avoid such problems not by finding better staff but by getting along without them. Indeed, there is some evidence of a strong antistaff bias among the volunteers.

Another notable difference between the volunteers' responses and the professionals' responses relates to the selection of organizational strategies to achieve their goals. While forms of direct political action rank high on the lists of both staffed and volunteer organizations, the volunteers tend to use more kinds of political action and rely on them to a substantially greater degree. The reasons are unclear. It may be that the volunteer sampling technique tended to select people who are more prominent and visible—and the greatest source of visibility among conservationists is usually the political arena. It may also be that organizations staffed by professionals, relying as so many do on tax-deductible contributions to augment their budgets, are more severely limited in their political activities by federal tax codes: For example, if they raise a greater proportion of their funds through private philanthropy, chances are that they lobby less. Another contributing factor might be the generally wider range of the staffed groups we surveyed. As noted ear-

TABLE 69   Comparison of Volunteers' and Professionals' Leading Choices Among External Resources

	Ranking by Volunteers	Ranking by Professionals
Lawmakers' forum for legislators and conservation leaders	1	3
Conservation planning forum with industry leaders and regulators	2	4
Discussions with leading thinkers in resource policy	3	2
Field studies with leading ecologists	4	11
An ongoing leadership development program	5	6
Discussions with leading thinkers in environmental ethics	6	8

lier, many of the staffed groups have no memberships and few volunteers affiliated with them. Policy research and environmental law centers, for example, tend to use volunteers far less, and in a much narrower field of capacities; they are virtually designed to rely more heavily on staff; and the activities of these groups, while hardly apolitical, often carefully avoid such tactics as lobbying and letter-writing campaigns. Moreover, the volunteers' sample included a higher proportion of membership-based organizations (85 percent versus 75 percent for the staffed groups). Membership groups tend to be more political.

It may also be the case that the volunteer organizations may simply attract more politically oriented people. Volunteerism in the environmental movement might be characterized by the desire to accomplish goals through direct political action, regardless of its consequences to one's chosen profession.

Whatever the reasons, the volunteer organizations appear to encourage political activism to a substantially greater degree but, like their staffed counterparts, they similarly eschew election campaigns and ballot issues (initiatives and referenda)—the latter due primarily to the fact that fewer than half the states use ballot issues to any substantial degree (indeed, many states forbid their use). Interestingly, international-national organizations in our sample tend to use ballot issues and try to influence elections to a significantly greater degree than their regional, local, and state counterparts. This finding has nothing to do with organizational *size* (where such differences were examined but not recorded), but strictly with geographical focus.

Finally, the staff and volunteers differ substantially in their evaluations of organizational effectiveness and problems. Especially with respect to relations between board and staff, there are stark disagreements between the volunteers and the professionals. While the volunteers gave their organizations the highest marks for their ability to treat staff well, the staff leaders told us repeatedly that their relations with their boards of directors are among their most troubling and persistently frustrating problems. It would appear that there is a lack of honest, direct communication between the board and the staff of many conservation groups: The staff may be willing to say in a confidential questionnaire or interview what they would never dare say to their board. But, indeed, their problems and anxieties over their boards of governance are myriad. They tend to believe that their board members, though knowledgeable and very well-meaning, are much in need of training in the subtle arts of serving well within the convoluted apparatus of nonprofit organizations. Common sense would concur: The typical board member of a U.S. environmental organization, though a highly educated professional, has no training and little experience in nonprofit governance. Too many lessons must be learned the hard way, and the person in the toughest position while the learning is taking place is the staff director of the organization. It is that person—and usually that person alone on the staff—who reports directly to the board and works at the pleasure of the board, and is therefore the one most vulnerable when things go awry.

We will now leave the thickets of quantitative data behind and address the meaning and future of leadership in the United States conservation-environmental movement.

Chapter 4

Key Issues of Conservation Leadership

Longevity counts. In trying to influence public opinion and policy, to create and sustain the work of conservation as a public work, longevity is the key to our effectiveness. . . . Our failure to create a base of healthy, mature advocacy groups throughout the states translates into a failure to achieve longevity. We are in effect running out of capacity to address our losses, let alone move into a new agenda. These are the skeletons in our closet, and we would just as soon keep the closet doors closed.

— Executive director of a statewide environmental organization

The problem with the environmental movement tends to be with the machinery, not with the cause—it's with the tools and the institutional structures. There are just far too many ways in which these organizations, instead of increasing people's power and facilitating their cause, are impediments to the cause.

— Environmental journalist

The data presented in chapters 2 and 3 represent a distillation of the issues and concerns expressed through staff and volunteer responses to mailed questionnaires, but like most data capable of statistical manipulation, these findings leave many important questions ambiguous or unaddressed. In order to buttress and enrich what we had learned from the copious information gathered from the questionnaires, we also went out into the field to interview thirty conservation leaders representing many kinds and sizes of organizations. The careers of some we interviewed reach back prior to Earth Day, while others are in their first two years as conservation professionals. Many had worked in government agencies and private businesses prior to taking positions in environmental groups. The backgrounds of these leaders were as varied and rich as those we encountered though the questionnaires. We talked to people trained in biology, geology, physics, law, journalism, forestry, social work, anthropology, languages, art, literature, engineering, and other fields. But while their educational backgrounds were kaleidoscopic, the leaders were almost uniformly persons whose work in conservation could be traced to childhood experiences. Nearly all of them professed an early and enduring love of nature, and agreed that a lifelong commitment to environmental ethics is what drives them in their work.

We were careful to select representatives from the broadest possible range of organizations and to seek insights from various levels (or programs) of larger organizations. In one instance we interviewed the CEO, the lobbying coordinator, and a regional office director of the same national organization; in another case we heard from a vice president, a field staff leader, and a board member of a fast-growing international organization. We were careful also to gather comments from the heads of state-based coalitions, local and regional grass-roots groups, national organizations that came into being since Earth Day 1970, policy centers, national clearinghouses that work primarily with local grass-roots groups, and other NGOs that stand firmly within the spectrum of American conservation. In addition, we sought out leaders who stand somewhat outside of conservation activism but are in key positions to critique the activists. These included leaders of various centers for dispute resolution or consensus policy-making; the head of a large, national foundation that gives grants to conservation groups; and environmental journalists. To the extent possible, we tried to conduct the interviews following receipt of a completed questionnaire from the subject.

Through the interviews, we were able to gain deeper insight into the demands, problems, and future opportunities for conservation leaders, as expressed by the leaders themselves. While we intended the completed questionnaires to frame our discussions with individual leaders, we found that the best interviews were the most far-ranging—the ones in which the leaders spoke from their own rich experiences working within the NGOs. We heard stories of epic political struggles, of the great but unheralded achievements of volunteers, of successful and unsuccessful campaigns to develop and strengthen organizations, of hiring practices (good and bad), of power struggles and turf battles, of the day-to-day pressures of management, of the grandest hopes and most dismal prospects for the future. We were told by many leaders that we had given them an opportunity to think afresh about their organizations and their own roles—that their participation in the Leadership Project had provided a moment to pause and reflect on many of the decisions and operating patterns that they had long ago internalized or subsumed beneath the daily pressures of running their organizations.

Not all of the interviews were positive. We wanted the leaders to reflect on the future of environmental reform, not merely by spelling out their own versions of the great issues that would constitute "an environmental agenda for the future," but with reference to the *capacity* of the environmental movement to accomplish long-range goals. We wanted to hear their ideas as to how that capacity could be improved. Where are the opportunities to reform the reformers and their movement? What must conservationists do to make sure that individual citizens are trained and empowered to lead in all levels of government, society, and private enterprise? How can the organizations of the movement achieve long-term stability and simultaneously remain dynamic, vital, and capable of change? As organizations grow into stable institutions, how can they avoid the trap of existing for the sake of their own continuing growth—the ubiquitous "tendencies toward ineffectiveness" that, according to management expert Peter Drucker, characterize the nonprofit sector? How is the nature of leadership evolving among conservation NGOs?

In addition to interviews, we collected a large volume of non-quantifiable information from the questionnaires themselves. We encouraged respondents to write copious comments—and many did. Some attached long pages of commentary, virtual essays reporting on their experiences as conservation leaders; others wrote epigrammatic comments, distilling their wisdom with the brevity of Zen masters. These were all extremely helpful as we searched for the key issues of conservation leadership.

Due to the sensitive nature of many interviews and questionnaires, we stipulated that we would quote no one by name (even if they were willing to be identified), but rather use salient statements and leave them all anonymous. The statements embedded in the narrative to follow are taken from interviews, questionnaires and, in a few instances, from the transcriptions of meetings with the Conservation Leadership Project Advisory Council, its members being themselves outstanding leaders in conservation. From the data we recovered through the questionnaires and the interviews conducted with NGO leaders in various parts of the country, we offer the following analysis.

The Evolving Movement

Twenty years after Earth Day the national environmental movement, long accustomed to the role of prominent social critic, suddenly found *itself* under the hot lamp of criticism, for despite every earnest effort for environmental reform, both the planetary environment and the environment of the United States itself continued to be degraded. By the late 1980s, many prominent scientists, writers, and politicians were sounding alarms seldom heard since the original Earth Day. Little or no progress had been made on what biologist E. O. Wilson has called the "four horsemen of the environmental apocalypse": global warming, ozone depletion, toxic waste accumulation, and mass extinction caused primarily by habitat destruction.[1] These planetary issues now loom over the coming century; many believe that they will become the predominant social, political, and economic issues, and that many other pressing issues—war and peace, poverty, overpopulation, economic stagnation—will come to be viewed increasingly within the context of these and other environmental problems. Moreover, the very issues that many consider to be fundamental to the post-1970 environmental movement—air and water pollution and the spread of industrial contaminants into the U.S. environment—not only had not been resolved but were beginning to appear intractable. Despite every earnest effort, levels of most major air and water pollutants were at least as severe as they were in 1970, and many had risen. Meanwhile, the world population continued to explode, and while the birth rate of the United States and other industrial powers had slowed, American cities were becoming increasingly unlivable due to crowding, noise, and increasing levels of pollution.

Long in the vanguard of worldwide environmental reform, the U.S. conservation-environmental movement found itself in a new cross fire of public opinion. Despite the enormous growth of national and worldwide interest in environmental issues, the organizations designed to lead in resolving those issues were being accused of not doing enough, or of pursuing wrongheaded strategies as they tried to achieve environmental goals. Some accused the environmental movement of "going soft"—of pursuing organizational growth strategies at the expense of effective (but less popular) advocacy. In the midst of all the environmental alarms both old and new, the environmental reformers made easy targets for those who cry out in frustration. There were many who would kill the messenger.

On the twentieth anniversary of Earth Day 1970, many commentators set out to review the environmental accomplishments of the past two decades. Not a few found the movement wanting. Critics from outside charged that the environmental movement was no less elitist than its conservationist forerunner—that it continued to be a movement of the rich, powerful, and well educated whose true motives stop at the preservation of nature and environmental quality for selfish gains.[2] Critics from within portrayed environmentalism as a movement that had failed to accomplish its central aims of pollution abatement and widespread environmental cleanup yet claimed great progress, mostly for the sake of recruiting new members. One prominent movement leader, Barry Commoner, charged that mainstream environmentalists had learned to compromise and negotiate away any chances for real environmental reform in a effort to appear reasonable at any cost—to guard the hard-won, precious capital of political influence and credibility, no matter what that would mean to the environment.[3] Another critic, former Greenpeace staffer Richard Grossman, went even further, claiming that the refusal of mainstream leaders to come to grips with the widespread failures of environmental reform constituted "a masterpiece of denial . . . that is rampant within our own movement."[4] Still other insiders took pains to protest the "professionalization" and "corporatization" of the mainstream environmental movement. Earth First! founder Dave Foreman saw his former colleagues at The Wilderness Society and other environmental SWAT teams donning business suits, purchasing lavish office buildings, and scribbling out organizational business plans and quickly concluded that the movement's heart had gone cold. Foreman deplored the new generation of incoming leader-managers—the institutionalizers—who had not paid their dues beneath the starry skies of the wilderness. He wondered how anyone who had not tasted huge drafts of wild nature could be an effective advocate for it, or for any other environmental goods that had not been experienced firsthand.[5]

Critics from other social movements got into the act, too. Civil rights leaders, reviewing the racial and ethnic composition of several mainstream environmental organizations, charged them with racism.[6] Caught off guard, the mainstream environmentalists searched for an intelligent response, but could scarcely provide anything but partial agreement. Even among those for whom the word *racism* seemed too strong an indictment, many were troubled over the obdurate "whiteness of the green movement."

Not surprisingly, the various assessments of the successes and failures of environmentalism often reflected the biases of the assessors at least as much as they portrayed the movement's achievements; indeed, some did not bother to recount any achievements, but rather attacked the overall record of environmentalism as a failed experiment in social policy. Broad axes were ground on a few narrow stones.

It is instructive that these indictments came from social movement activists, many of them within the camp of conservation itself. Where environmental leaders had once been excoriated for their idealistic forays into national and state policy and accused of being ignorant of economics, they were now finding members of their own camp worrying that all the topmost leaders ever *thought* about were economics—including the economics of their own organizations—at the expense of real progress in the issues.

While these arrows sting, it is important to remember that the conservation-environmental movement has always been a contentious one, precisely because it is dynamic. Disputes and competition among various factions of the movement date back to the earliest days of conservation when Muir feuded with Pinchot and both pulled at the ear of Roosevelt. Today, many decry the conflict and multiplicity of opinion, the heated arguments over strategy and approach that continue to punctuate the efforts of environmental and conservation organizations; they argue that the only important battles are outside, not within, and that environmentalists should not waste time, effort, and precious resources on intertribal disputes. But disagreements are inevitable, because conservation and environmental protection involve great ambiguities; conservationists have always lived in a green world marbled with gray. It is not surprising that they fight with each other over matters ranging from scientific facts to the deepest philosophies about humans' place in nature to the best way to diversify organizational income.

Contrary to what many say, conservation leaders in every quarter are asking themselves many of the same tough questions about effectiveness. There is a sense that despite the phenomenal growth of the environmental movement, the NGOs are not doing enough (or perhaps they are not doing the right things) to galvanize the electorate and make environmental protection a matter of first principle in governance, business practices, and community and individual behavior.

What much of the critical debate over effectiveness obscures, however, is the question of *capacity*. Framed as simply as possible, the question comes down to this: Given its resources and its methods of operation, what can any given conservation group effectively achieve with respect to the issues it attempts to resolve? Given the collective resources of the many groups working on environmental issues, what can the movement achieve? It's easy to attack environmentalists on their failures, and just as easy to obscure or negate their many successes. It is much more difficult to suggest practical ways in which the scanty resources available to environmental NGOs can be more effectively leveraged to achieve worthy goals.

From the copious data we recovered through the Leadership Project, one outstanding fact is clear: The great majority of conservation-environmental organizations in the United States do not have the resources, and do not know how to leverage the resources they possess, to accomplish their long-range goals. Indeed, only a minority of the organizations we surveyed even *have* long-range goals—that is, goals set by an acknowledged planning process. Even fewer report having methods to evaluate their own progress. Without the ability to leverage their scanty resources while they effectively pursue greater levels of support, many U.S. conservation groups continue to drift along willy-nilly, pursuing strategies dictated more by circumstance and financial necessity than by strategic imperative; in far too many instances, they are driven by the perceived demands of competition with groups that are seen to be rivals instead of allies. The movement is adrift precisely to the extent that each organization looks out for its own good instead of the public good. The conservation community is missing opportunities to leverage its resources by creating partnerships among organizations—and to make the United States into a truly conservationist nation by planting the seeds of effective action in the many places where it does not now exist.

These concerns might not seem as important as the great issues of global warming, ozone depletion, and all the rest; indeed, discussions of organizational capacity make many conservation leaders impatient. Yet these internal issues are the very substance of reform, and they go to the heart of our national environmental leadership. Everyone agrees that the movement "cannot afford to fail," yet it fails every day by refusing to address questions that are germane to its own capacity. Most of the leaders we surveyed are aware of these internal problems within their movement, and they are confused and divided about how to resolve them.

Leaders' Concerns

From the data we gathered, leaders' concerns about effectiveness and their own self-critique can be summarized as follows.

The environmental movement at the international-national level has learned how to prosper, grow, and institutionalize; but at all other levels, the movement is generally mired in organizational malaise. High rates of staff turnover, the failure to achieve financial stability, constant struggles to raise funds, and stagnant levels of membership support characterize most environmental and conservation groups (including many national organizations). While the increasing complexity of environmental issues calls for much greater resources and technical firepower from the NGOs, most groups remain woefully unable to provide them. These are not merely *organizational* problems, for they adversely affect the ability of these groups to influence public decisions, ensure the enforcement of good environmental management practices, and enhance voter support for environmental issues. Chronic organizational problems circumscribe the horizons for both conservationists and conservation issues, and everyone loses in the process.

Conservation advocacy is weak in about half of the states; indeed, in a few states it is nearly nonexistent. Practically no one seems to be paying attention to this problem. The national organizations with decentralized field offices, chapters, affiliates, and programs, while performing very well in a limited range of issues, do not create the synergy of activism needed to solve environmental problems at state, local, and regional levels. Many international-national organizations effectively recruit local members, but they rarely organize or assist coalitions for statewide advocacy across a full range of environmental issues. Many independent, state-based or regionally based organizations that could catalyze statewide advocacy are mired in an organizational swamp—too little money, faint local support, staff and board burnout, and the failure to plan and act on a positive vision of the future. Moreover, there are several regions of the United States in which conservation-environmental organizations are unable to operate effectively due to an inherently poor base of local support, coupled with the invisibility of these regions to nationally and internationally focused environmental funders. Merely getting groups started in these "conservation barrens" is not enough: Like small businesses, they must be shepherded through several years of early development until they are able to achieve reasonable levels of self-sufficiency. Until these regions are identified and the problems with their NGOs addressed, the United States cannot rightfully claim to possess a national environmental movement. It will continue to have states and regions that, due to the absence of environmental advocacy, continue to be environmental sacrifice areas, most of them within the increasingly forgotten rural quarter.

The U.S. environmental movement lacks a "central nervous system." It has no way to process or act on information fed from its "extremity" organizations out in the field. Thus, in very practical terms, it cannot and does not consistently link the intimate knowledge and political strength of the grass roots with the technical and legal competence of the topmost national organizations. While horizontal collaboration occurs very well in Washington (among various elements of the national environmental lobby), and in some states among strategically linked groups and coalitions, vertical collaboration among local, state, regional, and national organizations occurs only sporadically and usually with little planning or forethought. Effective, strategically planned vertical collaboration is the exception, not the rule. Until a central nervous system is created, the national environmental organism will stumble along dysfunctionally, failing to harness the considerable public support that already exists. A few individual organizations will prosper—some very greatly—while the opportunity for a cohesive local-to-national environmental movement languishes.

The mainstream environmental movement, including many well-established groups at the regional, state, and local levels, has perfected the art of "preaching to the choir" but is far less able to recruit new constituencies. As a result, the movement remains politically weak. In most regions of the country, it has not galvanized the electorate to judge candidates (federal, state, or local) very carefully or knowledgeably on the basis of their environmental records and agendas. Despite its great gains before Congress and the overwhelming public support for environmental issues expressed through national opinion polls, the movement remains an oddly impotent political force. Candidates for office are left to define environmentalism merely in self-serving terms, and the electorate in many regions lacks the capacity to judge them. Indeed, so many fakers have appropriated the label that the very word *environmentalist* is beginning to lose meaning. This strange political impotency is a precise reflection of the weakness and inefficiency of most environmental organizations, for these are the only entities positioned to induce accurate public judgment about issues of such daunting complexity.

The environmental movement is both divided and divisive. It is now a movement widely split between haves and have-nots—between a handful of well-heeled flagship organizations and the great majority of groups struggling along from balance sheet to balance sheet. The organizations of the movement, while exhibiting a healthy variety of advocacy approaches, are finding themselves increasingly at odds with each other over fundamental strategies and competing political philosophies. Debilitating polarities exist between policy technicians and political street fighters, environmental elitists and social justice advocates, check-writing memberships and grassroots activists, consensus-oriented national and state-capitol organizations eager to compromise and small, grass-roots groups "back home" who feel increasingly undercut by deals negotiated in Washington or the statehouse. The stage is now set for environmentalists to begin battling each other at least as furiously as they battle their traditional antagonists in big business and government.

Many leaders of the "new environmental movement" complain that they and their organizations seem to be invisible to mainstreamers. They receive little or no acknowledgment or assistance. This new movement—we prefer to view it as a new branch of the old movement—takes its cue not from the scientific-technical debate of the settled conservationists but from the well-thumbed workbooks of direct-action politics. It is making radical departures from mainstream conservation and environmentalism: Its organizations are often racially mixed groups that tend to focus on environmental issues not for their own sake but as elements of a broader, older campaign to promote social justice. They are growing fast, but their growth tends to be based on neighborhood and grass-roots organizing rather than on expensive direct-mail campaigns. The emphasis rests more on membership activism than on mere membership support in the form of contributions. There is increasing potential for conflict between the mainstreamers and the "invisible environmentalists," since the latter often view the former as elitist, even racist entities.

For most organizations, the tasks of management and fund-raising create debilitating inefficiencies that lead to ineffectiveness. Most conservation leaders in the United States are not the delegating captains of large, stable NGO institutions, but rather the jacks-of-all-trades who manage tiny groups with fewer than five staff and 3,500 members. The staff leaders of these groups generally rise to their positions precisely because they are so good at issues-oriented work. They end up as fund-raisers and NGO administrators essentially by default: Their knowledge of the *organization* as well as the issues becomes an irreplaceable asset. In such small organizations—the great majority of conservation and environmental groups—the inefficiencies of management are deadly. And they are very difficult to correct, since most are caused by a plethora of small, seemingly insignificant tasks that accumulate into a managerial morass and lie beyond the control of the leaders themselves. The myriad and diverse application and reporting requirements of foundations, the daily demands of servicing members, the resolution of tensions and disputes with board and staff members, the need to diversify income in order to survive, the unending and exhausting struggle for operating funds (especially among the unendowed organizations), and a hundred other internal factors press the movement leadership into the unwelcome posture of stoop-shouldered administrators. The average conservation leader spends over 70 percent of his time engaged in the internal business of the organization and less than one-fourth of the time in the substantive, issues-driven work that probably led him to his job in the first place. Yet correcting this imbalance will be extremely difficult, since on average these staff leaders spend only 2 percent of their time in professional or midcareer training, and many say that effective management support and training services are not available to them. Too often, leaders report that the issues and the organizations have become detached from one another. The leaders often feel that they must choose for the good of the organization regardless of the impact that choice will have on their ability to make progress on the issues. This problem has its correlate in even the largest, wealthiest conservation NGOs. Said one senior staffer of a prominent international organization: "Our agenda used to be dictated by the issues, but increasingly it is dominated by the development department. The money changers are telling us what we must do."

Opportunities for midcareer training and refreshment virtually do not exist for most professional staff leaders among the NGOs. On average, these leaders spend less than 2 percent of their time engaged in training. In many regions of the country, leaders report that the needed training does not exist, but more frequently they say that their organizations simply cannot afford in-service training for staff or volunteers. Moreover, both professional and volunteer leaders report dangerous tendencies toward burnout. It is personal refreshment and rejuvenation they long for, not professional training. The staff and volunteer longevity demanded by the issues is not being planned into the operations of many conservation NGOs.

We will now turn to a more detailed examination of these and other issues affecting the quality of leadership in the U.S. conservation movement, based on what the leaders themselves told us.

The "Gulf"

Conservation leaders at all levels, both professional and volunteer, perceive a "gulf" between the large, institutionally stable organizations on the international-national scene and the grass-roots groups working at state, local, and regional levels. Many describe the gulf as troubling but inevitable—a logical and expected outcome of the evolution of environmentalism, and a problem only to those who pay attention to interorganizational disputes. Success, according to some, is bound to breed discontent among the less successful. Others are less sanguine, pointing out that the organizational isolation which many leaders decry has an enormous impact on the issues as well as the people involved; for these leaders, the gulf between national and local environmental advocates has everything to do with a perceived lack of effective advocacy.

Since national NGOs rarely unite their talents and power with their state and local counterparts, environmentalists often fail to muster the critical mass needed to move important issues. As a result, local activists feel increasingly undercut and undervalued.

State and local leaders we interviewed complained that too many issues are being compromised by NGO "power brokers" in Washington. Accusations fly back and forth. Institutionalizers of the movement accuse activists of naïveté and point out that power looks a lot different from the inside. The self-described street fighters complain that the mainstreamers in actuality represent no one but themselves. Said one:

> Most of these Washington organizations are paper-issue people. They don't ask the grass roots, and they don't educate. They are not accountable. I would argue that they have no constituency. They have paid support, paid memberships—my God, some of them have millions of members!—but they don't have a constituency. If NRDC [the Natural Resources Defense Council] wanted to turn out a hundred people in D.C., they'd probably have a tough time doing it.

Given the recent history of the environmental movement, it is little wonder that the so-called gulf exists. Whether it is a terrible problem or an inconsequential inevitability is a matter of much debate among environmental leaders at all levels. What few dispute, however, is that the gulf is a direct result of an unconditional good: the phenomenal growth in the U.S. environmental movement. The following is a composite of what several leaders told us about the consequences of growth in their movement.

The 1970s and the 1980s were both decades of great success for the national environmental movement, but the successes of each decade, according to the leaders we surveyed, were quite different. While the late 1960s and early 1970s were productive years of environmental policy formation, driven by the ground swell of support crystallized on Earth Day, the 1980s were a decade of institution building. New policies and laws did not proliferate then as they had during the two prior decades; indeed, it was all environmentalists could do to hold the line. Given the hostility of the Reagan administration toward the goals of the national environmental movement, and a corresponding conservative shift among many state governments, holding the line was itself no insignificant achievement. Neither were the movement's efforts at institution building.

Many national and international organizations managed to consolidate their support through the 1980s by paying as much attention to organizational development as they paid to policy, law, and enforcement. The growth of NGO memberships and budgets, aided by the administration's awkward attacks on environmentalism, was in many cases remarkable. But new growth created new problems. Competition for members and funders intensified. As federal dollars dwindled, conservation NGOs, along with their counterparts in other wings of the American social change movement, flocked to the offices of national foundations. Environmentalists found themselves honing their entrepreneurial skills as they never had before; many began to see their organizations not only as crusaders but as *businesses* operating in the nonprofit economy. In many instances the freewheeling and often spendthrift patterns of operation that characterized the glory years of the 1970s, the "Environmental Decade," were abandoned.

The eighties were also a time of expansion and restructuring. Several leading organizations became decidedly more centralized in both operations and focus; they eliminated and consolidated field offices while expanding their lobbying programs in Washington, launching new endeavors in the media, and mobilizing resources in international conservation. Financial success was reflected in the rapidly changing patterns of staffing. Staffs grew, diversified, and departmentalized. In response both to their own motives for growth and to the changes mandated by the creation of major environmental policies and agencies, a new legion of legal, technical, scientific, and marketing experts began to enter the ranks of the conservation NGOs. While the use of experts was nothing new in American conservation, the numbers of technically trained professionals entering positions of staff leadership were without precedent. Meanwhile, significant mergers occurred, as did the creation of new organizations, especially policy development and research centers with international missions. While established environmentalists did not lose their focus on domestic issues, many of them hastened to create or improve programs in international conservation. U.S. dollars and expertise began to flow abroad.

Foundations and other philanthropists both led and followed these trends; money tended to flow "upward" toward international and national concerns. The elimination of much federal support, coupled with the increasing competition for funds, pushed a number of young organizations to the brink of extinction. The institutions that survived and prospered tended to do so either by growing their own memberships or quickly learning how to market themselves more effectively to philanthropists or (usually) both. The most successful saw their budgets skyrocket during the eighties; two of them—The Nature Conservancy and the National Wildlife Federation—are already near the $90 million annual income mark.

Many conservationists now point to the great growth of their own organizations as evidence that environmental advocacy is thriving; some are so exuberant over institutional growth that they seem to mistake the health and vitality of various conservation organizations for effective conservation itself. Recent assessments place combined memberships of the major national groups at around 8 million; counting lapsed members, the number of Americans who have recently belonged (or still do belong) to national environmental organizations soars to more than 10 million.[7] Some have argued that these impressive figures bear unequivocal evidence of a healthy movement. Conservation and environmentalism, they proudly contend, have never enjoyed such widespread support; environmentalists must be doing a great deal right. And they are. The growth of the most popular and successful organizations has been phenomenal by any standard. In 1989 two environmental organizations—the World Wildlife Fund and Greenpeace—stood among the ten fastest-growing nonprofits in the country. As *World Watch Magazine* reported, the late 1980s were indeed a "boom time for environmental groups," with growth in some memberships leaping by 50 percent in a single year and many national organizations doubling and tripling their numbers during the decade.[8]

Nevertheless, not all is well within the movement, and not all conservationists are pleased with the institution-building focus of the international-national organizations. Many leaders of smaller grass-roots organizations observe that the engine driving much of the institutional growth of environmentalism is direct-mail membership recruitment, which brings in great numbers of "check writers" but pays little attention to membership activism. Such leaders also express frustration with the centrism that often seems to accompany growth. Many we surveyed complain that the leaders of the topmost organizations have lost touch with the grass roots.

These critics do not view the national environmental movement as having evolved creatively since Earth Day 1970; they seem not to accept or favor the new roles required by the increasing institutionalization of environmentalism, nor do they embrace the new responsibilities of leadership that come with growth and the achievement of power. While the topmost leaders would dispute these complaints, some we interviewed chafe against their new roles as managers of growth-oriented businesses. They fear that their organizations have strayed far from their origins among the grass roots.

Some leaders whose careers reach back into the early seventies offered interesting and helpful perspectives on how and why the evolution of the conservation-environmental movement took place. Here are three short histories of environmentalism in the United States offered by leaders of three national organizations, the first from the president of a fifteen-year-old group with 10,000 members and a $1.2 million budget:

The conservation movement is at least eighty-eight years old, and probably older if you take a longer view of historical influences. The environmental movement, however, is only twenty years old. And the environmental movement is immature. It's like the civil rights movement or the feminist movement. It starts out as a bandwagon idea— something noisy, must generate attention for itself and its issues. But it has evolved. It's going through a phase right now where it's not ineffective, as some suggest, but less visible, less outspoken. That's because of something very good: The noise of the sixties and seventies became the impetus for institutionalizing, mostly in the form of laws. Whole agencies were created, and the laws, of course, become the province of the agencies. Environmentalism followed the work into the agencies—and work in bureaucracy is not, by anyone's definition, sexy. All the things we concentrated on over the years are now in the hands of professional, appointed stewards. Now environmentalism has a lot to do with how you manage the managing agencies.

In a way, that leaves us with some questions about our role. A lot of groups just haven't been able to adapt to that new role. They see no percentage, for example, in the inevitability of development. But conservation is a many-lobed movement. It's like a glacier, you know— this foot happens to be Earth First!, and that foot over there is The

Nature Conservancy, and there are all these feet in the middle. Part of the maturation of the whole glacier is that people are beginning to ask, "What kind of development is inevitable, and what can we do to work with the people we never converted back when we were so noisy?" That's what my organization is trying to do. A lot of my board still doesn't understand that. In fact, a lot of them resent it.

Next, from the president of a twelve-year-old, $500,000 public lands organization, is another version of our environmental history:

The environmental movement has gone through two or three little evolutions since the beginning. And it had to be this way—it's the same with the civil rights movement, the same with the women's liberation movement. Earth Day kicked off the period I'm talking about. When the Ohio River caught on fire, that ignited the whole thing. It was a real conflict approach. It was them or us—you know, sue the bastards. Then as we evolved into the grass roots, there came a clustering of individuals who saw the likelihood of being in this thing forever. It wasn't like the Vietnam War, where you knew someday it would end. The environment turned into a movement for the longtimers. There were plenty of others, of course, but those who didn't see it as a life's commitment fell out. When that happens, you have this clustering of the professionals—the managers, the long thinkers, the policymakers, the scientists. Then, instead of the grass roots tug-of-war, we moved into the policy arena. Now we're moving again, this time into something that resembles aikido [a martial art based on converting the opponent's force entirely to one's own advantage]. There are still factions out there polarizing, of course, but the evolution of the movement is toward a cooperative approach. I don't mean that the bottom line or our objectives have changed one degree. But society has changed.

Finally, from the head of one of the largest and most prominent conservation organizations in the country, is a third version:

There are so many more organizations today than when I began—a tripling or quadrupling of the number at the national level. There are many more outlets and niches for leadership. The increases created more diversity in the community and more opportunity for entrepreneurialism and experimentation. I think that's very healthy. But the quality of leadership? Well, you get into the Stephen Fox thesis, that the earlier leaders came out of a volunteer tradition and tended to be stronger, more assertive. They were outspoken, risk takers. On the flip side of the coin, they were less good at being managers. Many weren't managers at all.

Many of the groups, of course, have become substantial enterprises at the national and state levels. They require a lot of management. . . . I think the movement has had a very hard time, particularly in the large organizations, in combining a successful track record in management with people who are inspiring or have a larger vision. There seem to be a lot of people sort of stumbling as managers with a very bittersweet track record and not much in terms of a breadth of vision. Though, I must say, it's hard to dwell on breadth of vision when leaders are ground down by the cares of everyday management and personnel problems to solve and budgets to meet and meetings that go on endlessly.

I suppose Fox's supposition is true, but there are people in recent years who feel strongly and care deeply, too. Trouble is, there is this crisis as organizations grow. They keep outgrowing themselves—their leaders are not good enough as managers. And you have this general tendency of all nonprofits in which the businessmen on the boards keep thinking that they don't see the orderly, systematic business managers they're used to. People who know conservation are pushed out, and the groups start getting a new kind of leader. Most don't get too much in the way of strokes for being good at their real business, being good environmentalists and having convictions. They get their strokes by keeping the money coming in and having staff be harmonious and productive and the membership going up and getting publicity.

Most of the leaders we surveyed clearly agree that the hydra-headed nature of the environmental movement is healthy, as is the debate it engenders. They agree that despite the forms of evolution described above, many organizations, especially at the grass-roots level, will and must hew to the more radical approaches which many describe as leftovers from the 1970s, while the "leading edge" groups, operating in the new "cooperative mode," must attend to the compromising and deal cutting that come with the turf of real political power. These are profound philosophical differences, not mere matters of style. Conservation is indeed a "many-lobed movement," and in the minds of most leaders we surveyed, that is a sign of health and robustness.

Still, the gulf grows wider, and into it fall many of the very issues that galvanize and activate the grass roots and others who support environmentalism. Stories now abound of local groups feeling undercut by environmentalist deals made without their input in Washington, while the national leaders defend the "realism" of the negotiations they have had to perform. Said one national environmental leader:

> There are people in our business who don't want to negotiate compromise because it gets their hands dirty. It's dirty to get in there and cut the deal. I think we need more people willing to go into organizations where they're going to cut deals and get aggressive. People will then begin to see the conservation business as a business. Washington is the only town I've been in as a practicing conservationist that esteems conservationists in the way other towns esteem businessmen. . . . It's one of the few places you can go and have a conservationist looked at the same way someone else would look at a corporate chief or a doctor or a lawyer or somebody that's halfway important in day-to-day life.

There are other differences, besides philosophy and style, that separate international-national organizations and the local grass roots. Leaders of environmental NGOs are often so busy meeting the demands of their own organizations that they rarely look beyond the immediate horizon—past the next board meeting, the hurried attention to the budget, the hour-by-hour dramas on the Hill—to see their own position in the larger picture. Meanwhile, if they are fractious, territorial, and uncommunicative, perhaps they can be excused. NGOs compete tooth by jowl for talented new staffers, members, philanthropic dollars, influence in the public arena, and sound bites on the nightly news. National groups compete with local ones for members, recognition, and support. Local and statewide groups compete with each other, hoarding donor lists and philanthropic contacts as if they were the last drops of water on a desert island.

Among our sample of staff and volunteer leaders, and the thirty we interviewed more in depth, the gulf was decried not only by local leaders who feel left out of the national agenda, but by leaders of some of the major organizations as well. The gulf reaches in both directions. CEOs of the large organizations often complain of the distance and isolation they feel from local conservationists, and indeed from their own members. While many national and international groups in the United States have field programs and make deliberate efforts to work in partnership with groups at the state and local levels, even the most ambitious volunteer programs of the national groups cannot possibly cover all the environmental issues emerging at the state and local levels. Many national group leaders find themselves torn between the needs and demands of their own local volunteers and the exigencies of managing a complex, multi-programmatic enterprise. Said one:

> I'm always worried about bureaucratizing an operation, but you can't run a $32 million enterprise out of your hip pocket with a budget on the back of an envelope. That's something our chapter people frequently have trouble understanding.

Moreover, some national and international groups are now so specialized in their missions and approach that there is no room on their agendas, and no time, to consider any issues outside their own, very narrow scope. Leaders in these groups, even the ones whose work is close to the local arena, sometimes feel isolated not only from other conservationists but from the larger issues affecting the planet. A field office director for an international organization put it this way:

> I feel like I'm operating in a vacuum. I'm so stressed out with the things that we're trying to accomplish here in one state, and I have little time for personal development or understanding what other people are doing, including working on the greenhouse effect and other broad environmental issues. My job forces me to stay in this office writing letters, making phone calls, or going out on the road fund-raising, negotiating land deals. . . . I just don't have the time to know what others are doing, not even right here in the state capitol.

Conversely, groups focused on issues before the state legislature or local boards of governance often cannot find the means to contribute much to a national environmental agenda, even though many realize its critical importance in the context of local activism. Said one CEO of a state-based environmental coalition:

> The thing that makes our work possible at all is that we do have national environmental protection laws. There's no question . . . that were it not for what happens within the federal government and the national groups, we would be floundering here in the states. It's not just the law, either. It's the ideas, the research, the talent, the education

and training opportunities—all those kinds of resources require the equivalent of an urban center. As far as the rest of us are concerned, struggling with environmental policy out here in the sticks, Washington, D.C., is *the* urban center.

Inevitable or not, the chasm separating the institutionalized wing of the environmental movement from its less stable counterpart at the state, regional, and local levels is growing wider. The gulf contributes to the sense of personal and organizational isolation, but its more significant effect is far more insidious: At its worst, it contributes to a failure to ensure healthy environmental activism across the country. The absence of healthy environmental activism across the United States is a national problem that has long been ignored by both national NGOs and the philanthropic community. It cannot be ignored much longer.

The Haves and Have-nots

Partly as a result of the growth and increasing dissension, the environmental movement in the United States has taken on many characteristics of a stratified class system of haves and have-nots. The larger, centralized organizations nestled within the Washington Beltway or strategically located in New York and San Francisco are able to attract nationally focused philanthropy and can simultaneously take advantage of national demographics as they recruit members, especially through direct-mail. Though still small institutions by the standards of American nonprofits, many of these groups enjoy relative prosperity; they are well-established actors on the international-national stage, possessing financial endowments, stable bases of funding, and great confidence in their ability to grow. Their days of mere survival are long past.

Yet the rest of the environmental movement—and most particularly the organizations found in poorer areas and predominantly rural states—continues to struggle mightily with the fundamental issues of existence. Unwittingly, environmentalists have managed to follow the trend of national demographics strongly favoring urban-suburban growth and leaving rural regions behind. While the 1970s saw a "rural renaissance" of economic and population growth—much of it tied to dubious forecasts in the energy, minerals, and timber industries—the 1980s saw one of the greatest out-migrations of rural citizens in U.S. history. During 1986 and 1987 alone, over 750,000 Americans moved from rural environs into the cities.[9]

The national environmental movement seemed comfortable with this trend. An urban location has logistical advantages for an organization working on large-scale problems. And for demographic reasons the memberships of large conservation organizations are predominantly urban. More people live in cities, and a higher percentage of them fit the upscale profile of the larger groups' memberships.

The ironies are thick. So much environmental activity continues to focus on rural places—energy and mineral regions, public lands, wilderness and open spaces, wildlife habitats, and literal and figurative wastelands where garbage of all sorts can be disposed of. Yet many organizations *located* in rural places have stagnated, while their urban-based counterparts have grown like gangbusters. Partly as a result, many rural conservation organizations experience increasingly strained ties to the national environmental movement. As time passes, these organizations could become the movement's forgotten stepchildren.

But there are other manifestations of the rift between the haves and have-nots. The mainstream environmental movement has perpetuated the pattern of the earlier conservation movement in regard to poor and minority citizens. In some instances the mainstream movement has ignored them and their issues; in others it has been concerned but has not found effective action.

There are now myriad examples of nonwhite organizations all over the country that are working on environmental and natural resource issues without much assistance or even acknowledgement from the mainstream movement. Indeed, there is a virtual minority environmental movement that exists beyond the ken of both mainstream environmentalists and the national media. These are the "invisible environmentalists" who are working very hard to ensure environmental reform on their own terms and in their own communities.

Nearly every leader we surveyed expressed the belief that the national environmental agenda has not trickled down adequately to the state and local levels. Leaders of the flagship organizations with vigorous field programs, chapters, affiliates, and decentralized staff admit that they cannot possibly cover all the emerging environmental issues at the subfederal levels—indeed, they can cover only a small fraction. Leaders at all levels maintained that while new federal and international initiatives will be required to address emerging issues such as climate change, extinction, and sustainability, a much greater amount of environmental action will also have to occur at the subfederal level. And that is precisely where the American environmental movement faces its greatest disabilities. U.S. conservationists could hardly be more poorly equipped to tackle state policies. About half the states lack strong statewide coalitions or state capitol–based environmental organizations to coordinate lobbying and other advocacy efforts for various groups. Of the coalitions and independent groups that do exist, the majority are grossly undersupported; many possess nightmarish records of managerial malaise: rampant turnover of senior staff, poorly diversified and unreliable streams of income, memberships too small to support more than basic administration (and many too small to provide even that much support), poor or nonexistent track records of philanthropic support (especially from national foundations), troublesome or nearly nonexistent relations with national conservation groups (who as often as not are viewed as ineffective or irrelevant in the pursuit of a broad, statewide environmental agenda).

National organizations and their funders tend to focus primarily on federal issues; indeed, in order to qualify for funding at many private foundations serving the environmental community, the ability to demonstrate "national impact" is a common requirement. Local and state-based groups by definition do not qualify. In fact, the environmental era is yet to dawn in most states, and in others (several Rocky Mountain states, for example) the era dawned bright in the early seventies but has dimmed considerably, as an ongoing grass-roots backlash has now matured into a full-scale countermovement of citizens whose livelihoods depend on natural resource exploitation and whose political power is rapidly outstripping that of the environmentalists. Said one leader from Montana:

> I believe that many of our gains of the seventies are in jeopardy—many were temporary, and many never trickled down to the local ground.

We've been through a period now in the last five or six, maybe eight, years that for each of those gains we're so proud of from the "good ole days," we've suffered some pretty mighty losses—in issues and in public attitudes. As far as grass-roots organizing is concerned, we're getting beaten at our own game.

Virtually no one doubts the critical and growing importance of state and local governments in environmental management. Indeed, the key decisions affecting most aspects of environmental protection are now made by state and local agencies. They are the primary regulators of land use, water resources, wildlife management and protection, industrial-facility siting, energy development, mining, and air and water pollution. They are critical players in the designation and regulation of natural areas, federal wilderness areas and parklands, toxic and hazardous waste disposal, forestry, agriculture, and other key determinants of environmental quality. Moreover, the greatest growth in American government during much of this century has occurred within the states, not within the mossy halls of the federal bureaucracy. Between 1947 and 1987, employment in state and local governments grew by 82 percent, while federal employment grew by only 18 percent.[10] Three-fourths of all government jobs in the United States and 70 percent of all government domestic spending—excluding military jobs and spending—occur in state and local agencies. These facts add weight to the ubiquitous rhetoric about the increasing prominence of state and local governments in domestic affairs, including environmental affairs. Yet in relative terms, money and members continue to pour into the international-national organizations, while those groups focusing on subfederal issues often continue to languish.

The Tattered Map of American Conservation

On the map of effective U.S. conservation, one finds a great many gaps—regions, states, and locales that are virtual conservation barrens where the seeds of environmental protection have never been planted or watered and effective NGOs have either failed to grow or remain weak and in constant threat of collapse. One also finds states where early-1970s experiments in environmental policy failed or were subsequently eroded by the force of special interests, leaving the experimenters divided, bereft, and untrusted. In these places, local and state-based environmentalists and their counterparts from the national organizations will not be afforded much credibility in future efforts to craft new policy. Here, the vaunted "Environmental Decade" is not now dawning; it has already come and gone. And there are far too many places where the great new wealth of the international-national environmental movement—the dollars, the knowledge and expertise—is seldom, if ever, shared. The "boom time" has not ticked for all; no one should be celebrating the tattered map of American conservation.

One national leader, summarizing his experiences meeting with activists in the vast, public lands states of the conservative American West, said this:

> It's amazing how few activists there are in some places. Take Arizona. Arizona is about 90 percent public land. When you add up all the Indian reservations and state forests, the private land is only about 9 percent. The Wilderness Society has one full-time person there; the Sierra Club, one full-time person to cover several states; The Nature Conservancy has a couple of people. And that's it! Those are the only paid people I know working on 90 percent of the state of Arizona. There was a coalition for the BLM [Bureau of Land Management] wilderness battle . . . but the conservation leadership there basically consists . . . of eighteen or twenty people. I met them all in somebody's living room.

Arizona's key environmental issues might be oddly tied to the destiny of its vast public lands, but outside of that peculiarity, the same statement above could be made accurately for more than half the states: The "legion" of conservation professionals and stable, staffed organizations, outside of the District of Columbia and a handful of coastal cities, is small, indeed. And the corps of active volunteers, while growing substantially, is too often an ephemeral phenomenon.

Perhaps the single greatest challenge to conservation leadership in the United States is to fill in that map—to ensure that every region, every state, every local government begins acting effectively on behalf of conservation and environmental protection. That goal vastly exceeds the importance of developing any single conservation group or any particular sector of the movement. History tells us that the goal will not be achieved in the absence of a healthy legion of activist conservation groups of many sizes and types. But achieving that goal will be extremely difficult, precisely because of the rampant parochialism of the U.S. environmental movement. The hot competition among the empire builders of the national movement has forced most of its leaders to attend to the good of their own organizations and to pay less attention to measurable progress in all of the states and across the full range of environmental issues.

State, regional, and local organizations have proliferated, but the overwhelming majority of them continue to be all-volunteer associations. While these are critical contributors to environmental advocacy, and the principal "keepers of the agenda" in many places, they are all too often ephemeral entities. Keenly focused on the issues or opportunities that led to their founding, they trouble less over the demands of developing institutions or the management of their own growth. Lacking staff, they have had the freedom to proceed without considering their organizations in the light of career or professional development, and while finances and budgets often trouble them, they are not strapped with the responsibility of making payrolls. However, they are not apt to live very long, vulnerable as they are to the vagaries of change and the loss of energy, enthusiasm, and talent that occurs when the founders leave or the founding issues are resolved.

In between the handful of international-national organizations that have become bona fide institutions and the all-volunteer associations lie a number of small, staffed groups operating at the local, state, and regional levels. They are as diverse in outlook and interests as their staffed counterparts on the international-national scene. Some are focused on specific places or habitats and possess names that demarcate the group's primary interest (Idaho's Committee for the High Desert; Rhode Island's Save the Bay Foundation; the Louisiana Coastal Zone Protection Network). Others are advocates for a broad range of issues that evolve over time, but focus their attention on a particular policy arena, such as the state legislature or a regional commission empowered to make important public decisions affecting a specific geographic area (the Illinois

Environmental Council; the Northwest Power Planning Act Coalition in Seattle; the Southwest Research and Information Center in Albuquerque). Still others exist primarily to protect traditional, grass-roots communities against the onslaught of disruptive forms of industrialization (the Dakota Resource Council; the Western Colorado Congress). And there are many other kinds of groups besides: advocates for rare species (Save the Manatee; The Peregrine Fund), regional policy research centers or think tanks serving a particular locale (Designwrights Collaborative in New Mexico; the Texas Center for Policy Studies), regional centers combining environmental field education with advocacy on environmental policy (the Meadowbrook Project in Arkansas; the Atlantic Center on the Environment in Massachusetts), and state-based, regional, or issue-specific environmental law clinics (LEAF in Florida; the Arizona Public Interest Law Foundation; the Colorado Land and Water Conservation Fund). These examples only begin to describe the diversity of independent, staffed environmental organizations that citizens have founded all over the country.

What many of these groups have in common, other than their focus on environmental issues, is a strong desire to inject democratization into public decision making; their leaders seldom see environmental issues as an end and a cause in themselves, but rather as an opportunity to enhance the power and authority of individual citizens against the seemingly all-powerful state and the commercial interests that dominate it. Many of these kinds of organizations have effectively internalized their emphasis on the processes of decision making: They try to empower their volunteer leaders and not merely make their volunteers into subservient supporters of an expert staff.

Like their highly successful international-national counterparts, many of these small, staffed groups have spent years trying to diversify and consolidate their financial support; they, too, have tried hard to mature into established, long-lasting institutions managed by an appropriate mix of volunteers and professionals. They have struggled with the question of optimum staffing arrangements, done their best to achieve technical and legal expertise (on staff or board or both), expended great effort in developing a stable corps of philanthropic backers, and sometimes spent scarce dollars on campaigns to recruit new members through direct mail, canvasses or, more often, the development of chapters and affiliates. They often line up with their more established counterparts on the doorsteps of national foundations, but for the most part they enjoy considerably less grant-making success.

Unlike the handful of prosperous national organizations, most of these staffed groups have not achieved stability. Most remain small according to parameters devised by nonprofit management specialist Jonathan Cook: They have annual budgets far below $1 million, few staff, and no endowments capable of sustaining them indefinitely.[11] While many of these groups have been enormously adept at influencing policy and achieving other substantive goals, the business side of their operations can often be characterized as perpetual crisis management. They often suffer from high rates of staff and board turnover—we encountered one state-based lobbying group that had had ten executive directors in its fifteen-year life— and thus lack a clear sense of their own histories. Most of the ten- to twenty-year-old groups we examined possess no financial endowments (or very paltry ones), do not spend significant resources on the training of their staff or board, lack long-term planning procedures (or, worse, blatantly ignore the plans that were carefully created by volunteers and instead fight endless brush fires), and often do not clearly demarcate roles and responsibilities among the staff and between the staff and the board. In such an organization, a CEO with more than five years on the job is a rarity; regardless of the professed philosophy of these groups, their practices prove that they do not—or cannot—value longevity. The makeup of their boards and staffs often shows that they also mistrust true diversity: They frequently lack the critical synergy of skills and personal backgrounds that creates the foundation for successful institutional development.

One might argue that through processes tantamount to natural selection, NGOs thus troubled will—even should—eventually cease to exist, for the failure to grow into stable institutions is the kiss of death for nonprofit groups in all sectors. Says Jonathan Cook:

> The nature of small organizations in the nonprofit economy is that they depend upon a small number of special people. Small is a fragile, un-

stable condition. Small is temporary. Although small business is also fragile, there are no stable nonprofit equivalents of the small family business that passes on from generation to generation. . . . Small nonprofit organizations, many using volunteers and/or a key leader as their form of subsidy, have produced some of society's greatest achievements and progress. But unless they then developed fundraising skills and connections after they lost their initial leadership, chances are they are no longer with us (which may be good or bad). Nonprofits that fail to grow become extinct. . . . There are no "old," small nonprofits.[12]

But the extinction or continuing malaise of many of the small, independent environmental organizations dispersed across the country will be a great loss, for these are the very groups that provide much of the "glue" holding successful environmental advocacy together, especially at the state and regional levels. It is precisely the absence of such organizations—the coordinating councils and conservation coalitions especially—that keeps environmental progress at bay in many states. Particularly the staffed, statewide coalitions (of which there are about two dozen nationwide) offer environmentalists the opportunity to magnify their power greatly. In states possessing an independent, staffed environmental coalition, enormous opportunities exist for the proper coordination of skills, the orchestration of effective lobbying and agency monitoring activities, and the education of the electorate across the broadest possible range of emerging environmental issues. Moreover, the various staffed coordinating councils and state-based coalitions help incubate new organizations to fill in the gaps of activism across a given state or region. They can also work effectively to help link local organizations with national ones and to coordinate communication with national, and even international, groups in a way that brings maximum pressure and expertise to bear on issues of common concern. The very presence of a staffed, independent group working at the state level often serves as an inspiration (not to mention a provider of technical support) to emerging local groups.

Yet leaders of these metalevel organizations themselves often feel divorced from the international-national movement. They complain of isolation and often decry the efforts of national organizations to build support around local or regional issues without reference to the groups already hard at work on the same problems. They are not the only leaders who recognize this problem. Said one national leader:

> The national organizations look down their noses at the smaller state groups. The state groups would love to be supported by and are supportive of national groups. I can think of a group in Wisconsin [names the organization] that would love to work with The Nature Conservancy, but the [TNC] director in Wisconsin felt they were a threat and competition for funds and didn't want anything to do with them. That's just one little example of something that happens all the time all over the country.

For most practical purposes, the institutionalized, growth-oriented organizations in the coastal cities and the small, under-supported, often stagnant organizations operating in the states now comprise two distinct branches of the conservation-environmental movement in the United States. They discuss the same issues, read the same professional literature, decry the same egregious problems, pay attention to the same planetary trends, pursue the same national funders, and speak the same language of resource management and environmental protection, but in their daily operations, where questions and decisions unfold hour by hour for their leaders, they too often remain isolated from each other. As time passes and the issues become more intense and complex, these two branches of the environmental movement seem to be growing farther apart. They are studiously ignoring each other at the very moment when they should be seeking ways to combine their own best talents. As they continue to pull in opposite directions, they inadvertently guarantee that the deserts of American conservation—the places nearly devoid of effective activism—will continue to grow.

It is easy to be simplistic about the split between national and local groups, to see it as a matter of the distant national behemoths versus the sensitive local activists. The reality bears just enough resemblance to that picture to make the truth seem deceptively simple. These two branches of environmental advocacy have much to learn from each other. In the most basic terms, the state-regional-local organizations can learn from their international-national counterparts effective patterns of achieving institutional stability, including the critically important tasks of diversifying internal skills to make organizations effective at business as well as on issues and programs. Larger organizations can also offer technical help with local issues, on which they often do groundbreaking work. And some national organizations mobilize thousands of local volunteers year after year—to write their congressmen, to take care of preserves, to raise money for conservation. Their well-groomed members might not fit the conventional perception of environmental activists, but they can be tremendously effective.

Conversely, the larger organizations can learn some things, too. Their smaller counterparts understand the close-range use of the grass roots—the motivational factors that can turn distant check-writing members into active participants in social and political action. Their members don't just write their congressmen; they show up at the state legislature or county planning board to testify and lobby. Conservation action is ultimately local action, and local organizations can make it happen.

What both wings of the movement readily acknowledge (but less readily act upon) is that environmental advocacy must flow in both directions, from the national to the local level and vice versa. No one can seriously believe that the passage of federal legislation—or the enactment of a few state codes—is sufficient to guarantee the success of environmentalism. As the Reagan years should have taught everyone, new policies and laws might be difficult to enact but they are certainly easy to ignore, especially when environmentalists remain fragmented and politically impotent.

We will now turn to the nuts and bolts of organizational leadership, highlighting the key problems and opportunities we uncovered as we performed the surveys and interviews.

The Tasks of Management and Leadership

In the typical conservation group with a budget of a few hundred thousand dollars or less, staff serve in multiple capacities and must develop a staggering range of skills. As our data and interviews show, the CEOs of these groups are unmistakably the principal organizational leaders and are granted a full array of executive powers, but they are also, just as often, the development officers and fund-raisers, the public relations staff, the writers and editors of publications, and the chief implementers of at least some programs. In the universe of environmental management, the typical NGO conservation leader is the least specialized player of all. There is virtually no one in government service, for-profit business, or education in natural resources who must possess as many different skills and use them all effectively. One founder and CEO of a regional land-conservation organization described his job in this way:

> What I do really amounts to four jobs. There is the administrative job of just managing the organization from day to day—the staff, the budget, et cetera. There is what I would call the leadership job, which is conceptual—finding the direction for the organization. There is project work, which in our case usually means research and land management. And there is the fund-raising job, which I do mostly alone. In a group like this, the leader needs to do a little of all those things. I can't afford not to do them all well.

For the conservation leaders we surveyed, especially in the smaller, staffed organizations, these are literally skills of survival: The life of the organization depends on them. The ensuing stress on these leaders is enormous.

This is not to say that the leaders of the "large" conservation groups have it easy. In the midst of American enterprise, a large conservation outfit is still a very small business. Missoula, Montana, population 40,000, has stores selling cowboy boots that are larger businesses than many international conservation groups. For a nonprofit that can afford a greater division of labor and skill, much more depends on the CEO's ability to choose and empower a top-notch staff. Leaders of large conservation NGOs thus have a deep interest—again, an interest tantamount to organizational survival—in the quality of talent emerging in conservation. Moreover, leaders of the very largest organizations ($10 million and up), where departmentalization is a necessity, run the risk of becoming insulated from their own staff and alienated from many of the important decisions made throughout various levels of the organization. These organizations, while less prone to the eclipse that threatens small groups, possess plenty of size-related problems of their own; and, again, these are by no means unique to conservation but rather occur throughout the nonprofit sector. According to Jonathan Cook, common examples include the inability to act quickly in response to problems and opportunities (often due to conflicting internal constituencies or donor restrictions); "fossilization," or the inability to act at all; forgetting the purpose of the organization and beginning to exist for the sake of institutional prosperity; and the "conglomerate syndrome" of trying to grab too much turf and be all things to all people.[13] These problems accompany the "tendencies to ineffectiveness" that plague public sector organizations and that management expert Peter Drucker has described in detail.[14]

In the largest conservation groups, the tasks of management are often so complex, and the speed with which even the ablest leaders can move on to new agendas is so slow, that leaders of these groups often see their tenure of effectiveness as a very protracted affair. As the chairperson of one national organization put it:

> In the larger, more complex organizations it takes three years to really begin to get up to speed. At four years you have a chance to start to leave your mark on the organization. You know, that's the average situation. It takes seven or eight years to really begin to have a substantial influence on its character—having shown substantially increased membership or made it much more productive or changed its direction in some significant way.

It must be said here that in most *small* organizations, the leader has not merely "left his or her mark" after four years, but has probably just left.

In both large and small organizations, everything depends on the ability of a few leaders to perform the many tasks of managing so that the organization has an impact on the world and simultaneously prospers or at least survives as a business.

The peculiar skills required by NGO conservationists are not taught in colleges and universities. Indeed, schools of forestry and natural resources, departments and programs in environmental studies and environmental sciences report that on average only about 6 percent of their students (graduate and undergraduate) find jobs within the conservation NGOs. Of the many placements of newly graduated environmental professionals, the NGOs rank at the very bottom—far below state and federal agencies, private industry, and even below placements into academic (teaching and research) positions.[15] Only 11 percent of more than 150 academic training programs in environmental fields report offering a thorough curriculum in organizational management.[16] Nearly one-third have no offerings whatever in organizational management.

Moreover, academic programs specializing in nonprofit management—most of them new—tend to emphasize the kinds of skills required to run very large, settled, and noncontroversial institutions, such as hospitals, programs for the elderly, and national youth organizations. Even if aspiring conservation leaders were interested in them, they would find that these programs fall far short of providing the requisite skills for running social-political movement groups, especially those at work on issues as scientifically and politically complex as environmental issues. Nor is there a wealth of literature on the successful management and leadership of social-change organizations, large or small. There are myriad manuals and how-to books on various aspects of management—a virtual library of fund-raising guides, for example—but there is little of a comprehensive nature on running social-change groups. Said one national leader:

> People who write most of the manuals on management and leadership of nonprofit organizations don't come from the cause-advocacy side. I think they're fairly insensitive to it. They tend to be people who have worked for traditional charities—hospitals, social service fund-raising drives, things of that sort where if you're not looking entirely at a profit bottom line, you're still looking at things that are more like widgets, that can be measured in terms of hospital beds, occupancy rates, hungry people fed. They're very insensitive to the whole motivational aspect of a cause-advocacy organization—why people join, why they work their fingers to the bone as volunteers, how they get their rewards.

These findings lead to the inevitable conclusion that conservationists are left to themselves, and perhaps to support from other wings of the social-change movement, to incubate and train their own leadership. No one will do it for them.

There is another motivational aspect to cause-advocacy organizations as well—the motivation of the leaders themselves. The fact is, practically none of the people in key positions of conservation leadership were in any systematic way trained for the actual jobs they perform. Indeed, some told us that they can trace their difficulties in running organizations back to the lack of a fit between their own training and personal motivation and the realities of leading a nonprofit organization, with all its managerial complexity. Said one leader of a $300,000 regional environmental policy center:

> No one told me, when I first went to work for an environmental organization, that what I was *really* doing was becoming the CEO of a small, nonprofit corporation. We didn't think about it in those terms, but that's exactly what it was. It took me by surprise when I finally understood the magnitude of it—and what it meant. My training and experience were somewhere else. I think this all has something to do with people's ideals clashing with institutional behavior. Our mind-sets coming in govern a lot of the outcome—and we're seeing some fallout from our lack of preparation, especially in the smaller organizations. They are very often lacking the very tools and processes, the organizational dynamics that need to be grown, in order for them to become stable institutions. No one there is prepared to provide these things.

Said another, in this case the leader of a $500,000 national organization:

> Who the hell ever got into conservation in order to run a nonprofit organization? Forty-two percent of my time goes for fund-raising, 7 percent goes into conservation. I'm not a conservationist—I'm a professional fund-raiser.

Funding and Fund-raising

Leader after leader told us that the single greatest problem they face is the pursuit of money—not the advancement of issues before recalcitrant politicians, not access to the media, not the effective use of the scientific base underlying conservation, but dollars. Many took pains to describe their difficulties in raising money and the way those problems divert them from what they are trained and impassioned to do on behalf of the environment. Said the head of a national organization:

> I spend at least 30 percent, and probably should spend 70 percent, of my time raising money. I have a fairly stable list of 10,000 members who contribute $200,000 toward a $700,000 budget. That leaves me with a half million to raise from foundations. I get grants from twenty-five to thirty foundations, so you can see the grants tend to be small. Each foundation has a slightly different format, different requirements for reporting. I spend as much time getting $10,000 as I do getting $50,000. You see, you wind up with eighteen-hour days in order to spend a little time on what you're organized to do.

But the litany of woes over fund-raising is not limited to national leaders who must constantly hustle to meet six- or seven-figure budgets. Even the leaders of all-volunteer associations, some with budgets of less than $10,000 annually, complain that the time involved in fund-raising diverts them from their real work. Concerns over the pursuit of money stretch across all camps of conservation and, indeed, as most conservation leaders readily acknowledge, these concerns are not unique to conservation. They are ubiquitous throughout the nonprofit sector. Behind each of the "thousand points of light," there is a throbbing headache over money.

However, the most serious problems in fund-raising and financial stability seem to occur among the staffed organizations working at the state, regional, and local levels. Many of these groups have teetered for years on the brink of financial collapse. Unlike the all-volunteer associations, whose principal capital is donated labor, and the endowed, relatively stable organizations on the national scene, these groups occupy a very precarious position. Since most of them are unendowed, they rely solely on annual (in reality, perpetual) fund-raising efforts designed to tap the continuing goodwill of a small membership. Donor-patron gifts and small foundation grants are used to supplement the core support from membership dues, but the base of support tends to remain small—usually too small to carry more than two to six staff members—and the difficulties in making ends meet tend to plague these organizations without cessation.

Even when they do not underpay their senior staff—one of their most common ailments—these groups report that the fund-raising pressures on their leaders often prove impossible to endure. We encountered several grass-roots staff leaders who reported spending over half of their time on fund-raising, in many cases to achieve annual budgets of less than $150,000. One head of a prominent, twenty-year-old statewide coalition said she spends 70 percent of her time to raise an $80,000 budget. In the context of her minuscule organization (two professional staffers) such an enormous amount of time tied up in fund-raising effectively neuters the principal leader, and cannot help but render the group less effective. Survey data indicate that the smaller the organization, the more rapidly staff cycle through it. It is not uncommon to find NGO staff leaders who have worked for three or more environmental nonprofits, moving along just ahead of complete and final burnout but staying with one organization for no more than three or four years. The ensuing loss of institutional memory and the tendency to keep sending "green stock" staffers into the local and regional policy arenas conspire to make these local, state, and regional organizations less effective over time. These groups generally have not succeeded in achieving the ordinary formulations of long-range staff support that the more institutionalized groups have achieved. Yet that is precisely what their arenas of activity call for.

Like their larger international-national counterparts, local and state-based groups struggle to remain both credible and professional. For example, in the arena of the state legislature, where so many key environmental policies are made and broken, these mid-size, staffed organizations compete eye to eye with the well-paid professional lobbyists from industry, trade associations, and other special interests who aim to keep environmental progress at bay. Over the past twenty years, state-based environmentalists have learned the value of seasoned professionals who can challenge the propaganda of the exploiters with hard facts and well-conceived policy initiatives. But maintaining the conditions needed to keep experienced professionals on staff has eluded too many of these groups. Most have not made the successful transition from treating staff as if they were aging Vista volunteers to building the kind of institutional support and stability required by professionals over the long term.

But other leaders—they might be called the hardest of the hard core—look at the situation quite differently. Without a trace of irony, one field staffer of a struggling national organization said this:

> I just can't figure out why recruiting new staff to work here has gotten so damned hard. They just won't come any more for room and board and $30 a month.

As state and regional groups have come to grips with the need to create stronger financial bases, they have naturally turned to foundations and other outside funders for help. To their dismay, they have often found that while foundation grants can help meet the budget, grantsmanship—even within the fast-moving, fluid, and often innovative world of private foundations—is not without its pitfalls. As many leaders have discovered and reported to us, foundation grants are a very mixed blessing; the pursuit of this deceptively "easy money" can become a new treadmill ready to exhaust even the ablest of leaders. Some leaders we encountered complained of the subtle but definite pressures exerted on their organizations when they began to rely more heavily on foundation grants and other forms of institutional philanthropy. The fact that most grants are "restricted" to conform with the issues of interest to funders prompts some conservation leaders to complain that accepting foundation funds—something they feel they must do—subtly alters their own selection of issues, until in the worst cases, according to one leader "we're just the gofers doing what X, Y, and Z foundation officers want to see happen in the world." Another leader said this:

> The foundations move in herds, and there's that temptation to follow the herd yourself. If they're funding water, you're trying to repackage your mission so that some of that water money trickles down to you. Some of our local supporters have been real critical of that tendency with me and just in general. They think it's important to set organizational goals and stick to them. But for an organization like ours out here in the hinterlands, there's obviously a downside to that: no money. The fact is, time is a luxury we just don't have. I'm looking for the quickest path to my budget.

Ironically, leaders of staffed *grass-roots* groups are often more firmly tied to the foundation-funding treadmill than their counterparts among the larger organizations (some of which have no memberships at all). The mythic view of the environmental grass roots is of small, high-powered organizations comprised of self-sacrificing staff and volunteers and supported almost entirely by a devoted corps of activist-members, whose constant trickle of dollars somehow makes the organization hold together. The reality is quite different. In many parts of the country, staffed grass-roots groups learned long ago that they cannot rely entirely (or even substantially) on their members and stay afloat. Like their larger counterparts on the national scene, they have learned to capture what might be best described as philanthropic subsidies—that variety of donor-patron income, foundation grants, and in a few peculiar cases corporate contributions that together with membership support make for a diversified balance sheet. That they often tend to concentrate on philanthropic subsidies rather than increased support from the membership is a reflection more of demographics than of their sophistication as fund-raisers: The numbers often fail to support them and they know it.

The fact is that many of these organizations, especially those located in predominantly rural states, remain unable to garner levels of membership that can provide even half of their budgetary needs. While national organizations can take advantage of economies of scale and favorable demographics in their nationwide direct-mail campaigns (usually focused on urban-suburban prospects), most groups in rural or poorer urban areas find that the demographics simply don't work in the same way for them. Still, the costs of running their organizations are rising, just as they are in places where the membership base is richer.

Few organizations with paid, professional staff can operate credibly on a budget below $100,000—even in the poorest regions of the country where business and living expenses remain low—and, indeed, only 24 percent of the independent, staffed organizations in our sample operate with less than that. The median salary of primarily executive officers in our sample is about $40,000. Other professional staff in an organization that pays its CEO that much would probably be paid between $25,000 and $35,000. Thus, it is clear that staffing an organization well enough to manage several major programs, perhaps lobby and work with agencies, produce a newsletter and other publications, and tend to the administrative demands and the ordinary legal and fiduciary responsibilities of running a nonprofit corporation would most likely take $200,000 or more, regardless of location. If such a group were to exist on memberships alone, it would need around 8,000 active dues payers per year (at $25 per member). Given a 30 percent annual drop-off rate, the base from which the membership must be drawn would have to be over 10,000 people. To environmental leaders in large, urban-based organizations, achieving a membership base of 10,000 would seem easy, but in many states, especially the rural ones, this is not the case.

For example, the Rocky mountain and Great Plains states report remarkably similar experiences with respect to the ability of resident environmental groups to increase local memberships. In organization after organization from the Dakotas across the northern and southern Rockies and into the desert Southwest, leaders told us the same story about memberships: In most cases, their organizations had managed to achieve membership levels ranging from 500 to around 3,000 and then plateaued. Most of these groups have not seen significant increases in their memberships over one to two decades of existence, despite many earnest efforts to increase them. Canvasses have failed to add to these memberships significantly; direct mail has not worked (except for replacement); the institution of chapters, field offices, and community organizing programs has done little to raise membership levels beyond the apparent peak. It is easy to dismiss these failed efforts as nonprofessional or misguided, but there is probably another factor at work. Given the demographics of their states, these groups, by and large, have already achieved what in any normal circumstance might be considered their peak levels of membership. And these levels of indigenous support are simply not enough.

Take Montana as an example. Among the Rocky mountain states, Montana is an outstanding exception to the environmental quietude that characterizes much of the American West. With a population of only 800,000 and the third largest landmass in the lower forty-eight, Montana ranks among the lowest in population density. Yet its history of environmental activism is long, rich, and exemplary. Montana boasts a dozen homegrown environmental groups with full-time, paid staff, including a wilderness advocacy organization that predates The Wilderness Society. Moreover, Montana possesses a very active corps of national environmental group members; a host of highly active and effective chapters of the Sierra Club, the Audubon Society, and other national organizations; and several professional staff and field offices of major national organizations. For all of this, a homegrown, statewide environmental organization in Montana would consider itself fortunate to have more than 2,000 dues-paying members (about 1 percent of the state's households). In fact, hardly any of the state-focused organizations have that many members. At an average cost of $25 per family membership, those 2,000 supporters would yield only $50,000—barely enough to cover a single full-time professional and his or her office expenses at the median salary paid by NGOs nationwide. Finding the new corps of members out on the margin beyond the readily achievable peak demands a level of recruitment sophistication that these organizations do not possess and feel they cannot afford. The easier path toward their annual financial goals leads them through the thickets of philanthropic subsidy.

The common complaint that environmentalists register about states such as Montana is that the competition among organizations is too fierce to allow any of them to grow sufficiently: They each capture a small portion of the potential membership pool, with no one organization able to achieve a critical mass of local support. Thus, like density-dependent fish, their size is limited by the available food supply. But that conclusion is both facile and false. In fact, if the offending competitors disappeared tomorrow, the survivors would probably still not fare much better, at least not without alterations in both structure and focus. Many donors habitually give a fixed amount to any one organization, unless that organization works assiduously with individual donors to increase their giving. Some organizations do succeed in highly competitive environments by using at least one of three strategies: intensive individual fundraising, finding a niche with few competitors and a strong constituency of its own, or collaborating well with other organizations.

Although we have no relevant hard data, our interviews and observations indicate that organizations chronically in jeopardy use none of those strategies.

Apparently more important than the number of competing organizations is the state or regional climate for support of conservation action. Even some heavily populated states simply lack the tradition of environmental advocacy that serves as an inducement for broad public support of environmental organizations. Indeed, nonmetropolitan states such as Alaska, Maine, Montana, and Vermont, with their impressive numbers of tough, lean environmental organizations, outperform many highly populated states with respect to citizen support merely because the citizens of those states learned long ago to appreciate the benefits of organized environmental advocacy. Conversely, there are many other states in which the conservation message has been meager, practically nonexistent, until as recently as the last two to five years—including some, such as Arizona, where population growth, real estate development, or rapid industrialization dominate the economy. In many of the places where they are needed most, conservationists find the least support.

As a result of their stagnant memberships, many small to midsize conservation groups ($80,000 to $500,000 organizations) in all regions of the country rely heavily on national and local philanthropy for programmatic support. But they are not alone. Indeed, their reliance on organized philanthropy mirrors the national trend. The average conservation group in the United States receives 44 percent of its annual income from philanthropic sources (primarily foundation grants and gifts from individuals). Even among membership organizations (comprising three-fourths of our staff survey), only 32 percent of the average income accrues from membership dues, while a full 40 percent is philanthropic income.

Across the board, organizations both large and small reported to us that personal philanthropy—individuals' gifts and contributions beyond membership dues—is vital to their continued existence. And this form of philanthropy is usually tied directly to the membership base: With the exception of those rare environmental groups that tend to attract a predominantly low-income constituency, the more members an organization possesses, the greater the likelihood that substantial individual philanthropy can be garnered. The importance of these donor-patron gifts can hardly be over-stated. When asked which sources of philanthropic support the leaders considered crucial to their organizations, over 40 percent listed small individual contributions (under $5,000 each) as their leading choice, ahead of all other forms of philanthropy, including foundation grants and corporate gifts—even though foundation grants comprise a slightly higher proportion of the organization's budgets on average (21 percent versus 19 percent from individual gifts). We assume leaders prefer individual contributions because once committed to an organization, individual people are more re-liable supporters than are foundations. They yield a better return on time invested in fund-raising. For that reason, conservation leaders have spent a great deal of time and effort cultivating indi-vidual donors who can give substantial gifts beyond membership dues, although they continue to hold a deep stake in the foundation world as well.

What is missing from the national philanthropic agenda is an organized, strategic effort to nurture grass-roots organizations where they are most needed. As discussed earlier in this chapter, about half the states lack the peculiar network and variety of con-servation groups that stimulate successful advocacy across the full range of environmental issues. It can be argued that the states that possess the best records of environmental management (and the states with what might be described as the highest environmental standard of living) are those with a strong and diverse fabric of con-servation groups.

The development of a strong fabric of environmental advocacy can usually be traced from the grass roots upward (this is not a trickle-down phenomenon). For example: Numerous all-volunteer grass-roots groups working at the city, town, and country levels eventually realize that they need consistent, expert representation in the state capitol. This need gives rise to a statewide environmen-tal coalition, located in the capital city, staffed with professionals and supported by its grass-roots member organizations as well as its own independent membership (individuals). Because of its larger size and geographic reach (and the presence of a paid, pro-fessional staff), the coalition can begin to import philanthropic sub-sidies to supplement its core of support from the membership. It can provide some staff support to its all-volunteer members and perhaps even serve as a broker to leverage funding to grass-roots groups for the resolution of precedential issues. In addition, many states now need their own legal and scientific professionals who concentrate on environmental issues. In some cases (Maine is a good example) these professionals serve on the staff of the leading statewide coalition. But in other cases they might serve through independent organizations of their own (public-interest law clinics, for example, or organizations such as the newly formed Land and Water Conservation Fund, a Colorado-based group designed to offer free legal services to grass-roots environmentalists in seven states). Serving with these homegrown efforts, the chapters and field offices of national organizations can add greatly to local firepower. Indeed, in some of the leading public-lands states, a great deal of legal and some technical-scientific assistance is provided to the grass roots through local offices of national organizations. These efforts are crucial in making sure that leading environmental laws are obeyed and that natural resource agencies (both state and federal) do their jobs well. With these resources in place, the more specialized conservation groups will find that they can benefit from advocacy and activism, sometimes by offering a more conservative alternative to it. For example, land-trust and natural-areas protection groups often report that they willingly exploit the political spoils that occur naturally in states with strong traditions of environmental activism. Said an executive in the national office of The Nature Conservancy:

> We can't be who we are without the hard-core activist groups. They allow the Conservancy to be as conservative as it is. It's pretty far at one end of the spectrum. In terms of issues we involve ourselves in and don't involve ourselves in, I'm absolutely convinced that if it wasn't for the more activist groups, there's no way we could get support from corporate America. We don't look good to corporate America—we look good in comparison to other people. We need those organizations, and we need that spectrum to successfully occupy our niche along the way.

Moreover, some regions of the country have learned that they can benefit from the addition of multistate (often regionally focused) policy research centers. Since many economic activities in the United States tend to revolve around regions and their central cities, and since many regions are distinguished by their peculiar endowments of natural resources, conservationists have learned that it makes sense for the states of a given region to learn from one another's best policy initiatives. Hence, in the northeastern, southwestern, northwestern, northern Rocky mountain, and Great Lakes states, environmentalists have managed to develop policy centers designed to examine the future needs and trends of their respective regions. When compared with the state-based coalitions, these multistate groups (some with memberships, some not) tend to be even more capable of reaching out for philanthropic subsidies from national funders.

These are all healthy patterns, exhibiting the diversity, sophistication, and dynamism of the U.S. environmental movement. What the movement needs now is a central nervous system. Its leaders— in established organizations, in sympathetic government agencies, in academia, and most importantly in the funding community— need to pay attention to the imperatives of making environmentalism into a truly *nationwide* movement, instead of a federally focused movement with a plethora of "national" organizations. It is time to rethink the directions of grant making and the flow of "seed money," or philanthropic capital. The states and regions where environmentalism has not taken root need special attention; if they were capable of organizing themselves along the lines described above, they would have done so by now. Some would argue that the fact that they haven't is good reason to avoid them, but that would be a mistake. Healthy patterns of environmental activism can be replicated (or enhanced) in all states and regions, and there is no good reason why they should not be. Through the Leadership Study, however, we learned of the existence of many poor reasons: Too many leaders of the international-national groups and "competing" local and statewide groups fear the fallout from a truly nationwide environmental movement. To some, expansion threatens hegemony.

The Failure to Diversify

Interestingly, conservation and environmental groups, despite their firm reliance on private sources of philanthropy, receive little (4 percent) in the form of corporate gifts, until recently one of the fastest-growing sources of philanthropy nationwide. This avoidance of corporate funding clearly fits with the overwhelming tendency of environmentalists to distrust business, undoubtedly coupled with similar feelings on the other side. But it is also indicative of a larger problem: the failure to diversify. In our interviews, conservation leaders repeatedly challenged the notion that American business might be persuaded to join their movement with any meaningful motivation beyond mere public relations benefits. Indeed, many found the very notion of "corporate environmentalism" oxymoronic and repugnant. Many conservation leaders see corporations as their intractable enemies and would never seek corporate funding for fear it would co-opt their efforts or at least lead members and supporters to distrust the motives of the organization. The prospect of placing corporate and business leaders on the boards of conservation and environmental groups elicited an even stronger response from many of the leaders we surveyed. Given the strength of these attitudes, it is little wonder that conservationists reap so little income through corporate philanthropy. Only 10 percent of the leaders said that corporate gifts were crucial to their organizations.

But too many conservationists have learned to paint business with too broad a brush. While the desire to remain free of the potentially tainting influence of natural resource exploiters might be an honorable motive, it makes sense to recognize that most businesses and corporations are not necessarily in the business of resource exploitation; moreover, for many conservation NGOs struggling mightily with the balance sheet, sympathetic business leaders placed on the board might bring exactly the right skills and insights to the organization. Many groups obviously suffer from the absence of managerial and business acumen. Yet many of them act as if that is their destiny, and nothing can or should be done about it. They disagree with the notion of midcareer training for their staff (one leader called it "frosting;" another, who leads a $300,000 organization, described our questionnaire list of organizational management tools as irrelevant). Bound to the prejudice that businesspeople by definition are hostile to conservation, they eschew even beneficial relations with true conservationists who manage businesses. This tendency contributes to organizational weakness even though it reaffirms a sense of solidarity among the homogeneous board and staff.

When organizations have proven themselves unsuccessful—when they chronically fail in the policy arena, when they sputter along financially, lurching from crisis to crisis and unable to control their own destinies—it is often the case that they have learned to refuse the benefits of internal diversification or believe they have diversified when in reality they have not. Such groups, when examined closely, are usually revealed to be a social hall of mirrors. Their board members come from the same socioeconomic strata; they do not comprise a team representing diverse skills and interests. Without diversity, they usually exhibit a predictable response to new issues, opportunities, or threats: They resist new ideas and the regenerating influence of new people. While such groups might score astonishing victories early on, outmaneuvering opponents of enormous size and capability, they usually fail over the long run. They become odd little environmental clubs instead of dynamic, functioning organizations.

As John Gardner has argued persuasively, organizations and their leaders both need renewal.[17] They need systematic ways to examine themselves, and they need periodic tune-ups. As one sixty-five-year-old volunteer told us:

> Some of the organizations that got going so strong pursuant to Earth Day 1970 are suffering "founders' disease," in that they are playing musical chairs on their boards with the same people over and over—not developing new leadership or a built-in changing of the guard. They need leadership-recruitment training and help in how to gracefully "retire" those people who are merely "caretakers."

In addition to suffering from inbreeding based on political prejudices, most mainstream conservation-environmental groups lack racial, ethnic, and cultural diversity as well. Compared with other social-change movements in the United States, the whiteness of the green movement is one of its most troubling—and telltale—characteristics. We address this critical problem at length in the second Island Press book resulting from the Conservation Leadership Project: *Voices from the Environmental Movement: Perspectives for a New Era* (1992).

Membership Development

The presence of a membership colors the styles of leadership required by the organization. Members are constituents; in many (but not all) instances their views must be reflected in the workings of the organization. Still, simply having a membership is no guarantee that the organization is a grass-roots group. Said one national leader: "Grass-roots activism is not the same as grass-roots membership. Today especially, with the growth of direct mail, these are two different phenomena." Indeed, many conservation groups have members who are entirely inactive in the affairs of the organization; their views are seldom if ever sought and have no bearing on the agenda. They are passive check writers who applaud and support the decisions made by an elite board and staff, but expect no role in decision making and do not use the organization as the launching pad for their own volunteer activism. In many instances, the development of such a membership is entirely appropriate: The organization *is* a confederation of experts and not a grass-roots activist organization. Expecting all environmental organizations to be structurally and philosophically the same is anathema to a healthy movement. Leading an organization with an active membership is different from leading a group of check writers— and different again from leading one with no membership at all. No single prescription of responsible leadership covers all three kinds of groups, but all three could work hand in hand on an identical set of issues, and indeed each has its place. What is most important is that these various kinds of organizations learn how to use each other constructively, making the most of complementary talents in pursuit of a bona fide public good. This requires mutual respect, constant communication, and a willingness to work out any disagreements.

Behind the scenes, conservation leaders criticize each other over such matters. Some leaders of activist grass-roots groups look askance (and often jealously) at those with large but inactive memberships. Conversely, some leaders of the "expert" organizations accuse grass-roots groups of political naïveté or failure to comprehend and act on technical information in a manner that increases the credibility of environmentalists among developers or regulators. Many conservation leaders seem unable to come to grips with fundamental questions arising from the never-ending debate between ideology and pragmatism, or between grass-roots activism and executive-level decision making, and nowhere is this failure more apparent than in the use of and attitudes toward members.

In some organizations, the membership is often a most awkward appendage. Staff leaders sometimes look upon members as if they are a necessary evil: necessary for finances, clout, and credibility, but a nettlesome threat to staff or board hegemony and a potential source of diversion away from the mission. Other groups take membership participation to such an extreme that they virtually gridlock themselves: They set organizational goals that are impossible to achieve but are worded in ways that satisfy various segments of their constituencies; their efforts at strategic planning and programmatic evaluation are subverted by powerful but uninformed members. Fortunately, most surviving membership organizations have struck a balance between these two extremes and have learned how to use membership input to enhance planning, implementation, and evaluation.

How to recruit and *use* members effectively is one of the key challenges facing conservation leaders and their organizations. As the dramas of national environmental politics and issues are acted out increasingly at state and local levels, and as earnest members of local, grass-roots organizations develop issues that they want to see "the nationals" address, the question of effective use of members looms ever larger. This question has everything to do with effective leadership, for if conservation leaders cannot marshal their constituencies, beginning with their own members, it is doubtful that they will be able to achieve one of the most widely professed goals on their agenda: to move their issues more deeply into the communities, decision-making arenas, and homes of the nation. Now that so many egregious environmental issues have left the realm of theory and forecast and have come home, literally, to roost, how can conservationists achieve a much broader base of public support and action? How can they deepen their effectiveness in the arenas of government, private enterprise, and the individual choices and behaviors that affect the quality of the environment? Said one national leader:

We in the national environmental organizations aren't doing a very good job of reaching out to locally based environmentalists, but we're doing an even worse job of reaching out beyond the people who are already interested in the environment . . . those who are not identified as environmentalists. It's comfortable to spend five or ten years working in an organization like this one, just talking to friends . . . but the mandate or challenge of leadership is to reach that broader constituency and cast wilderness protection, pollution control, the stewardship of public lands in a broader context, including an economic context. . . . The trick is to do all that without losing the edge of advocacy . . . to do it without copping out or becoming a corporate bedfellow. You've still got to articulate what you think is right. . . . We don't simply want to become the businesspeople of the environmental movement.

But how are conservationists attempting to reach the interested but unconverted? The great majority of organizations we surveyed rely heavily on public education through the use of various media as their principal strategy. That strategy scores far ahead of direct political action, litigation, influencing elections, lobbying, performing and disseminating research, mediation, and other broad strategies available to nonprofit groups. Given that many conservation groups run their substantive programs with philanthropic dollars (foundation grants and tax-deductible gifts), the overwhelming emphasis on education—rather than other, more activist strategies—is not surprising. By federal law, philanthropists are restricted in their support of lobbying and other forms of political action. But looking at leaders' widespread frustration with the effectiveness of their organizations, one wonders whether the great emphasis on public education is getting the job done.

Many leaders complain of their movement's failure to alter public and private behaviors in favor of conservation and simultaneously move public opinion in ways that guarantee the election of conservationist policymakers. What passes for public education is, in many instances, a form of preaching to the converted: Those who have already heard and believe the conservation message are getting it again and again in a numbingly familiar refrain through newsletters and other movement publications as well as sympathetic media sources (usually print media) that regularly report on environmental and conservation issues. The message, delivered with increasing frequency, force, and sophistication, may be leaving the electorate well informed but passive, even hopeless. Voters do not seem to be rushing to the polls to bring conservationists into power, nor do they seem very able to judge the actual records of elected officials—records so easily obscured by the "smoke and mirrors" of spin-doctored campaigns. Everyone now claims to be an environmentalist; the term is in danger of losing its meaning.

Some leaders we interviewed expressed strong opinions about the educational focus of so many groups. Some feel that the era of mass public education has now passed: At least in the United States, they argue, the environmental agenda has largely become institutionalized, and the real battles are being fought through negotiation, litigation, and an emphasis on direct enforcement of laws and regulations. Others question whether conservation NGOs are even appropriate vehicles to educate beyond the "choir of the already converted." Said one national leader:

> I question whether we ought to be in the education business at all—or whether so many of us ought to be. I sort of wonder if there isn't a lot of money going down the rat hole for education. . . . All conservation organizations ought to be able to say to donors what happened to their money. We in the conservation business are just as susceptible to bureaucratic flabbiness as any other business is. Education is very difficult to measure. You have to make sure that all your resources as much as possible are going into producing a conservation product as opposed to merely talking about it. . . . I think the public is damned unsophisticated about this. . . . The National Audubon Society is not going to educate people about conservation. It's going to happen because Mom and Dad care about it, and the schools have done something about it, such as nature study. That's out of the realm of nonprofits' essential influence.

Several leaders we surveyed pointed out that educating and activating are not the same. Public education might be a necessary precursor to action, but is not action itself. What conservationists clearly lack in nearly every region, state, and locale are legions of well-informed, highly motivated volunteers who consistently and effectively advocate environmental causes before planning and zoning boards, town councils, city and county commissions, state legislatures, regulatory bodies, and other decision-making authorities. Certainly there is already much effort in this arena, and organizations such as the Sierra Club, some chapters of the Audubon Society, affiliates of the National Wildlife Federation, and scores of independent state-based and local groups have been fostering such activism successfully for many years. Still, it is not nearly enough. All over the country, polluters are being granted variance after variance, developers are destroying wetlands and prime agricultural lands, waterways are being depleted and degraded, and waste disposal facilities are sited next to the neighborhoods and homes of the least powerful people in society. And these issues, serious though they are, barely begin to touch on the more daunting perils we face in the coming century, the "four horsemen of the environmental apocalypse" as they are described by E. O. Wilson: global warming, ozone depletion, toxic waste accumulation, and mass extinction. How can these be reversed?

There is a reflexive nature to conservationists' widespread cries for public education, and an equally reflexive response that their organizations, and theirs alone, should be providing it. But important questions need to be asked. What groups or sectors of society do conservationists think about when they ponder campaigns for outreach? Are these the right groups? Are decisions for member recruitment based on carefully crafted strategies to achieve outcomes in the appropriate decision-making arenas, or are they more often based on the desire merely to increase organizational memberships and revenues regardless of the issues? How can organizations who recruit members largely, or solely, through the device of direct mail ensure any significant level of activism among the membership? These are questions that campaigns in public education, broadly cast as they are, frequently ignore. And they are the stuff of much internal, but mostly hidden, debate among conservation leaders.

Presumably, broad-scale education, while focusing attention on environmental issues, is expected to serve double duty as an effective recruitment tool as well. The more "surgical" or "strategic" techniques of moving issues, ranging from direct political action through litigation and mediation or direct acquisition and management of land and water resources, are used far less than broad-scale education. Yet often missing is a focused, long-term strategy for combining leadership and highly motivated volunteers in coordinated action for institutional change.

U.S. NGOs are uniquely positioned for strategic action, combining effective campaigns on the issues with organizational growth so that one feeds the other. This is a task requiring both commitment and strategic planning, yet, as we learned through our surveys, strategic planning is either weak or lacking among most NGOs. Hand-to-mouth survival will allow hundreds of conservation groups to plod along indefinitely, but survival is not nearly enough. Leadership implies the constant search for excellence. Strategic planning is one of the watersheds currently dividing excellent from merely good conservation leadership.

Leaders' Use of Time

Leaders of conservation and environmental NGOs often lament their failure to recruit new constituencies and new kinds of supporters, including foundations and other funders, into the movement. Many organizations whose leaders we surveyed and interviewed report that their memberships have remained stable for several years—in some cases for more than a decade—while their ability to move issues, extraordinary during the 1970s, has slowed to a kind of chronic stalemate with the opposition. While some attribute this common stasis to the historical "elitism" of the natural resource field, others have observed that it is the logical outcome of the way that conservation leaders actually spend their time and their organizations' money.

How effectively do conservation leaders use the very little time that they delegate to outreach? Clearly, most spend little time in this arena, perhaps believing that the educational focus of their organizations is enough. Staff leaders spend on average about 75 percent of their time in project implementation and issue development, fund-raising, planning, and board and staff development. While each of these activities can have strong outreach components, and each is certainly necessary to running a nonprofit organization, none is outreach per se. Many leaders complain that the pursuit of money combined with a plethora of daily administrative chores binds them to their offices. They are often frustrated that their work on the issues is truncated—that they cannot spend more time meeting with new constituencies and taking their messages into unexpected quarters. Some readily admit that even when they are performing substantive work on the issues, they are doing so in association only with their own members and staff, so that, in a very important sense, even their issues "never leave the office." One result: little time left over to develop the organization by meeting new people. Given the hard-bitten nature of most conservation groups, these findings should surprise no one. But considering that the great majority of leaders we surveyed are the CEOs of their organizations—and likely to be performing many of the duties of outreach themselves—their inability to get out and meet the public is especially troublesome.

Many conservation leaders describe outreach activities as a luxury that they can only afford to pursue in the odd hours between fund-raising junkets, administration, and other activities which press more heavily on their time. Membership development and active recruitment are especially neglected components in the organizations of many we surveyed—except for those that aggressively pursue members through direct mail.

Several leaders reported that the absence of seed money prevents them from the aggressive pursuit of new members. Many now view organizational growth campaigns as another luxury that they cannot afford and that funders, after supporting a brief flurry of "development campaigns" a few years ago, have largely stopped supporting. This change of heart is particularly disturbing now, when most of the easily recruited public has already joined the movement.

Finding out what the larger public wants and will support from the environmental movement is a difficult task. It requires research, strategic thinking, and creativity. Where these tasks have been done well, the rewards have been great for both the organization and the cause. But most organizations lack the resources and the opportunity to learn what will work for them. As described above, there are remarkably high numbers of state-based and regional conservation groups whose memberships have not grown significantly since the middle 1970s, when many of the organizations were founded. The foregoing might help explain why.

Moreover, the data show that remarkably little time is spent on the leaders' own professional development (2 percent on average). Leaders report that they have no time and too little money to pursue needed training, and complain that even if they had the time and the money, the training services are not available. This is a serious problem faced by the leader-managers of growing organizations. Most conservation groups would benefit from additional in-service training for their staff.

Leaders' Personal Needs and Rewards

From the survey data and interviews, a clear portrait of the NGO conservation leaders emerges, and their needs become clear. These leaders are very committed professionals who enjoy their work and plan to stay in the field of conservation for the rest of their lives. Although staff leaders definitely feel overworked, they are not as likely to feel underpaid. A substantial raise would be welcome, but it's not among the first choices of rewards. (Obviously, this question is moot for volunteers, the great majority of whom do not desire wages for their conservation work.)

Many staff leaders report a sense of discomfort with their boards of directors—a discomfort that certainly runs through many nonprofit organizations, not merely conservation groups. The CEOs' relations with their boards present a paradox: They are often expected to lead the very boards that hold full authority over their jobs; they must direct the groups that supposedly exist to direct them. Conservation CEOs acutely feel the pressures caused by a board of well-intentioned volunteers who scarcely have time to discharge their many responsibilities as directors. The CEO often complains that the board does too little work or fails to discharge important responsibilities on time or at all; the staff is left to perform many of the board's unfinished tasks. Leaders of smaller organizations in particular complain that managerial duties and responsibilities are not clear-cut; there is no clear line marking where the board's authority ends and the staff's begins. In these instances, the board is often viewed, in the words of one staff director, as "working the boiler room instead of steering the ship."

Conversely, the volunteers, most of whom serve on NGO boards, see the situation very differently. They overwhelmingly pride themselves on their successful communication with staff and tend to see far fewer problems in the relationship between staff and board. Clearly, communication on these matters is not going well: The problematic relationship between the conservation CEO and his or her board is one of the great blind spots of the conservation movement.

These data and the interviews that buttress them suggest that in order to gain the greatest impact from a volunteer board, there is a strong need for more and better training of board members and a wider dissemination of information on successful nonprofit management. At their worst, conservation group boards virtually strangle their staffs, choking off their sense of authority and autonomy and reducing their willingness to go the extra mile for the organization. At their best, boards delegate great responsibility to their staffs and evaluate them on the basis of clear objectives: Goals and ends are expected to be met, while the means, if ethically and honestly pursued, are left to the staff. Making for better board-staff relations is clearly one of the greatest challenges among most of the organizations.

Another great challenge concerns the personal renewal of staff members. Conservation leaders again and again report a sense of personal stagnation. It is not professional training they seem to want as much as opportunities for *personal* growth and renewal. This demand presents a dilemma. While professional training seems clear-cut, involving such straightforward matters as board-staff training, fund-raising assistance, financial-management tutorials, and so forth, personal growth and renewal are ambiguous concepts. They touch on the realms of spiritual refreshment and probably require opportunities for leaving the professional setting.

Dealing as they do with nature and natural environments, conservation leaders would seem to have abundant opportunities to renew themselves with the tonic of the wilderness. Yet many apparently do not. They take vacations, but that is not enough. What they seem to require is the opportunity to enrich the spiritual dimensions of their lives and work—to take new steps into some unknown territory that will help renew and refresh them, regardless of whether it provides new skills. This is a healthy longing, and one which might be satisfied by the provision of three resources: First, organizational policies that not only allow for but demand substantial leaves and sabbaticals for staff. Second, a modest amount of funding and perhaps a new, national granting program for mid-career fellowships to allow seasoned conservation leaders to pursue some dream, or structured regime, of personal renewal. Third, the provision of information on options that leaders might pursue to achieve renewal and growth—a kind of resource guide outlining options for successful sabbaticals.

These suggestions are clearly radical in the context of the U.S. conservation-environmental movement, where personal martyrdom is still rampant. In some quarters, one's net worth to the movement is measured by how close one veers to emotional and physical collapse on the job. The abuse (or loss) of one's family, the damage to oneself, the visage of the lonely warrior whose life exists only for The Cause are still not only acceptable but desirable "attributes" for far too many workers in the movement.

The suggestions outlined above rest on two premises: first, that the *whole* environmental movement is critical in crafting a benign future for humans and other species and, second, that the environmental movement is no healthier than the people who run it. The genuine good of the movement rests on effectiveness that can be planned for and measured, and that effectiveness demands long service by individuals. The issues that conservationists care most about are long-term, many of them multigenerational, issues. Their resolution virtually demands long service and, indeed, conservation leaders profess every intention for long service. Clearly, the commitment is not lacking. The question that remains is this: Under what conditions will today's leaders and future leaders achieve their greatest levels of effectiveness? We believe that the leaders must be strong, refreshed, spiritually active, and overwhelmingly positive in their outlook. They and their organizations must constantly seek renewal.

Still, many conservationists will refuse to accept the organizational therapy of leaves and sabbaticals. One complaint will be that even when an organization has a policy encouraging them (fewer than 2 percent of U.S. conservation groups do), the organization cannot possibly afford extended leaves for staff. Given the willy-nilly manner in which most conservation groups operate, this belief is probably correct. But the point is that the pattern of operations is fatally flawed, and this is but one bit of evidence. Planning for the systematic renewal of key staff is not an insurmountable problem, but must be handled within the context of the whole. There are examples of small, nonprofit organizations that make sabbaticals work. The Native American Rights Fund, an Indian legal-aid organization based in Boulder, Colorado, not only allows for but *demands* staff sabbaticals. They are budgeted and executed within the context of the long-range plan; they are not exceptional or unusual, but normal behavior in this and some other organizations. The fact that sabbaticals are unimaginable to most conservationists is merely testimony to a lack of imagination. Some will complain that sabbaticals are nothing more than an "extended vacation," not a time of enhanced personal productivity. A resource guide to help conservation leaders design productive sabbaticals would be most helpful to the few who will pursue this option. Some will want to teach; some will want to write; some will pursue religious or personal growth experiences; some will disappear into the wilds and not be seen for days, weeks, or months—a commonly accepted practice of personal growth in many healthy cultures.

These kinds of resources aimed at personal renewal will prove more useful over time than any number of professional training experiences. Their net benefit may even exceed that of additional substantive programmatic grants to organizations—particularly if these chances for personal renewal keep the finest leaders on the job, refining their own skills and becoming evermore graceful and convincing in their arenas of advocacy.

Chapter 5

Academic Training

Leaders have always been generalists. Tomorrow's leaders will, very likely, have begun life as trained specialists, but to mature as leaders they must sooner or later crawl out of the trenches of specialization and rise above the boundaries that separate the various segments of society. Young potential leaders must be able to see how whole systems function, and how interactions with neighboring systems may be constructively managed.

—*John Gardner*, On Leadership

$\mathbf{A}$s we went about the tasks of surveying the professionals and volunteers of the conservation NGOs, we were struck by the extraordinary variety of the leaders' academic backgrounds. While 99 percent of the professional staffers possess at least one college degree, the variety of degrees they possess forms no very coherent pattern. Slightly less than half of the professionals we surveyed have degrees in the sciences (with about one-fourth of all bachelor's degrees in various biological sciences); the rest of the bachelor's degrees are in liberal arts (22 percent), social sciences (25 percent), and technical fields (6 percent). About one-quarter of the professionals possess master's degrees, but again no clear pattern emerges. While 60 percent of the master's degrees are in the sciences, no one major predominates. Forestry is the most common degree mentioned, but it accounts for only 9 percent of the professionals who hold master's degrees; another 8 percent hold an M.S. in biology, and 7 percent have an M.S. in environmental sciences. Among the 21 percent of staff leaders who hold doctorates or professional degrees, law is the most common field. Forty-one percent of the advanced degrees are in law. Still, given that only about one-fifth of the professionals possess doctorates or professional degrees, the proportion of lawyers among the staff leadership, contrary to much popular opinion, is insignificant: Only 8 percent of the professional staff leaders we surveyed hold degrees in law.

Among the volunteers, college education is a somewhat less prominent but still significant feature of their educational backgrounds. Seventy-nine percent of the volunteers surveyed possess at least a bachelor's degree, but in the case of the volunteer leaders, the arts and social sciences prevail. Fifty-five percent of the respondents possess B.A.'s, while 40 percent have degrees in the sciences. The remaining degrees are in business, education, and general studies. Once again, there is no predominant field of study in the undergraduate backgrounds of these conservation leaders. The leading bachelor's degrees are in biology and history, with 7 percent each. Interestingly, more than one-third of the volunteers we surveyed possess master's degrees—a higher percentage than we found among the professional staffers. Fifty-three percent of the master's degrees are in the sciences, 24 percent are M.A.'s, and 12 percent are in business or public administration. The remaining 11 percent were unspecified. Once again, the pattern is diffuse. The most prevalent among the forty-six master's majors recorded is geology, with 7 percent of the sample.

Law degrees predominate among the 18 percent of the volunteer leaders who possess a Ph.D. or equivalent professional degree: A full 48 percent of the advanced-degree holders have law degrees. Seven percent are medical doctors; 34 percent possess doctorates. Again, no doctoral major predominates, but one-third of the doctorates are in scientific fields. While law dominates the sample of advanced-degree holders, just as it did in the staff sample, only 9 percent of the entire volunteers' sample hold law degrees.

These findings firmly demonstrate that no single academic arena can begin to contain contemporary conservation leaders. The heads of environmental and conservation groups emerge from nearly every imaginable academic background. What is more important to stress about the NGO leadership—both professional and volunteer—is its extraordinary level of education. This is a movement that attracts (and holds) highly educated, though not necessarily highly specialized, leaders. The demands of leadership in nonprofit organizations, including conservation groups, do not require intense specialization on the part of executive-level staff and volunteer leaders, but over time the conservation movement has demonstrated that leaders must know where to look in order to find the specialists they need. Increasingly, these organizations demand the services of experts in both substantive issues and programs, and in management and administration. Thus, it is fair to inquire about the academic training of current and future specialists in conservation sciences, and it is not unreasonable to be concerned with the preparation of managers who will come to work in the conservation NGOs.

Two broad, recent trends frame this inquiry. First, as we have observed in earlier chapters, conservation and environmental management are rising professions, subject to increasingly intense public scrutiny and accountability. Worldwide public concern and the complexity of the tasks associated with environmental protection are growing apace and cannot be separated. While "official" conservationists early in the twentieth century might have wanted their movement to remain a primarily scientific venture, led and dominated by trained specialists,[1] most contemporary conservationists now agree that the politics of conservation and environmental protection cannot and should not be rendered technically arcane. Indeed, growth of the profession and enhancement of public interest in natural resource management are but two sides of the same coin.

Second, as the natural resource professions grow and deepen, so does the profession of nonprofit organization management. Nonprofit groups form a substantial sector of the national economy. In 1990 charitable contributions to nonprofit groups (donations given beyond membership fees and other forms of subscription) exceeded $100 billion.[2] While conservation-environmental groups form a very small segment of the not-for-profit enterprise (less than 2 percent), the critical importance of the issues they address, coupled with their unmistakable power in Congress, greatly enhances their stature within the nonprofit domain. The quality of management among conservation groups is therefore an issue of concern to people both within and outside of the movement.

The trajectory of programs in academia has somewhat mirrored these two trends. During the 1960s and 1970s, programs designed to train emerging environmental scientists and policy advocates proliferated; more recently, there has been a burst of academic interest in training nonprofit executives, chiefly through the promulgation of new programs in the business schools. Most of these latter programs are very new and seem to tend toward training executives for careers in large, stable nonprofit institutions. How well such efforts will prepare students bound for jobs in nonprofit organizations committed to social change and its attendant and inevitable controversies is an open question.

Many of the natural resource training programs are not new, however. Some U.S. forestry schools date back to the beginning of the century; most programs in environmental sciences, environmental studies, and natural resource management are at least fifteen years old. Many were born of the political fervor that accompanied Earth Day 1970, when conservation NGOs proliferated in every region of the country. It is thus fair to inquire how well these academic initiatives have served the needs of leaders in the conservation NGOs.

Method

In order to answer this question, the Conservation Leadership Project identified and queried 390 academic programs designed to train natural resource and environmental professionals. We devised a seven-page questionnaire to perform three functions:

1. To create a body of baseline data on these programs. How large are they? What aspects of natural resource management do they emphasize? What degrees do they offer? Where are their graduates typically placed?

2. To perform a brief health assessment of these programs, most of which we believed to be relatively recent in origin. How have they weathered the 1980s, when student interest in environmental issues and natural resource fields reportedly declined? What do their recent patterns of enrollment show with respect to student interest? How securely are they positioned on campus?

3. To determine to what extent these programs deliberately serve conservation NGOs. Do any of them include the training of NGO

professionals as an integral part of their mission? Do they offer midcareer training opportunities that benefit NGO staffers or volunteers? How many of their graduates emerge in jobs among the NGOs? Do these programs place much emphasis on organization management for students looking for careers in positions of institutional leadership?

The sample we drew included natural resource programs covering a variety of emphases. Our focus rested on broadly cast programs in natural resource management and environmental sciences. We made sure to include forestry schools, which are among the oldest academic institutions designed to train natural resource professionals. We also looked for "schools of natural resources," and forestry programs that have now been merged or converted into broader missions (some of them, for instance, have become programs in forestry and environmental studies). In addition, we sought out the interdisciplinary programs in environmental sciences, environmental studies, and natural resource management. We tried to avoid the more narrowly cast, traditional programs covering individual aspects of natural resource management and science. For example, the sample did not include agricultural specialties such as range science, specialized divisions of biology, or technical specialities such as environmental engineering, nuclear engineering, or waste management. (The questionnaire is included in appendix C.)

The Respondents

The questionnaire, mailed to 390 heads of academic natural resource programs, received 141 responses. Sixty-three percent of the respondents were program directors, deans, chairpersons, heads, or assistants. The remainder of the people who responded occupied positions as faculty, program advisors, "coordinators," or administrative assistants. Some of the questions required insight and information pertaining to the history and mission of the program, and on that count we were pleased to note that 55 percent of the respondents had been in their current job for more than five years, with nearly 30 percent holding their job for eleven or more years. With these relatively long careers in place, the leaders of these programs tended to possess greater insight into the backgrounds of their programs. Just as we discovered among the corps of staff and volunteer leadership in the NGOs, the academic natural resource programs are also dominated by male leadership: 89 percent of the respondents were male.

The Nature of Academic Natural Resource Programs

Our supposition about the age of these programs proved to be accurate: 74 percent of them came into being between 1961 and 1980. Only 8 percent were products of the 1980s. As to their missions, we found through an open-ended question that one-third of the programs exist to train environmental scientists. Another 13 percent offer training specifically in marine or aquatic science, 10 percent train students to solve environmental problems, and 10 percent are general forestry programs. Only 2 percent of the re- spondents said that their central mission is to prepare students for natural resource management roles. Tables 70 and 71 summarize these data.

The programs surveyed are a balanced mix of graduate and undergraduate programs. Thirty-seven percent reported that they are entirely undergraduate, while 11 percent are entirely graduate. Twenty-eight percent are about equally graduate and undergrad- uate in emphasis. The degrees awarded are as broadly named as the programs themselves: 67 percent of the bachelor's degrees, 39 percent of the master's degrees, and 27 percent of the doctorates awarded through these programs are in environmental science. The

TABLE 70   Academic Programs Questionnaire—Period of Origin

	Number of Respondents	Percentage of Total
1903–1930	12	9%
1931–1960	13	10%
1961–1970	38	28%
1971–1975	38	28%
1976–1980	24	18%
1981–1988	11	8%

TABLE 71   Academic Programs Questionnaire—Mission of Program

	Number of Respondents	Percentage of Total
Train environmental scientists	41	33%
Train marine or aquatic scientists	16	13%
Train students to solve environmental problems	12	10%
Train foresters	12	10%
Provide an interdisciplinary environmental studies program	11	9%
Trains students in biological aspects of the environment	5	4%
Provide scientific basis for environmental studies	4	3%
Provide liberal arts studies for environmental students	3	2%
Train geographers for government agencies	2	2%
Prepare students for natural resource management roles	2	2%
Provide program for ecology in agriculture	2	2%
Other	13	10%

next most common degree awarded is in forestry, followed by natural resources. Tables 72 and 73 summarize the nature of these programs and the degrees they award.

Table 74 summarizes the formal administrative standing of these various natural resource programs within their respective institutions. Notice that over 50 percent of them are either interdisciplinary programs or "adjunct institutes" of study. The departments and colleges or schools presumably enjoy the greater benefits of

TABLE 72   Academic Programs Questionnaire—Level of Academic Training

	Number of Respondents	Percentage of Total
Entirely undergraduate	52	37%
Primarily undergraduate	26	19%
Entirely graduate	16	11%
Primarily graduate	7	5%
Equally graduate and undergraduate	39	28%

TABLE 73   Academic Programs Questionnaire—Degrees Awarded*

	Percentage of Bachelor's Degrees	Percentage of Master's Degrees	Percentage of Doctorates
Environmental science	67%	39%	27%
Forestry	21%	28%	32%
Natural resources	11%	20%	15%
Biology	11%	13%	12%
Wildlife-fisheries	7%	10%	6%
Geography	7%	4%	6%
Marine science	6%	10%	15%
Other	12%	18%	23%

*Many programs offer more than one of each kind of degree. Therefore, percentages in the table exceed 100.

TABLE 74   Academic Programs Questionnaire—Administrative Status of Programs within Their Respective Institutions

	Number of Respondents	Percentage of Total
College or school	26	18%
Department	52	37%
Interdisciplinary program	66	47%
Adjunct center or institute	8	6%
Program within a department	2	2%
Other	7	5%

stability that come with their standing. We will return to this topic in a later section of this chapter.

Trends in Student Enrollment

When we initiated research into the recent evolution of academic natural resource programs, several commentators told us that many of these programs were in trouble. The obscurity of environmental issues during the early 1980s, they said, had led to declining enrollment and a general lack of student interest in environmental careers. Gone were the days of student and faculty fervor over environmental issues; gone were the prominent campus environmental organizations that seemed to sprout all over the country following the end of the Vietnam War, when national peace activism turned to domestic issues. With these cautions in mind, we expected to find evidence of rapidly declining enrollment during the Reagan years, coupled with despair for the future of these programs on the part of academic leaders. Instead, we found stability during the 1980s and hopefulness for the 1990s. The leaders of these programs predict sharp increases in student interest and enrollment, at least over the short term.

At the undergraduate level, median enrollments run between forty-five and fifty-eight students per year. The much higher average enrollments (more than 100 undergraduate majors per program) are due to the exceptionally large size of a few leading programs, such as the University of Michigan's School of Natural Resources. The graduate-level programs are not much smaller, running at around thirty majors per year.

What is most telling about these enrollment data, however, is not the number of students but the solid stability of enrollment during a six-year period that by all counts was not a time of soaring national interest in the environment. Table 75 summarizes student enrollments in academic natural resource programs between 1982 and 1988.

When asked what trends the program leaders see in their programs now and in the near future, the response was optimistic (see

TABLE 75   Academic Programs Questionnaire—Student Enrollments, 1982–88

Academic Year	Undergraduate Majors		Graduate Majors	
	Mean	Median	Mean	Median
1982–83	117	54	48	30
1983–84	122	58	46	30
1984–85	110	49	46	28
1985–86	105	45	47	28
1986–87	103	47	46	28
1987–88	108	54	48	30

Table 76). Nearly three-quarters of the leaders surveyed said that enrollment would increase or remain relatively stable. Only 16 percent observed declining enrollment. The reasons cited for these optimistic responses were unequivocal. Increased enrollment will come not as a result of internal improvements in the programs, but because of external factors—chiefly, increased public concern over the issues, coupled with a greater availability of jobs in the environmental field. Table 77 summarizes responses on the reasons for increasing enrollment.

In addition to the numbers of students increasing (or at worst remaining stable), the quality of students entering the programs during the past five years is also on the rise. Over 40 percent of the

TABLE 76 Academic Programs Questionnaire—Program Leaders' Views on Trends in Future Student Enrollment

	Number of Respondents	Percentage of Total
Enrollment will increase.	61	47%
Enrollment will be stable.	31	24%
Enrollment will decrease.	21	16%
No response/irrelevant	17	13%

TABLE 77 Academic Programs Questionnaire—Factors Underlying Trends in Enrollment*

	Number of Respondents	Percentage of Total
Increased public concern over issues	62	56%
More environmental jobs available	24	21%
Fewer jobs available	14	13%
Increased visibility of environmental issues	12	11%
Decreased public concern over issues	9	8%
Program made more attractive by improvements	8	7%
Improved student recruitment	6	5%
Student demand for new technical skills	5	5%

*Some respondents listed more than one reason for trends; thus, the percentage of responses exceeds 100.

academic program leaders reported an increasing quality among their new students, while another 34 percent reported that the quality remains stable. Only 17 percent observed a general decline in student quality. When the leaders offered comments on specific trends they see in student quality, the most common had to do with commitment to environmental issues: 11 percent said their recent students are more committed to environmental issues, 2 percent said the opposite, and another 5 percent said that their new students are less prepared in math and science. Still, the academic leaders seem generally pleased with the increasing quality of incoming students. Table 78 summarizes these data.

Job Placement

Few academic natural resource programs keep careful track of job placements for their graduates. In many instances, students graduate without knowing where they will get their first jobs; their subsequent contacts with faculty weaken; they wander off into the world, loosening their ties to their alma maters. Still, most leaders of the academic natural resource programs have a good sense of where their students find at least initial job placements; some

TABLE 78 Academic Programs Questionnaire—Trends in the Quality of Incoming Students

Trends in Quality	Number of Respondents	Percentage of Total
Student quality is improving.	47	42%
Quality is about the same as always.	38	34%
Quality is declining.	19	17%
Other	7	7%
Additional Comments		
New students are more serious about and committed to environmental problems.	12	11%
New students are less prepared in math and science.	5	5%
New students are more money-oriented.	3	3%
Students are less committed and serious.	2	2%

have hard data, updated as their graduates move through their careers. We asked these academic leaders to provide us with the best information they could offer on the placements of their graduating students, and here is what they said. The great majority of students who graduate from natural resource programs find employment in their field of study—80 percent of the undergraduates and 89 percent of the graduate students, according to the leaders of their academic programs. The largest number of all graduating students go to work for state agencies, followed closely by consulting firms, other kinds of for-profit businesses, and the federal government. Very few students (6 percent of the undergraduates, 6 percent of the graduates) take jobs among the NGOs. About as many become school teachers. Table 79 summarizes job placement data for the undergraduates of these natural resource programs.

Most likely, government agencies and for-profit businesses are better recruiters than their counterparts among the NGOs. In most instances, they are able to offer better salaries, greater stability, and a sense of long-term institutional support, reflected in such measures as retirement plans, better long-term employee benefits and, in the case of the for-profit world, incentives unique to private enterprise. They are also more likely to define jobs more clearly and narrowly. Most important, however, there are simply more jobs available outside the nonprofit sector. For all of these reasons,

TABLE 79 Academic Programs Questionnaire—Annual Job Placements

Sector of Placement	Average Percentage of Students Placed	
	Undergraduates	Graduates
State government	20%	19%
Federal government	12%	17%
Consulting firms	14%	15%
Other for-profit businesses	18%	11%
Academia (higher education)	5%	15%
NGOs	6%	6%
Other educational institutions	6%	5%
Placements outside of field	14%	4%
Unknown	6%	7%

placement outside the NGOs will be a more common occurrence. There is simply a greater job market elsewhere.

The implications of these findings extend beyond placement, however. The job market partially dictates the nature of student training and education. With so few of their graduates going to work in the NGOs, there is little incentive for academic natural resource programs to offer any special preparation for students to meet the unusual challenges they will face when they go to work in nonacademic NGO environments. Most NGO leaders we surveyed told us that their jobs were often less about conservation, environmental protection, and influencing natural resource management, and more about fund-raising, volunteer development, and nonprofit organization management. While it is also true that jobs in government agencies and for-profit businesses often involve revenue raising, personnel management, and administration, the tasks and risks involved are really quite different. Prospective heads of, say, state natural resource agencies could be fairly well trained in good schools of public administration; the same would not be true for the executive director of the Sierra Club or the staff coordinator of the Western Colorado Congress.

Moreover, the job market creates a series of practical expectations that are bound to influence the direction of the educational experience. For instance, many forestry schools virtually train students for jobs in the Forest Service and private timber companies. Some interdisciplinary programs in wildlife management train primarily for jobs in state fish and wildlife agencies. The outcome of such preparation is as definite as it is predictable: Students learn the parameters of natural resource management according to the contemporary dictates of the field. That is, of course, a good and necessary endeavor, but it also means there is much that students are *not* encouraged to learn. Students may very well graduate with honors but with little or no grasp of conservation history, or even the history of their field. They are probably not well schooled in environmental philosophy. They may have, at best, a nodding familiarity with the emerging field of environmental ethics. Most likely, they do not become internationalists prior to graduation; nor are they likely to be at all well schooled in the emaciated branch of political science that applies to the evolution of social and political movements. As a result, students probably don't know much about the NGOs and the unique culture of management found among them, even as they emerge in fields in which the NGOs will likely lead public efforts to challenge prevailing resource management objectives.

It is likely, however, that these same students will have been exposed to the exigencies of natural resource agency management. The majority of our academic leaders report that their programs offer various incentives (or requirements) for students to receive offerings in natural resource agency management. While nearly one-third of the programs have no management offerings at all, 11 percent offer a very thorough curriculum in management and administration, and another 36 percent offer their own courses in these areas. The most popular form of training in agency management and administration is internships. Over half of the programs use them. Only 2 percent of the program leaders report that agency management and administration is the primary emphasis of the program. Table 80 summarizes these data.

In-service Training

Professions in natural resource management undergo rapid change. New scientific information adds to the understanding of natural systems and must be accommodated by professional

TABLE 80 Academic Programs Questionnaire—Emphasis on Training in Natural Resource Agency Management

	Number of Respondents	Percentage of Total
Program has no such emphasis	44	31%
Program offers its own courses in management and administration	51	36%
Program encourages students to take management courses outside the program	57	40%
Program encourages students to take internships to learn about organizational management	84	59%
Program has its own very thorough curriculum in management and administration	15	11%
Primary emphasis of program is management and administration	3	2%

resource managers. New public demands lead to the rapid alteration of public policies that affect management decisions. Resource professionals often report that regardless of the technical-scientific aspects of their management missions, they increasingly find themselves "managing people instead of resources." Their in-service training needs are therefore immense, and are often quite different in kind from the training they received as undergraduates at a university.

Academic natural resource programs are apparently trying to respond to the needs of midcareer professionals, but only 41 percent of the programs we surveyed offer any in-service training at all. The most common vehicle for the offerings that do exist is the short course (see Table 81). About half of the programs offering inservice training prepare short courses for professionals in the field. Another 20 percent offer training in the form of internships, while 16 percent of the programs are dedicated to recertification. Only 6 of the 141 institutions we surveyed offer a full-scale graduate program in in-service training. Virtually none of the programs we're aware of have offerings tailored to the needs of professionals in the NGOs.

What does the foregoing mean to NGO conservation leaders? It means that the national environmental community cannot expect academic institutions to take very seriously—or even understand— the training needs that are peculiar to the management of conservation NGOs. The great majority of academic natural resource programs are clearly directed toward training and educational goals

TABLE 81   Academic Programs Questionnaire—Availability of In-service Training for Professionals

	Number of Respondents	Percentage of In-service Programs
Short courses	24	56%
Internships	10	20%
Recertification program	7	16%
Graduate program for midcareerists	6	14%
An established training institute	1	2%
Faculty assistantships	1	2%

that are tailored to a different market. NGO leaders may very well rely on academic natural resource programs to help prepare candidates for technical and scientific specialties needed by the NGOs, but they should not (and do not) expect these programs to deliberately train students to become leaders of organizations within the environmental movement. Whatever specific training the prospective NGO leaders receive that will be helpful to them on their jobs will be mostly accidental or incidental. The NGOs simply do not constitute a market for emerging students that is sufficient to cause a redirection of emphasis in the academic natural resource programs. The message coming from the academic programs we surveyed is clear: The conservation-environmental community of NGOs must grow its own in-service training entities; and it must continue to rely on the satisfaction of employment in the not-for-profit sector to lure aspiring leaders into the movement.

Stability

Academic natural resource programs provide valuable educational experiences for aspiring environmental professionals. Everyone concerned with natural resource and environmental issues has a stake in the health and longevity of these programs. Not surprisingly, the question of long-term stability is a key question for many leaders of these programs. While the forestry programs tend to be very stable and long-lived (most of them long ago having achieved the status of accredited schools within their respective institutions), the younger programs seldom enjoy such favor. Indeed, their leaders report many of the same kinds of stresses that affect the leaders of the conservation NGOs: chronic shortages of funds coupled with concerns over long-term financial security, concerns over the capacity to grow, and a sense that the goals and objectives are not fully supported by the parent institutions they are part of. One program director described his interdisciplinary studies program as "the defiant bastard child of the university."

Many of the programs we surveyed suffer from problems endemic to new, nontraditional activities at American universities. Since they are interdisciplinary programs, not colleges, schools, or departments, they often recruit faculty from related disciplines in an ad hoc fashion and sometimes cannot depend on the pool of willing faculty to continue with voluntary interdisciplinary responsibilities. They are sometimes accused of lacking academic rigor, and in some instances—with the clear exception of the forestry schools—they lack systems of accreditation and certification. Still, they have proven themselves to be resilient and long-lived, despite their chronic problems.

Stability is an important issue for many natural resource program leaders, who feel somewhat precariously perched atop the departmental bedrock of American colleges and universities; yet most of these leaders feel their programs are no less stable than other, comparable programs within their respective institutions. When asked about the stability of their funding, only 1 percent report that it is very unstable. Twenty percent describe it as very stable, while 61 percent describe their funding as comparable to that of similar programs in their institutions. (Table 82 presents these findings.) Still, there is widespread concern with the sufficiency of funding.

When asked about institutional obstacles that block the development or improvement of these programs, over three-quarters of the leaders cite funding woes. They report a general lack of funding to support or enhance their programs and a lack of direct financial support to students. About 70 percent of them also say they lack adequate facilities for their programs, and slightly over half of them are concerned about adequate student enrollment. Low on their list of obstacles is a lack of public support or a negative public perception of their programs. They are also less concerned with the employment possibilities for their graduating students. Forty-nine percent say that a scarcity of jobs is not a problem. (But 52 percent say that it is.) Forty-four percent say the same about low-paying or low-prestige jobs for their graduates.

TABLE 82   Academic Programs Questionnaire—Stability of Funding

	Number of Respondents	Percentage of Total
Very stable	28	20%
About as stable as other, comparable programs	84	61%
More uncertain than most	25	18%
Very unstable	1	1%

When asked about the greatest single pressure affecting the *quality* of their program and the greatest single pressure affecting its *future stability*, the leaders answered unequivocally: 62 percent listed lack of funding as the principal pressure working against program quality, and 50 percent said that lack of funding will damage their future stability. Concern about enrollments (another underpinning of funding) came in a distant second. Like their counterpart leaders of the NGOs, when these resource professionals apply their own thinking to the impediments they face in pursuit of higher-quality programs, their concerns rest chiefly with money. Tables 83 and 84 summarize these data.

Summary and Conclusions

Ever since the Pinchot family fortune started the first great American forestry school at Yale at the turn of the century, academic programs in natural resource management have flour-

TABLE 83 Academic Programs Questionnaire—Evaluation of Selected Obstacles to Program Enhancement

	Major Problem	Somewhat of a Problem	Not a Problem
Lack of funding to maintain or enhance program	33%	53%	14%
Lack of financial support for students	30%	47%	23%
Lack of adequate facilities	27%	41%	32%
Lack of adequate enrollment	20%	33%	41%
Attracting and retaining top-notch faculty	14%	35%	50%
Shift of values in society away from our emphasis	14%	34%	52%
Isolation from natural resource programs at other institutions	13%	30%	57%
Failure to attract top students	13%	51%	36%
Competition with other programs	12%	33%	56%
Lack of professional identification	11%	40%	49%
Low-paying or low-prestige jobs for our graduates	11%	45%	44%
Too few jobs for our graduates	10%	42%	49%
Lack of public support or a negative public perception	9%	25%	66%

TABLE 84 Academic Programs Questionnaire—Greatest Pressure
Affecting Quality and Future Stability of Program

	Quality		*Future Stability*	
	Number of Respondents	*Percentage of Total*	*Number of Respondents*	*Percentage of Total*
Lack of funding	83	62%	62	50%
Low enrollments	28	21%	27	22%
Retaining faculty	7	5%	6	5%
Jobs for graduates	2	2%	4	3%
Institutional support	1	1%	3	2%
Other	14	10%	23	18%

ished in this country. There are now hundreds of them, doing the best job they can to educate future professionals in the rising fields of environmental management. The 1970s in particular saw a radical increase in national interest in these kinds of programs, but since then they have faced many of the common institutional difficulties encountered by interdisciplinary studies and training.

If a majority of these programs were born of the same charged political atmosphere that gave rise to Earth Day 1970, it is fair to say that the electricity flows less ardently in their 20-year-old veins today. Few of these programs deliberately seek to train the professionals who go to work on the leading edge of environmental reform; most see their role as training competent environmental scientists, not policy advocates and activists. To the extent that leading-edge organizations of the environmental movement are able to reach out to recruit environmental scientists and other technically trained professionals, these programs can be looked to to provide a steady stream of potential candidates. But they should not be relied on to "create" John Gardner's enlightened generalists who emerge to lead innovative public movements. Nor will they soon become the critical centers for training midcareer professionals from the NGOs. Most of them offer no in-service training at all, and the ones that do tend to create offerings that are mostly useless to leaders of social-change organizations.

It is abundantly clear from these data that the national conservation-environmental movement must continue to develop its own network of training programs for its own emerging leadership. The models created by academic natural resource programs can serve as a guide—just as the programs themselves can be trusted to educate incoming technical staff—but in order to help emerging NGO leaders to accelerate the long, arduous process of learning how to manage and lead their nonprofit advocacy organizations, the movement must develop its own customized training programs and seek to build a broader constituency.

Chapter 6

Recommendations

T he questionnaires and interviews from the Conservation Leadership Project reveal clear deficiencies in training, communication, and leadership-development strategies among both staff and volunteers of NGOs. The following recommendations speak to these deficiencies, and in some instances offer concrete solutions to problems described by the conservation leaders who were queried in the study.

Movementwide Recommendations

1. The NGO conservation community needs leadership-development and communication center(s) specifically designed for conservationists. The center(s) should serve both paid, professional staff and volunteers, particularly board members. It should offer training in various aspects of organization management, outreach, and mass communication. It should also serve as a meeting ground for organizations to develop integrated strategies to address problems of common concern, and for NGO conservationists to confer with scientists and other experts, academic leaders, policymakers, regulators, business leaders, and others who are instrumental in solving environmental problems.

Faculty for the above programs and activities could be drawn from the conservation community itself, from existing consulting centers, from academia, and from specialized fields as needed. Coordination, administration, and fund-raising would require a full-time staff. These functions should be centralized, but the training itself, to the maximum extent possible, should be conducted in various regions of the country.

2. Existing programs in conservation leadership development need to be coordinated and better publicized so that more staff and volunteers leaders around the country become aware of them. National, regional, and local programs are now proliferating, yet the leaders of the movement have little sense or knowledge of these efforts. The decentralized leadership center outlined above could help in this regard.

3. Staff exchanges among conservation NGOs would be helpful in reducing interorganizational conflicts and creating new opportunities for leaders to learn from each other. In order for such exchanges to occur, financial incentives must be offered. These might come in the form of honoraria or paid leaves of absence funded through a new philanthropic program.

4. In order to expand the effects of conservation throughout society, conservation leaders must take their cause to new constituencies. Leaders of national conservation groups and state coalitions and others representing the larger organizations should devise a national strategy to persuade clergy and school superintendents to teach conservation in churches and schools. They should devise a concurrent strategy to identify leaders in the national business and labor communities to proselytize their peers, delivering the message that good conservation is good business. Editorialists of powerful business journals would be of great help here.

5. Efforts need to be made to expand the national constituency for conservation through deliberate recruitment of leaders from minority and low-income communities and through focused efforts to address environmental issues of particular concern to these communities. Conservation has a well-deserved reputation as an elitist, Anglo-American, male phenomenon—not because of deliberate organizational policies or hardened attitudes, but largely as a result of omission, deeply engrained organizational habits in hiring and leadership recruitment, and the overweaning emphasis on direct mail as a membership recruitment tool (at least among the larger international-national organizations). Given the recent emphasis on important environmental issues in the neighborhoods and homes of middle-income and poor Americans, the time is ripe to alter the reputation of conservation groups among nonwhite citizens and to build greater constituencies by addressing these important issues. This effort could be initiated through the devel-

opment of a new conservation fellowship program designed to groom minority and low-income students for positions of professional leadership among conservation NGOs. But the effort must go farther and must include the deliberate engagement of environmental issues of greatest concern to nonwhite citizens, coupled with recruitment of leaders from the communities that have traditionally been omitted from the conservation constituency. These leaders can play an effective role as board and staff members, as well as general volunteers, in many kinds of conservation groups.

6. Conservation NGOs must redouble their efforts to bring qualified women into key positions of organizational leadership, particularly into appointments as chief executive officers and board chairs.

7. Conservation NGOs of all sizes need to spend time and resources helping to incubate leadership for the conservation movement. In some instances this might mean assisting academic program leaders in the orientation, education, and placement of outstanding student conservationists or in devising curricula that would be helpful to students who wish to graduate into jobs with conservation NGOs. In other instances organizations might alter their own hiring practices in order to recruit distinguished professionals from nonconservation fields (who also have distinguished records as conservation volunteers) into positions of staff leadership. Still other instances might call for the recruitment and training of young people with outstanding leadership potential—a deliberate effort among conservationists to "grow" their own leadership. Volunteer recruitment and training is even more in need of attention than the recruitment of staff, and can be improved through effective use of consultants and training centers oriented toward volunteers. Each of these efforts and others like them would serve to get conservation NGOs thinking about the future demands of leadership and would begin to inculcate in them and their movement a "culture of leadership."

8. Conservationists representing local, state, national and international organizations need to expand their efforts to develop collaborative strategies where and when they are appropriate. Such "vertical integration" of conservation groups working on common issues has, at various times and in various places, made optimal use

of expertise and scarce resources, and simultaneously dissolved the mistrust that often exists among various sectors of the movement. The first step in fostering greater collaboration is face-to-face communication among conservation leaders from various sectors and locales. Efforts should be made to sponsor national or regional gatherings of conservation leaders to share information and begin to devise joint strategies for action.

9. NGO leaders should assist in efforts to strengthen the infrastructure of conservation advocacy in those regions where it is weak. Conservation issues, according to those queried in the study, are moving "beyond and below" the national level in the United States and into international, state, and local settings. Serious investigations of the infrastructure of conservation advocacy should be undertaken nationwide and worldwide. In the United States, there are still many states that lack the number and diversity of NGOs that seem to create an effective synergy among advocacy groups across a broad range of issues. Assistance in this area, on the domestic front at least, could do much to begin deepening the effects of conservation policy while simultaneously helping to alleviate the isolation that national conservation leaders often claim to feel from issues and activists "in the field."

Organizational Recommendations

Most conservation-environmental groups in the United States are small organizations by any measure. Their leaders tend to engage in multiple tasks and often feel there is no hope of delegating responsibilities; hence the all-too-familiar pattern of personal burnout among the leadership. Effective management of small nonprofit groups calls for exceptional skills—among them, the skills of protecting and renewing the leaders of organizations in order to keep them vital and creative. Clearly, most of the following changes in leadership and management strategy will apply most effectively at the level of individual organizations.

1. Conservation NGOs, particularly the smaller organizations, need to budget more time and money for training and professional consultation. This applies to the following areas: strategic planning (including the drafting and use of effective short-term and long-

term operating plans); programmatic evaluations; board, staff, and executive performance evaluations; board-staff relations; and effective use of volunteers. Conservation NGOs need to develop a much clearer sense of how to set goals effectively and how to measure performance in achieving goals, including the internal goals of management. While the question of funding is widely discussed—and often lamented—among conservation NGOs, a disturbingly large number of them do not seem to understand the basics of organizational development, which leads to greater opportunities for funding. Thus, too many reach out for simpleminded "fund-raising training" when they should be making investments in long-term organizational development and planning.

2. At the same time, NGO leaders should learn to manage their organization's affairs so that they can concentrate more of their own time on public outreach and less on managing internal organizational matters that can be readily delegated. The average conservation leader queried in this study spends less than 10 percent of his time in outreach activities (public speaking, media relations, and so forth). Leaders who are serious about altering public opinion and behavior need to free themselves somewhat from management and administration and concentrate on stimulating public involvement.

3. Conservation NGOs must place a much higher priority on the midcareer training and refreshment of their leaders, both professional and volunteer. The average conservation leader queried in this study spends only 2 percent of his time on professional and personal development. In most instances this is clearly insufficient. NGOs must become aware of the thriving national market that offers training for nonprofit executives, staff, and volunteers, and avail themselves of the best support they can find. Once again, a decentralized, national center tailored to their needs would be most useful in pursuing this goal.

4. Conservation NGOs need to adopt policies to validate and implement staff sabbaticals and leaves of absence. One of the greatest obstacles facing many conservation leaders is a sense of personal stagnation. This problem cannot be solved merely by expanding conventional training opportunities or consultancies with management support groups. Several effective leadership-

development programs in the United States concentrate their efforts on personal (not strictly professional) development precisely by encouraging activities that leaders can pursue outside of their professional expertise. The wisdom of such efforts does not seem to have penetrated the conservation movement, whose organizations continue to see themselves as hard-bitten ventures run by martyrs to the cause.

Recommendations to Funders

Private philanthropy plays a crucial role in the advancement of natural resource conservation nationwide. In the United States, private foundations that give to conservation and environmental advocacy are key players in developing successful long-term conservation strategies. While funders and NGOs are strongly oriented toward substantive programs and issues, far too little attention is being paid to the preparation and support of conservation leaders across the country. Long-term commitment to conservation is absolutely necessary; there is no better way to ensure that commitment than to pay attention to the development of existing and new conservation leaders.

Foundations are best positioned to play the pivotal role in developing movement leadership through careful grant making. They lead partly by announcing programs in giving and support and by modifying new programs to meet urgent new needs. The following strategies on the part of conservation philanthropists would do much to improve the caliber of conservation leadership.

1. Institute new programs to underwrite consulting in management and leadership development. Several foundations now offer special grants to help conservation groups pay for specialized management consultations with distinguished firms that have proven successful in assisting conservation organizations. Especially useful are consultancies in strategic planning, board development, and organizational self-sufficiency campaigns.

2. Increase support to local, state-based, and regional organizations through direct grants and effective partnerships with national conservation groups. As emphasis shifts from federal policy-making to local and regional enforcement, local and state-based

conservation groups will become increasingly important. Yet many of them, weakened by the paucity of federal and state funding and by the permanent departure of their founding staff and board members, seem to be adrift into the 1990s. They are in need of recognition and support from funders and from their national counterparts.

3. Alter fundamental giving strategies by increasing grants for general support. Especially in regions of low population density and historically poor capital formation, conservation groups are often hamstrung by the reliance on "hard money" support from members and local donors. They look to foundations and other national funders to support critical programs, but they are often burdened by the lack of discretion that comes with restricted support. Greater flexibility will allow them to advance their own efforts to build leadership while making progress in individual, substantive programs.

4. Make new grants available for staff sabbaticals and leaves of absence. While many conservation groups have policies encouraging sabbaticals and leaves, few can afford to use them. The policies are useless without the ability to implement them; the critical missing element is often funding. Foundations and other philanthropists, while generously supporting students with special promise, generally overlook the midcareer needs of established conservation leaders. New programs should be created to help NGOs offer meaningful sabbaticals for their leaders. In addition, assistance in planning them would help ensure that they are productive and successful.

Recommendations to Academia

Data from the survey of academic programs in natural resource fields reveal that these programs place little emphasis on preparing students for careers in the nonprofit sector, and even less emphasis on midcareer training for NGO professionals. While the NGOs will continue to find well-trained specialists graduating from various interdisciplinary programs in environmental fields, these programs cannot be expected to provide meaningful training in the broader aspects of NGO leadership and management. To the extent that they train in agency management at all, their efforts clearly emphasize the administration of natural resource agencies of government and, to a lesser degree, private enterprise. Moreover, many of these programs seem to place little emphasis on humanistic and philosophical concerns related to working in the environmental professions. Most programs seem to be designed to follow the dictates of turn-of-the-century emphases on conservation as an emerging movement dominated by scientific resource management. Thus, they tend to pay much less attention to the evolution of policy and public concern over environmental issues, and to concerns that transcend efforts at scientific management. To be of greater use to the NGO community and, more broadly, to citizens and students concerned with the progress of environmental advocacy, academic natural resource programs could pursue the following strategies.

1. University programs in natural resources could place greater emphasis on conservation history (including the history of conservation and environmental protection as an emerging social-political movement), environmental policy, and effective writing for general audiences. Conservation leaders among the NGOs rate incoming staff as being weakest in these areas of skills and training.

2. Some few academic programs may see an opportunity in training students to lead conservation NGOs. For those rare programs the field is wide open. Attention could be given to the creation and refinement of a curriculum emphasizing nonprofit organization management in the context of environmental advocacy. Visiting faculty who possess practical experience could help design such programs and would be of great use in teaching (perhaps through sabbaticals or other leaves of absence from their NGOs) and in providing internships in their respective organizations.

3. Increased emphasis on placing interns at conservation NGOs would be very helpful in preparing students for recruitment into these organizations. But the NGOs themselves must share in this responsibility and make arrangements for satisfying educational internships. Using students as cheap "grunt labor" is too often the familiar pattern of NGO internship programs. A "mentors program" wherein promising young student leaders receive part of their academic training through exposure to accomplished conser-

vation NGO leaders would be most helpful, as would clearly defined assignments to assist in substantive organizational research or development programs.

4. Increased communication among NGO leaders and the leaders of natural resource programs at universities would foster more useful curricula and open new avenues for job placement and recruitment. Unfortunately, the situation as it stands today is that academic and NGO leaders hardly communicate at all. Efforts should be made to bring them together—nationally, regionally, and locally—to address ways in which academic programs can interface with conservation NGOs. Beyond questions of job placement and internships, university faculty and students could assist conservation NGOs in research projects and studies of various kinds that the NGOs are not equipped to perform on their own. The opportunities for productive synergy between these two sectors of conservation are enormous.

5. Student conservation organizations need to be revitalized nationwide. Many of today's conservation leaders made their own career commitments to the movement while they were students. The presence of a vigorous campus conservation group gave many of them their first exposure to the demands of leadership within an organization. Yet a great number of those student associations of the 1970s have languished. Efforts should be undertaken to reestablish the tradition of student conservation, particularly at those academies with strong programs in natural resources.

6. As NGO leaders and their allies in private philanthropy begin to orchestrate new training opportunities for emerging conservation leaders, seasoned faculty and administrators from the academic training programs will be of great use and should not be overlooked. The provision of enhanced education and training will demand the expertise of professional educators. Too many of the so-called nonprofit management support agencies do not include staff trainers who are well educated in the dynamics of natural resource organizations or who have a grasp of the rich history, politics, and scientific traditions underpinning the complex fields of environmental protection. What emerging conservationist leaders need is not mere training in aspects of nonprofit organization man-

agement; they need an enriched education (with opportunities to revisit the educational setting) in the great traditions of American conservation. The field tends toward narrowness; it must open up into the future. Thus, it demands leaders with vision to exceed their skills.

Introduction to the Appendixes

In designing and administering mailed questionnaires, an important objective is to achieve a high rate of return. In the Conservation Leadership Project, we knew that the challenge was made all the greater by the complexity and sensitivity of the information we were seeking. Volunteer and staff leaders alike are extremely busy people; we knew that our questionnaires would take most leaders at least an hour to complete. And many of them, we judged, would be loath to answer questions about the finances and internal management of their organizations. We thus tried to design questionnaires that were as intriguing and as user-friendly as possible: sophisticated but not slick; warm to the touch and eye. We also shared with our sample (cold term, isn't it?) our sense of mission in performing the project. We were not dispassionate observers studying movement leaders as if they were laboratory animals, and our materials said so.

We felt that the questionnaires needed to be the right size. A small booklet fitting nicely in most hands would be best. We chose an odd size (8½ by 6¼ inches) because it felt right. While some practitioners of the art of sociological surveys insist that the opening questions of the questionnaire should be challenging and intriguing (providing a "hook"), we largely eschewed this advice, opting instead for a more conventional opening: personal and organizational identification. Our hook was the risky cartoons we commissioned for the covers of the staff and volunteers' questionnaires. Some found the cartoons offensive and refused to fill out their questionnaires, or grumbled but completed them anyway. But most seemed to enjoy the droll humor of the cartoons, created by

224 Introduction to the Appendixes

Ellen Meloy, an environmental writer and illustrator from Helena, Montana. At the end of the questionnaires, we allowed respondents to critique our work; most did, but no one felt that the bias evident in the way the questions were framed would invalidate the results.

After administering the questionnaires, we followed up with postcard reminders and, as a last resort, telephone calls to the stragglers.

In designing and administering the questionnaires, we borrowed heavily from Dr. Don Dillman's "total design method" of sociological surveying. For more information about it, see Don A. Dillman, *Mail and Telephone Surveys: The Total Design Method* (New York: John Wiley & Sons, 1978).

Conservation Staff Questionnaire

Conservation Leadership Project
Sponsored by
The Conservation Fund
Conservation Staff
▪
Questionnaire

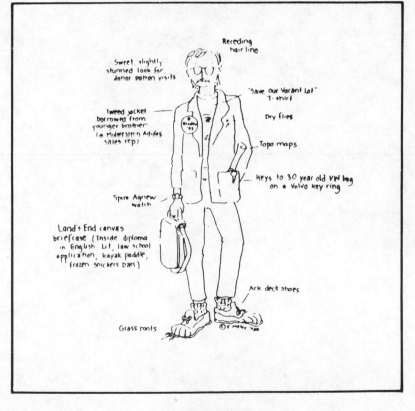

Urgent!
Please complete and return within two weeks of receipt.
(Return envelope provided)

Instructions: Please answer every question to the best of your ability and please follow the format of the questionnaire. Remember, if your organization is a subdivision of a larger organization, answer the questions in terms of your subdivision unless otherwise instructed.

PART I - IDENTIFICATION

1.   Name of Organization or Agency _____

2.   Name of Bureau, Department, Division _____

3.   Address _____

4.   Telephone _____

5.   Your name _____

6.   Your job title or position _____

7.   How long in current job? _____ years

8.   How long in current organization? _____ years

9.   Your sex: _____ Male _____ Female

10.   The year of your birth: _____

11.   Would you like to receive a complimentary summary of the survey results? __Yes __No

PART II - JOB DESCRIPTION

12.   Workers in conservation organizations or agencies often observe that their written "job descriptions" do not accurately represent the actual demands of their jobs. Please describe your actual job by filling in the percentages below. What percentage of your time during a typical six-month period do you spend performing the following?

Tasks	Percentage of your time
Planning (organizational, programs & projects, etc.)	_____ %
Program or project implementation	_____ %
Fundraising (including grantsmanship, donor-patron work, visitations, researching funders, etc.)	_____ %
Membership, volunteer, or constituency development (aimed at increasing numbers of them)	_____ %
Membership, volunteer, or constituency development (aimed at increasing the quality of their participation or involvement)	_____ %
Board development/relations	_____ %
Personnel recruitment or management	_____ %
Substantive programmatic research	_____ %
Press or media relations	_____ %
Public speaking	_____ %
Your own professional training, retraining, or development	_____ %
Other (please describe) _____	_____ %
_____	100 %

13. Which statement or statements below best characterize your <u>actual</u> job? (Check as many as are appropriate.)

   a. _____   Organizational manager and principal leader with executive powers; chief of staff; primarily responsible for the overall direction, plan and vitality of the organization or agency.

   b. _____   Executor, or "executive secretary" responsible for implementing the objectives of an appointed or elected governing body; less discretionary authority than in "a" above.

   c. _____   Programmatic vice president (or equivalent).

   d. _____   Administrative vice president (or equivalent).

   e. _____   Program, project or "division director;" primarily an implementor of goals, objectives, strategies established by others in the organization.

   f. _____   Fundraiser and/or organizational development officer.

   g. _____   Co-director, associate or deputy director of an organization with multiple or "split" management.

   h. _____   A "field officer or director" of a larger parent organization, but with extensive executive powers.

   i. _____   A "field officer or director" of a larger parent organization, but with few or no executive powers.

   j. _____   Other professional staff (please circle appropriate choice(s) below, <u>or add the appropriate position title(s) on the lines provided).</u>

Science officer	Researcher
Community organizer	Legal Counsel
Editor	Land acquisition specialist
Writer	Public relations

   _____

   _____

   k. _____   Other (please describe) _____

   _____

   _____

14. Which range of figures below best describes the annual salary or wages paid to you by your organization?

   _____ none   _____ $30,000 to $39,999 per year

   _____ less than $9,999 per year   _____ $40,000 to $59,999 per year

   _____ $10,000 to $19,999 per year   _____ $60,000 to $99,999 per year

   _____ $20,000 to $29,999 per year   _____ over $100,000 per year

15. Given your responsibilities and attributes, do you feel that your salary is adequate?
   _____ Yes _____ No

   If not, what should you be paid? _____

PART III - ORGANIZATIONAL DESCRIPTION

Please answer each of the following questions with respect to your organization. If you work for a field office, affiliate or subdivision of a parent organization, please answer with respect to your subdivision, unless otherwise instructed.

16.   Please summarize your organizational mission.

17.   In very general terms, which one word best characterizes your organization:
       _____ conservationist   _____ environmentalist
       _____ preservationist   _____ educational

18.   Which one of the following best describes the primary geographic scope or emphasis of your organization (or subdivision)?
       _____ international   _____ state
       _____ national   _____ local
       _____ regional

19.   What is the approximate annual budget of your organization? $ _____

       If you work in a field office, or subdivision, of a parent organization, what is the approximate annual budget of your field office or subdivision? $ _____

20.   Does your organization (or subdivision) have a dues-paying membership?
       _____ Yes   _____ No

       If so, how many members does it currently have? _____

21.   Most conservation organizations have diversified streams of income. Please indicate below the approximate percentages of your organization's annual budget by source:

Source of Funds	Percentage of Annual Budget
Membership dues (or equivalent subscriptions)	_____ %
Contributions from individuals, donors, patrons, etc. (beyond membership dues)	_____ %
Corporate gifts	_____ %
Foundation grants	_____ %
Federal grants and contracts	_____ %
State grants and contracts	_____ %
Other contracts	_____ %
Capital assets	_____ %
Sales of goods or organizational products	_____ %
User fees	_____ %
Other (please specify)_____	_____ %
	100%

CONSERVATION LEADERSHIP PROJECT   Page 4

Answer questions 22 and 23 only if your organization receives charitable contributions. If it does not, skip to question 24.

22.   Private philanthropy, in the form of foundation grants, corporate gifts, and donations from individuals, provides vital capital to many conservation groups while others use little or none of it. Regardless of the <u>amounts</u> of philanthropic support you receive, please indicate the <u>importance</u> of the following forms of support to your organization (or subdivision):

Unimportant to us	Somewhat important	Very important	Crucial
1	2	3	4

_____ Small foundation grants (less than $25,000)

_____ Large foundation grants (greater than $25,000)

_____ Corporate gifts

_____ Large contributions from individuals ($5,000 and up)

_____ Small contributions from individuals ($100 to $5,000)

_____ Other (please specify) _____

23.   The following statements express attitudes about private foundation giving. Please use the appropriate numbers to express your level of agreement with each statement.

Strongly Disagree	Disagree	Agree	Strongly Agree
1	2	3	4

_____ Foundation officials I've dealt with are generally well informed about the issues I've presented.

_____ Foundations ought to be more willing to give funds for general support.

_____ Foundations who fund conservation give too little money to local and state-based conservation efforts.

_____ Increased competition for funds has seemed to make foundations less responsive and accessible.

_____ Foundation officers often seem blind to the power they wield over grantees.

Are there any comments you'd like to make about your experience with private foundations?

24.   How many full-time, paid staff does your organization (or subdivision) employ? _____

How many part-time, paid staff? _____

Of these full- and part-time staff members, how many do you consider "professional" staff? _____

25. Many conservation organizations work on numerous issues, problems, or educational
     programs. Some have just one major area. Please indicate below the approximate
     percentages of organizational resources (staff, time, money, volunteer activity, etc.)
     which your organization spends in various issue areas.

Issue or Program Area	Percentage of Resources
Agriculture	_____ %
Air quality	_____ %
Economic/sustainable development	_____ %
Energy conservation/facility planning & regulation	_____ %
Fish/wildlife management/protection (including Endangered Species protection)	_____ %
Marine conservation	_____ %
Mining law/regulation	_____ %
National forest/national parks/public lands management	_____ %
Nuclear power/weapons	_____ %
Population control	_____ %
Private land preservation/stewardship	_____ %
Protection of waterways (rivers, lakes, coastal zones)	_____ %
Toxic/hazardous waste management	_____ %
Urban/rural land use planning	_____ %
Water quality	_____ %
Wilderness	_____ %
Zoological/botanical gardens	_____ %
Other (please specify) _____	_____ %
	100%

26. Conservation organizations use many different strategies and activities in order to reach
     their organizational goals. Please indicate below the relative importance, to your
     organization, of the following strategies:

Irrelevant to us	Very seldom used by us	Not a major strategy, but we use it sometimes	A very important strategy to us	This is our highest priority
1	2	3	4	5

_____ Direct litigation

_____ Direct management/stewardship of land or waterways

_____ Directly influencing elections of officials

_____ Educating people through encounters with nature (natural history, hikes,
       species identification, etc.)

_____ Educating the public through various media (print, video, TV, radios,
       self-publicity, conferencing, public speaking, etc.)

_____ Lobbying lawmakers

_____ Mediating environmental conflicts

_____ Mobilizing letter-writing and other political action campaigns

_____ Monitoring governmental agencies

_____ Performing and disseminating ethical or philosophical research

_____ Performing and disseminating policy research and analysis

_____ Performing and disseminating scientific research (including physical, biological, and/or social sciences)

_____ Placing issues on the ballot via initiative or referendum

_____ Preserving or protecting land (or other resources) through direct purchase or acquisition

_____ Organizing coalitions

_____ Training volunteers to act on behalf of our organization

_____ Other (please specify) _____

27. The relationship between paid professional staff and conservation volunteers is often a key factor in the success of organizational efforts.

   a. How would you honestly characterize your organization's use and involvement of volunteers?

   _____ We see them as integral to our mission and effectiveness, and use them accordingly.

   _____ We use them fairly well.

   _____ We tolerate volunteers, rather than using them effectively.

   _____ We look down on them, or even abuse their good will.

   _____ Given the nature of our organization, the use of volunteers is inappropriate or irrelevant.

   b. Any comments you'd care to make about your organization's use of volunteers or about volunteers generally?

28. Has your organization (or subdivision) hired new professional staff within the past year or two? _____ Yes _____ No - If no, skip to question 29.
   How many? _____

   a. If so, please use the appropriate numbers to evaluate the adequacy of incoming professional staff in the following areas:

Very poor	Poor	Good	Excellent	Not applicable to the job
1	2	3	4	5

   _____ Organizational management skills   _____ Technical skills

   _____ Interpersonal skills   _____ Writing skills

_____ Oral communication skills   _____ Scientific training

_____ Knowledge of conservation history _____ Training in environmental policy

_____ Overall rating

b. From which setting(s) did you recruit new professional staff? (Check all that are appropriate.)

_____ University programs in natural resources

_____ Other university programs   _____ Government agency

_____ Other non-profit organization(s)   _____ Business

_____ Other (please describe) _____

29. In recent years, conservation organizations and agencies have increased their emphasis on organizational management, staff orientation, and other "internals." Below, please use the numbers to indicate each of the items which appropriately describes your organization's use of various management tools.

We have it and use it	We have it but don't use it	We don't have it but need it	We don't have it & don't need it
1	2	3	4

_____ Strategic planning process

_____ A written statement of the organizational mission

_____ A written annual operating plan

_____ A written multi-year (long-range) plan

_____ A statement, or statements, of programmatic goals and objectives

_____ A process of formal programmatic evaluation

_____ Written job descriptions for staff

_____ Written job descriptions for board members

_____ Written job descriptions for volunteers

_____ In-house orientation or training program for new staff

_____ A formal process to evaluate executive's performance

_____ A formal process to evaluate staff's performance

_____ Regular salary or wage increases for employees

_____ Paid vacations for professional staff

_____ Paid vacations for non-professional staff

_____ A benefits package for staff, including health insurance

_____ A written policy regarding staff sabbaticals or leave

_____ A policy or program to encourage in-service professional training for staff (e.g., referesher courses, peer retreats, professional management seminars, etc.)

_____ A pension or retirement plan for employees

_____ A grievance policy for staff members

_____ A grievance policy for board members or volunteers

_____ Regular financial audits

_____ Regular management audits

PART IV - EDUCATION, TRAINING, AND PERFORMANCE

30. If you have completed college and/or graduate degrees, please indicate them below:

Bachelor of _____ in (major) _____

from (college or university) _____

Master of _____ in (emphasis) _____

from (college or university) _____

Ph.D. or other professional degree (e.g., M.D., LL.D, etc.) _____

from _____

Additional degrees or educational certificates? _____

_____

31. Is your current job directly in your field(s) of academic training? _____ Yes _____ No

32. The following is a list of educational experiences. Please indicate how much each experience prepared you for your current job.

Not at all	A little	Quite a bit	A lot	Did not have this educational experience
1	2	3	4	8

_____ Undergraduate major   Major: _____

_____ Undergraduate minor   Minor: _____

_____ Graduate school major   Major: _____

_____ Other undergraduate classes

_____ Formal training outside of academia such as professional conferences, training seminars, or professional consultation

_____ Other (please describe) _____

33. **Please describe the most and least important aspects of your education, with respect to your current job.**

34. In the past **two years**, have you attended any conferences, symposia, or training seminars for the purpose of professional enrichment? _____ Yes _____ No

If so, did your organization or agency sponsor your attendance (i.e., pay the costs of you attending? _____ Yes (always) _____ Yes (sometimes) _____ No (never)

35. If you have attended training seminars or conferences during the past two years, please indicate the primary areas of training you received. (Check as many as appropriate.)

_____ Advancements of scientific knowledge	_____ Leadership skills
_____ Communications/public relations	_____ Mediation/conflict resolution/negotiation
_____ Conservation history	_____ Organizational administration
_____ Ethics	_____ Personnel management
_____ Financial management	_____ Policy analysis
_____ Fundraising/membership develop.	_____ Political history
_____ Interpersonal relations	_____ Research methodologies
_____ Law	_____ Stress/time management
_____ Other (please specify) _____	

36. Of the professional training seminars or conferences you've attended, which one or two would you rate as truly outstanding in enhancing your effectiveness? Who conducted them?

       Seminar   Conducted by

1. _____   _____

2. _____   _____

37. Which one or two would you rate as very poor? Who conducted those?

       Seminar   Conducted by

1. _____   _____

2. _____   _____

38. The following is a list of consulting services commonly available for nonprofit organizations and other institutions for the purpose of improved management, administration, fundraising and organizational effectiveness. Of the services engaged by your organization (or subdivision) in the past two years, please use the appropriate numbers to rate the quality of services to your organization. Leave the rest blank, please.

Terrible services	Inadequate services	Adequate services	Excellent services
1	2	3	4

_____ Board or volunteer development

_____ Computers and software (consulting beyond acquisition)

_____ Dispute resolution

_____ Financial accounting

_____ Fundraising (including grantwriting or other contracted services)

_____ General management consulting

_____ Interpersonal communications

_____ Legal assistance

_____ Marketing

_____ Membership development

CONSERVATION LEADERSHIP PROJECT   Page   10

     _____ Office systems or design

     _____ Organizational planning

     _____ Program review or evaluation

     _____ Publications

     _____ Public relations/communications

     _____ Other (please specify) _____

     _____

39. The following is a list of "internal" resources and opportunities that might help conservation leaders and organizations perform more effectively. Please use the appropriate numbers to indicate which of these resources would be most, and least, useful to your organization (or subdivision). Also, please indicate if your organization has used these resources by placing a check in the "has used" column.

	Useless/worthless 1	Not very useful 2	Fairly useful 3	Extremely useful 4

	Evaluation	Has used	
a.	_____	_____	Participation in a training program for volunteers (other than board members).
b.	_____	_____	Training in the resolution of interpersonal conflicts among staff members.
c.	_____	_____	Participation in a training program for board members.
d.	_____	_____	Establishment of an in-house training or orientation program for staff.
e.	_____	_____	Assistance with organizational strategic planning.
f.	_____	_____	Hiring staff to help with management and administration.
g.	_____	_____	Hiring staff to help with fundraising & organizational development.
h.	_____	_____	Hiring staff to help with substantive organizational programs.
i.	_____	_____	A better office environment (physical workspace).
j.	_____	_____	Greater data processing and computer capabilities.
k.	_____	_____	Greater opportunities to hire or work with professional researchers (e.g., economists, biologists, earth scientists, etc.)
l.	_____	_____	Access to more, or better, information.
m.	_____	_____	A much larger budget.
n.	_____	_____	A financial endowment for the organization.
o.	_____	_____	Expert training in lobbying.
p.	_____	_____	Expert training in dispute resolution or mediation.
q.	_____	_____	A field program with full- or part-time staff.
r.	_____	_____	An organizational evaluation performed by the membership.
s.	_____	_____	Other (please specify) _____

40.   Of all items listed above in question 39 above (a through r), which <u>one</u> item would be your first and highest priority? (Please circle the appropriate letter above.)

41.   The following is a list of "external" resources and opportunities that might help conservation leaders perform their jobs more effectively. Please use the appropriate numbers to indicate which of these resources would be most, and least, useful to <u>you</u> in the future performance of your job. Also, please place a check mark in the space provided in front of each item of the ones you have <u>already participated</u> in at some time or another.

| | Useless/worthless
1 | Not very useful
2 | Fairly useful
3 | Extremely useful
4 |

<u>Usefulness</u>   <u>Participated In</u>

a. ____   ____   Open discussions about management problems and opportunities with my peers in other conservation organizations.

b. ____   ____   Open discussions about issues, programs and other matters of substance with my peers in other conservation organizations.

c. ____   ____   Discussions about management problems and opportunities with leaders of nonprofit organizations other than conservation.

d. ____   ____   Participation in a "loaned executive" or "executive exchange" program with for-profit corporations or businesses.

e. ____   ____   Participation in an ongoing leadership development program designed specifically for conservation leaders.

f. ____   ____   Travel to other countries to see for myself how they are dealing with natural resource and environmental issues.

g. ____   ____   A structured program that would expose me to the causes of and responses to poverty in the United States.

h. ____   ____   Receiving a fellowship for advanced training in relevant aspects of natural resource management.

i. ____   ____   A paid sabbatical that would allow me the time and independence to pursue some studies or creative work of my own design.

j. ____   ____   Participation in a "teaching sabbatical" that would allow me to share my practical knowledge with students.

k. ____   ____   Participation in discussions or courses conducted by leading thinkers in environmental ethics.

l. ____   ____   Participation in discussions or courses led by experts and scholars in the history of resource conservation.

m. ____   ____   Participation in courses or field studies led by experts in conservation biology and ecology.

n. ____   ____   Participation in discussions or courses led by leading thinkers in natural resource policy-making.

o. ____   ____   Participation in a "lawmakers' forum" with legislators/ Congressmen and conservation leaders on future needs for environmental law and policy.

p. _____   _____   Participation in a structured forum in which conservation
                             leaders, regulators, and industry leaders can seek out ways to
                             enhance planning and reduce conflicts over development.

q. _____   _____   Greater access to journals or newsletters related to the
                             conservation profession.

r. _____   _____   Other (please specify) _____

42.   Of all items listed in Question 41 above (a through r), which <u>one</u> item would be your first
      and highest priority? (Please circle the appropriate letter above.)

43.   The following is a list of statements describing some attitudes about the conservation
      movement in the United States. Please indicate your level of agreement or disagreement
      with each of these statements.

                Strongly disagree   Disagree   Agree   Strongly agree
                       1   2   3   4

_____ The large numbers of conservation groups and their millions of members and
       supporters are proof that the cause of conservation has never been healthier than
       it is today.

_____ Leadership and leading ideas of conservation have tended to emerge primarily
       from the nonacademic, nonprofit world.

_____ The leaders of conservation in the U.S. are more reactive than farsighted; they
       seem to be lacking in real vision or originality.

_____ The conservation movement is fragmented, territorial and uncommunicative.

_____ There is no longer any such thing as "the conservation movement"; in the sense
       that "movement" implies a unified effort of many people to achieve specific goals,
       the "movement" has gone out of conservation.

_____ National conservation organizations are generally unsupportive of unaffiliated
       local conservation groups.

_____ National conservation organizations are actually detrimental to local conservation
       efforts, because they soak up funds that end up having little local effect.

_____ Local conservation groups where I live are generally unsupportive of national
       conservation organizations.

_____ National conservation groups should expand their field programs at the local level.

_____ Many, perhaps most, minority and poor rural Americans see little in the
       conservation message that speaks to them.

_____ The conservation movement in the United States is generally bereft of new ideas;
       it is mired in a sort of business-as-usual approach to environmental problems.

_____ National conservation organizations have become altogether too "professional";
       they have come to resemble the very corporations they purport to fight.

_____ The real leadership in conservation lies in the grassroots, not among the
       professional conservationists.

_____ The fact that environmental issues seem, once again, to be absent from the current
       presidential debates is a sign of a political failure among conservation groups.

_____ Funding is insufficient to meet the enormous challenges faced by conservationists worldwide.

_____ Funding is insufficient to meet the challenges faced by local conservationists in my area of the country.

_____ Professional staff of conservation organizations are overworked and under-supported.

_____ The administrative, management and fundraising demands within conservation organizations distract their finest staff from what they ought to be doing -- namely, the substantive work of the organization.

_____ The contention that internal organizational demands distract conservation staff away from substantive effort is just another way of saying that these organizations tend to be poorly managed.

_____ Conservation is not a profession; it lacks the clear career paths, accreditation and rewards for real achievement that come with a real profession.

44. Some conservation leaders seem troubled by a "gulf" between urban-based national conservation organizations and the more local, grassroots groups. Do you perceive such a "gulf"? _____ Yes _____ No

If yes, how would you characterize it and what, if anything, would you do to close it?

45. Do you view your work in conservation as something you'll be doing for the rest of your professional life? _____ Yes _____ No

46. Please describe how and why you got started in conservation work. What made you become a conservationist?

47. Have you ever worked professionally in a governmental agency? _____ Yes _____ No
If yes, please name the agency and describe your responsibilities there:

Have you ever worked professionally in a for-profit business? _____ Yes _____ No
If yes, please name the businesses and describe your responsibilities there:

Were you ever (or are you now) a conservation volunteer? _____ Yes _____ No
If yes, please describe:

48.   What do you need to make your work as a conservationist more rewarding and effective? Please use the appropriate numbers to indicate how rewarding each of the following would be to you.

Irrelevant to me	Somewhat rewarding	Very rewarding	My top priority	This needs no improvement
1	2	3	4	5

_____   Substantially higher pay.

_____   A promotion within my organization.

_____   A new, or different, job within my organization. (Please specify) _____

_____   Leaving my organization for something new. (Please explain) _____

_____   A greater sense of organizational security.

_____   A more supportive staff.

_____   Greater participation by our members or volunteers.

_____   A stronger, better, or more involved board of directors. (Please explain) _____

_____   More support or recognition from my peers in the conservation movement.

_____   More support or recognition from outside the conservation movement. (Please explain) _____

_____   More time for myself.

_____   More, or better, training for professional growth.

_____   More opportunities for personal renewal and growth.

_____   Other (please specify) _____

49.   What are the most important obstacles you face in performing your work?

50.   Please describe the job or work you'd like to be doing five or ten years from now.

PART V - THE QUESTIONNAIRE AND FOLLOW-UP

51. Do you perceive a bias in this questionnaire? _____ Yes _____ No

    If yes, please describe the bias(es) and how extensive you perceive the bias(es) to be. How do you think such bias(es) will affect the results of the questionnaire? Do you have any other comments regarding this questionnaire?

52. Are you willing to be interviewed, either by telephone or in person, so that we can gain a greater understanding of your attitudes toward leadership in conservation?

    _____ Yes   _____ No

53. Is there anything else you'd care to say about leadership in conservation? Lengthy comments are encouraged. Please use additional pages if necesary.

THANK YOU FOR YOUR TIME AND COOPERATION IN COMPLETING THIS
LENGTHY QUESTIONNAIRE!!

Please mail to:

Joe W. Floyd
Department of Sociology, Political Science,
and Native American Studies
Eastern Montana College
Billings, Montana 59101

Conservation Volunteers' Questionnaire

CONSERVATION LEADERSHIP PROJECT
SPONSORED BY
THE CONSERVATION FUND

Conservation Volunteers'
■
Questionnaire

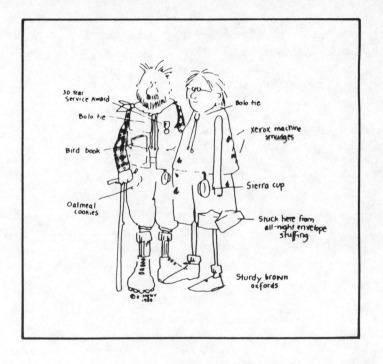

Urgent!
Please complete and return within two weeks of receipt.
(Return envelope provided)

PART I - IDENTIFICATION

1.   Your name _____

2.   Address _____

3.   Telephone _____

4.   Your sex: _____ Male   _____ Female

5.   Your date of birth _____

6.   Most of your conservation volunteer work is done with which organization(s)?
     _____

MORE INSTRUCTIONS: Many conservation volunteers serve more than one organization. If you listed more than one organization above, please choose the one you would consider your primary affiliate. Please list it below and answer the rest of the questions relative to that organization only.

If that organization is a field office, state affiliate, or some other kind of subdivision of a larger parent organization, please answer the questions relative to the subdivision, not the parent organization.

If your volunteer work is not affiliated with any organization, please skip to question #29.

7.   Primary organization _____

8.   Address and phone of organization (please include area code and zip code) _____
     _____

9.   Name and title of organization's staff person who serves as your primary contact
     _____

10. If you have a job title with the organization, please state it here:
     _____

11. Would you like to receive a complimentary copy of the survey results? ___Yes ___No

PART II - ORGANIZATIONAL DESCRIPTION

12.   Now that you have told us with which organization you are primarily affiliated, we'd like
      you to describe it. Which statement, or statements, below adequately characterize your
      "primary" organization? (Please check as many as are appropriate. If none of the
      statements accurately describes it, or if you want to add information to the description,
      please use the choices marked "other.")

      A.   With respect to geographic scope or emphasis, the organization is

           _____ international   _____ state

           _____ national   _____ local

           _____ regional   _____ other (please describe)

                                                   _____

      B.   I would characterize the organization as

           _____ a national or international organization with chapers and/or field offices

           _____ a national or international organization with no chapters or field offices

           _____ an independent regional or state-based organization

           _____ a coalition or "coordinating council" of organizations

           _____ a local organization focusing on local issues or concerns

           _____ a trade association

           _____ other (please specify) _____

                 _____

      C.   The offices to which I report directly represent

           _____ the central headquarters of the organization

           _____ a field office, chapter or affiliate of a parent organization

           _____ other (please specify) _____

                 _____

      D.   What is the approximate annual budget of the organzation (or the organizational
           subdivision) to which you report? _____

13.   In very general terms, which one word best characterizes the organization:

      _____ conservationist   _____ environmentalist

      _____ preservationist   _____ educational

14.   Does your organization (or subdivision) have a dues-paying membership?

      _____ Yes   _____ No

      If so, how many members does it currently have? _____

CONSERVATION LEADERSHIP PROJECT   Page 3

15. How many full-time paid staff does your organization (subdivision) employ? _____

     How many part-time paid staff? _____

16. Many conservation organizations work on numerous issues, problems, or educational
     programs. Some have just one major area. Please indicate below the relative importance
     of the following problem areas with respect to the efforts and activities of your primary
     organization.

	Unimportant 1	Somewhat important 2	Very important 3	Our highest priority 4

Issue or Program Area	Rating
Agriculture	_____
Air quality	_____
Water quality	_____
Energy conservation/facility planning & regulation	_____
Fish/wildlife management/protection (including Endangered Species protection)	_____
Marine conservation	_____
Mining law/regulation	_____
National forest/national parks/public lands management	_____
Nuclear power/weapons	_____
Population control	_____
Private land preservation/stewardship	_____
Protection of waterways (rivers, lakes, coastal zones)	_____
Toxic/hazardous waste management	_____
Urban/rural land use planning	_____
Wilderness	_____
Zoological/botanical gardens	_____
Naturalism/environmental education	_____
Other (please specify) _____	_____

_____

17.   Conservation organizations use many different strategies and activities in order to reach their organizational goals. Please indicate below the relative important, to your organization, of the following strategies:

Irrelevant to us 1	Very seldom used by us 2	Not a major strategy, but we use it sometimes 3	A very important strategy to us 4	This is our highest priority 5

_____   Direct litigation

_____   Direct management/stewardship of land or waterways

_____   Directly influencing elections of officials

_____   Educating people through encounters with nature (natural history, hikes, species identification, etc.)

_____   Educating the public through various media (print, video, TV, radio, self-publicity, conferencing, public speaking, etc.)

_____   Lobbying lawmakers

_____   Mediating environmental conflicts

_____   Mobilizing letter-writing and other political action campaigns

_____   Monitoring governmental agencies

_____   Performing and disseminating ethical or philosophical research

_____   Performing and disseminating policy research and analysis

_____   Performing and disseminating scientific research (including physical, biological, and/or social sciences)

_____   Placing issues on the ballot via initiative or referendum

_____   Preserving or protecting land (or other resources) through direct purchase or acquisition

_____   Organizing coalitions

_____   Training volunteers to act on behalf of our organization

_____   Other (please specify) _____

18.   Volunteers are often important actors in conservation organizations of all sizes   In organizations with paid staff, the relationship between staff and volunteers is often a key factor in organizational effectiveness.

A.   How would you honestly characterize your organization's use and involvement of volunteers?

_____   The organization sees volunteers as integral to its mission and uses them accordingly.

_____   The organization uses volunteers fairly well.

_____   The organization tolerates volunteers, rather than using them effectively.

_____   The organization looks down on them, or even abuses their good will.

B. In what capacities does the organization use volunteers? (Please check all that are appropriate below.):

_____ Board members

_____ Advisors (please describe): _____

_____ Lobbyists

_____ Fundraisers

_____ Organizers

_____ Programmatic assistants

_____ Office help

_____ Other (please describe): _____

_____

C. Any comments you'd care to make about your organization's use of volunteers or about conservation volunteers generally?

PART III - EVALUATION, NEEDS, AND ATTITUDES

19. The following is a list of "internal" resources and opportunities that might help conservation leaders and organizations perform more effectively. Of the services listed below, please indicate which ones you feel would be useful in improving the effectiveness of your organization.

Useless/ worthless 1	Not very useful 2	Fairly useful 3	Extremely useful 4	Organization already has this 5

a. _____ Participation in a training program for volunteers (other than board members).

b. _____ Training in the resolution of interpersonal conflicts among staff members.

c. _____ Participation in a leadership training program for board members.

d. _____ Establishment of an in-house training or orientation program for staff.

e. _____ Assistance with organizational strategic planning.

f. _____ Hiring staff to help with management and administration.

g. _____ Hiring staff to help with fundraising & organizational development.

h. _____ Hiring staff to help with substantive organizational programs.

i. _____ A better office environment (physical workspace).

j. _____ Greater data processing and computer capabilities.

k. _____ Greater opportunities to hire or work with professional researchers (e.g., economists, biologists, earth scientists, etc.)

l. _____ Access to more, or better, information.

m. _____ A much larger budget.

    n. _____ A financial endowment for the organization.

    o. _____ Expert training in lobbying.

    p. _____ Expert training in environmental dispute resolution or mediation.

    q. _____ A field program with full- or part-time staff.

    r. _____ An organizational evaluation performed by the membership.

    s. _____ Other (please specify) _____

21. Of all items listed above (a through r), which <u>one</u> item would be your first and highest priority? (Please circle the appropriate letter above.)

22. The following is a list of attributes that often affect the performance and effectiveness of conservation groups. Please use the number below to evaluate each attribute in the context of your organization today. (Written comments elaborating on any of these, or adding new ones, would be especially helpful to us):

Severe problems here	Serious problems here	We're doing well but could improve	Very good here	Excellent	Does not apply
1	2	3	4	5	8

a. _____ The clarity of the organization's mission and goals.

b. _____ The effectiveness of our strategies in reaching our goals.

c. _____ The board's ability to establish effective organizational policy.

d. _____ The board's ability to stay within its own boundaries, and not interfere with the staff.

e. _____ The organization's ability to raise sufficient funds.

f. _____ The use of tools of evaluation to measure the progress of our programs or projects.

g. _____ The effectiveness of our organizational planning.

h. _____ The effectiveness of our public communication.

i. _____ The diversification of our income, such that we are building organizational security.

j. _____ Relations between board and staff.

k. _____ Relations between staff and other volunteers.

l. _____ Relations among the staff.

m. _____ Overall effectiveness of our organizational management.

n. _____ Overall effectiveness of our organization.

Do you have comments about any of the above?

23. The following is a list of "external" resources and opportunities that might help conservation leaders perform their jobs more effectively. Of the services listed below, which ones do you feel would be useful in improving your performance as a conservation volunteer?

Useless/ worthless 1	Not very useful 2	Fairly useful 3	Extremely useful 4	I'm already involved in this 5

a. _____ Open discussions about management problems and opportunities with staff and volunteers in other conservation organizations.

b. _____ Open discussions about issues, programs and other matters of substance with staff and volunteers in other conservation organizations.

c. _____ Discussions about management problems and opportunities with leaders of nonprofit organizations other than conservation.

d. _____ Participation in an ongoing leadership development program designed specifically for conservation volunteers.

e. _____ Travel to other countries to see for myself how they are dealing with natural resource and environmental issues.

f. _____ A structured program that would expose me to the causes of and responses to poverty in the United States.

g. _____ Receiving a fellowship for advanced training in relevant aspects of natural resource management.

h. _____ A paid sabbatical that would allow me the time and independence to pursue some studies or creative work of my own design, relative to conservation.

i. _____ Participation in a "teaching sabbatical" that would allow me to share with students my practical knowledge of conservation.

j. _____ Participation in discussions or courses conducted by leading thinkers in environmental ethics.

k. _____ Participation in discussions or courses led by experts and scholars in the history of resource conservation.

l. _____ Participation in courses or field studies led by experts in conservation biology and ecology.

m. _____ Participation in discussions or courses led by leading thinkers in natural resource policy-making.

n. _____ Participation in a "lawmakers' forum" with legislators/congressmen and conservation leaders on future needs for environmental law and policy.

o. _____ Participation in a structured forum in which conservation leaders, regulators, and industry leaders can seek out ways to enhance planning and reduce conflicts over development.

p. _____ Greater access to journals or newsletters related to the conservation profession.

q. _____ Other (please specify) _____

24. Of all items listed above (a through q), which one item would be your first and highest priority? (Please circle the appropriate letter above.)

25.   The following is a list of statements describing some attitudes about the conservation movement in the United States. Please indicate your level of agreement or disagreement with each of these statements.

Strongly disagree	Disagree	Agree	Strongly agree
1	2	3	4

_____ The large numbers of conservation groups and their millions of members and supporters are proof that the cause of conservation has never been healthier than it is today.

_____ Leadership and leading ideas of conservation have tended to emerge primarily from the nonacademic, nonprofit world.

_____ The leaders of conservation in the U.S. are more reactive than farsighted; they seem to be lacking in real vision or originality.

_____ The conservation movement is fragmented, territorial and uncommunicative.

_____ There is no longer any such thing as "the conservation movement"; in the sense that "movement" implies a unified effort of many people to achieve specific goals, the "movement" has gone out of conservation.

_____ National conservation organizations are generally unsupportive of unaffiliated local conservation groups.

_____ National conservation organizations are actually detrimental to local conservation efforts, because they soak up funds that end up having little local effect.

_____ Local conservation groups where I live are generally unsupportive of national conservation organizations.

_____ National conservation groups should expand their field programs at the local level.

_____ Many, perhaps most, minority and poor rural Americans see little in the conservation message that speaks to them.

_____ The conservation movement in the United States is generally bereft of new ideas; it is mired in a sort of business-as-usual approach to environmental problems.

_____ National conservation organizations have become altogether too "professional"; they have come to resemble the very corporations they purport to fight.

_____ The real leadership in conservation lies in the grassroots, not among the professional conservationists.

_____ The fact that environmental issues seemed, once again, to be understated during the presidential debates is a sign of a political failure among conservation groups.

_____ Funding is insufficient to meet the enormous challenges faced by conservationists worldwide.

_____ Funding is insufficient to meet the challenges faced by local conservationists in my area of the country.

_____ Professional staff of conservation organizations are overworked and under-supported.

_____ The administrative, management and fundraising demands within conservation organizations distract their finest staff from what they ought to be doing namely, the substantive work of the organization.

    _____ The contention that internal organizational demands distract conservation staff away from substantive effort is just another way of saying that these organizations tend to be poorly managed.

    _____ Conservation is not a profession; it lacks the clear career paths, accreditation and rewards for real achievement that come with a real profession.

26. Some conservation leaders seem troubled by a "gulf" between urban-based national conservation organizations and the more local, grassroots groups. Do you perceive such a "gulf"? _____ Yes _____ No

If yes, how would you characterize it, and what, if anything would you do to close it?

27. Please describe how and why you got started in conservation work. What made you become a conservationist?

28. What are the most important obstacles you face in performing your work as a volunteer?

PART IV - OCCUPATION, EDUCATION AND TRAINING

29. Please check the item below which most closely characterizes your current occupation:

    _____ professional   _____ unskilled laborer

    _____ managerial   _____ unemployed

    _____ technical   _____ other (please describe) _____

    _____ skilled laborer   _____

30. Please describe your current job or occupation below. If you have a job title, please write it down, then briefly describe the functions of the job if you feel they are not self-explanatory:

Title or occupation: _____

Functions: _____

Length of time in current occupation: _____

CONSERVATION LEADERSHIP PROJECT   Page 1 0

31.   If you have completed college and/or graduate degrees, please indicate them below:

Bachelor of _____   in (major) _____

from (college or university) _____

Master of _____   in (emphasis) _____

from (college or university) _____

Ph.D. or other professional degree (e.g., M.D., LL.D., etc.) _____

_____ from _____

Additional degrees or educational certificates? _____

_____

32.   Have you ever worked professionally in a conservation or natural resource organization or agency? _____ Yes   _____ No

If yes, please describe your work and the organization(s) in which you performed the work:

_____

_____

Was that organization a:

_____   branch of federal government

_____   branch of state government

_____   branch of local government

_____   nongovernmental, non-profit organization

_____   for-profit business

_____   other (please specify) _____

33.   Do you desire to work professionally for a conservation organization?

_____ Yes   _____ No (if no, go on to Question #34)

With which organization? _____

Please describe the job you'd like to have there: _____

_____

What do you feel are your major obstacles in obtaining this employment? (Please check as many as are appropriate below):

_____   There are no major obstacles.

_____   I lack the appropriate educational background.

_____   I don't feel that I'm adequately trained for the job.

_____   The job doesn't pay enough to make the transition worthwhile.

_____   The job is too insecure.

_____   The job I want in conservation is not available.

_____   Other (please describe) _____

_____

34.   In the past two years, have you attended any conferences, symposia or training events for the purpose of enhancing your effectiveness as a conservation volunteer?

_____ Yes   _____ No (if no, go to Question # 38)

If so, did the organization or agency for which you work as a volunteer sponsor your attendance (i.e., pay the costs of your attending)?

_____ Yes (always)   _____ Yes (sometimes)   _____ No (never)

35.   Please indicate the primary areas of training you received at this, or these, event(s). (Check as many as are appropriate.)

_____ Board member training

_____ Communications/public relations

_____ Conservation history

_____ Ethics

_____ Financial management

_____ Fundraising

_____ Interpersonal relations

_____ Law

_____ Leadership skills

_____ Mediation/conflict resolution

_____ Organizational administration

_____ Personnel management

_____ Policy analysis

_____ Membership development

_____ Other (please describe) _____

36.   Of the training seminars or conferences you've attended, which one or two would you rate as truly outstanding in enhancing your effectiveness? Who conducted them?

Seminar   Conducted by

1. _____   _____

2. _____   _____

37.   Which one or two would you rate as very poor? Who conducted those?

Seminar   Conducted by

1. _____   _____

2. _____   _____

CONSERVATION LEADERSHIP PROJECT   Page 1 2

PART V - THE QUESTIONNAIRE AND FOLLOW-UP

38.   Do you perceive a strong bias in this questionnaire? _____ Yes   _____ No

       If yes, please describe the bias(es) and how extensive you perceive the bias(es) to be.
       How do you think such bias(es) will affect the results of the questionnaire?

39.   Are you willing to be interviewed, either by telephone or in person, so that we can gain a
       greater understanding of your attitudes toward leadership in conservation?

       _____ Yes   _____ No

40.   If there anything else you'd care to say about leadership in conservation? (Please feel
       free to use the backs of pages, if necessary.)

Thank you for your time and cooperation.
Please mail to:

Dr. Joe W. Floyd
Chair, Department of Sociology,
Political Science, and Native American Studies
Eastern Montana College
Billings, Montana 59101

Academic Programs Questionnaire

CONSERVATION LEADERSHIP PROJECT
SPONSORED BY
THE CONSERVATION FUND

ACADEMIC PROGRAMS QUESTIONNAIRE

URGENT!

Please complete and return within two weeks of receipt.
(Return envelope provided)

PART I - IDENTIFICATION

1. **Name** of university or college _____

2. **Name** of your school _____

3. **Name** of your department _____

4. **Name** of your program _____

5. **Address** _____

6. **Telephone** _____

7. **Your name** _____

8. **Your sex** _____ male _____ female

9. **Your job title or position** _____

10. **How long have you held this position?** _____

11. **Would you like to receive a complimentary copy of the survey results?**

     _____ yes   _____ no

PART II - PROGRAM DESCRIPTION

12. Please state the mission or purpose of your program.

13. Is the program: _____ Primarily an undergraduate program

                           _____ Exclusively an undergraduate program

                           _____ Primarily a graduate program

                           _____ Exclusively a graduate program

                           _____ Equally a graduate & undergraduate program

CONSERVATION LEADERSHIP PROJECT   Page 2

14. Please check the item, or items, below which most accurately characterize
    the administrative foundation of the program:

    _____ A college or school

    _____ A department

    _____ An interdisciplinary program

    _____ An adjunct center or institute

    _____ Other (Please describe) _____

    _____

15. What are the kinds of degrees and certificates awarded by the program?

    Bachelors degree(s)   _____   in (Major)   _____

                           _____   in (Major)   _____

    Masters degree(s)   _____   in (emphasis) _____

                           _____   in (emphasis) _____

    Doctorate degree(s)   _____   in _____

                           _____   in _____

    Additional degrees or certificates? _____

    _____

16. In what year did the program originate? _____

17. Have its purposes or emphases changed substantially since its year of
    origin? _____ yes   _____ no

    If so, please describe: _____

    _____

    _____

18. We are interested in trends in student application and enrollment in the program. During the past five years, the total student enrollment, as well as number of graduate candidates applying, has been:

Academic year	Enrolled undergraduate students	Graduate applications	Enrolled graduate students
1987–88	_____	_____	_____
1986–87	_____	_____	_____
1985–86	_____	_____	_____
1984–85	_____	_____	_____
1983–84	_____	_____	_____
1982–83	_____	_____	_____

19. What trends do you see in student interest and enrollment in the program, and what are the principal factors contributing to these trends?

      Trends   Factors

PART II – STUDENT INFORMATION

FOR GRADUATE PROGRAMS ONLY

20. Does the program actively recruit students for the purpose of maintaining the highest possible quality? _____ yes   _____ no

    If yes, what specifically does the program do to recruit?

268   Appendix C

21. If you have readily available data on the following, please provide.

    What are the average GRE scores of students currently enrolled in the program?

    _____ verbal   _____ analytical

    _____ quantitative   _____ field of study

22. What are the three most common undergraduate majors among graduate students enrolled in the program?

    _____

    _____

    _____

FOR ALL PROGRAMS

23. During the past two years, approximately what percentages of graduates from the program have found employment in the following areas? (Please make estimates if hard data are not available.)

	Percentage of baccalaureate graduates	Percentage of masters/Ph.D. graduates
Federal government agencies	_____ %	_____ %
State government agencies	_____ %	_____ %
Consulting firms	_____ %	_____ %
For-profit businesses (other than consulting firms)	_____ %	_____ %
Non-profit, nongovernmental organizations	_____ %	_____ %
Academia	_____ %	_____ %
Other educational institutions	_____ %	_____ %
In a field outside of their training	_____ %	_____ %

24. Are these percentages typical of placements during the past five to ten years? _____ yes   _____ no

    If not, how do they differ?

CONSERVATION LEADERSHIP PROJECT   Page 5

25. Please offer any observations you might have about trends you see in the
    quality of students who have come to the program over the past five years.

PART III - OBSTACLES, OPPORTUNITIES, FUTURE DIRECTIONS

26. By comparison with other programs at your university or college, your
    program's funding is:

    _____ very stable
    _____ about as stable as any other, comparable programs
    _____ more uncertain than most programs at the institution
    _____ very uncertain

27. The following is a list of obstacles which academic programs often face.
    Please use the numbers below to evaluate each of these obstacles relative
    to your program.

        A major problem   Somewhat of a problem   Not a problem
             1   2   3

    _____ Lack of financial support for students

    _____ Lack of adequate student enrollment

    _____ Lack of adequate funding to maintain or enhance programs

    _____ Lack of adequate facilities

    _____ Attracting or retaining top-notch faculty

    _____ Competition with other programs

    _____ Failure to attract top students

    _____ Low-paying or low-prestige jobs for our graduates

    _____ Lack of professional identification

    _____ Too few jobs for our graduates

    _____ Lack of public support, or a negative public perception

    _____ A values-shift in society away from our emphasis

    _____ Isolation from natural resource programs at other institutions

CONSERVATION LEADERSHIP PROJECT   Page 6

28. The greatest single pressure affecting the <u>quality</u> of our program is:

_____

_____

29. The greatest single pressure affecting the <u>future</u> <u>stability</u> of the program
    is _____ _____

_____

30. In what ways does the program emphasize training in the management and
    administration of natural resource organizations or agencies? (Check all
    that apply.)

    _____ It has no such emphasis.

    _____ It offers its own courses in organizational management and
             administration.

    _____ It encourages or requires students to take organizational
             management courses outside of the program.

    _____ It encourages students to take internships to learn about
             organizational management.

    _____ It has developed a very thorough curriculum in organizational
             management and administration.

    _____ The primary emphasis of the program is in organizational management
             and administration.

    Comments?_____

    _____

31. Are there plans to enhance curricular offering in management and
    administration? _____ yes   _____ no

    If yes, please describe._____

    _____

32. Does the program offer (or is it planning to offer) in-service training
    for natural resource professionals currently on the job?
    _____ yes   _____ no

    If yes, please describe. _____

    _____

CONSERVATION LEADERSHIP PROJECT   Page 7

33. Do you, or does anyone associated with the program, meet or correspond regularly with your counterparts at other institutions about matters pertinent to the further development of the program?

_____ yes   _____ no

If yes, please describe.

34. Is there anything else you'd care to say about the program, or about tends you see in the training of natural resource students? Lengthy comments are encouraged. Please attach pages if necessary.

THANK YOU FOR YOUR TIME AND COOPERATION IN COMPLETING
THIS QUESTIONNAIRE!!

Please mail to:

Joe W. Floyd
Department of Sociology, Political Science,
and Native American Studies
Eastern Montana College
Billings, Montana 59101

Notes

CHAPTER I *Introduction*

1. Stephen Fox, *John Muir and His Legacy: The American Conservation Movement* (Boston: Little, Brown & Co., 1981), 107.
2. John Gardner, *On Leadership* (New York: The Free Press, 1990), 81.
3. J. Clarence Davies, Frances H. Irwin, and Barbara K. Rodes, *Training for Environmental Groups* (Washington, D.C.: The Conservation Foundation, 1983), 3–5.
4. Barry Commoner, "The Environment," in *Crossroads: Environmental Priorities for the Future*, ed. Peter Borrelli (Washington, D.C.: Island Press, 1988), 162.
5. Robert Gottlieb and Helen Ingram, "The New Environmentalists," *The Progressive* (August 1988): 14.
6. Ibid.
7. Ibid.
8. Ibid., 15.
9. Ibid.
10. Howard Youth, "Boom Time for Environmental Groups," *World-Watch* (November–December 1989): 33.

CHAPTER 2 *Staff Leadership*

1. Jonathan B. Cook, "Managing Nonprofits of Different Sizes," in *Educating Managers of Nonprofit Organizations*, ed. Michael O'Neill and Dennis R. Young (New York: Praeger, 1988), 101–16.
2. Ibid., 107.
3. Ibid., 110.
4. Ibid., 111.
5. Ibid., 110.

CHAPTER 4 *Key Issues of Conservation Leadership*

1. Edward O. Wilson, "The New Environmentalism," *Chronicles of Contemporary Culture* (August 1990), 16.
2. William Tucker, *Progress and Privilege: America in the Age of Environmentalism* (Garden City, N.Y.: Anchor/Doubleday, 1982).
3. Barry Commoner, "Environment," 162–63.
4. Richard Grossman, review of *Crossroads: Environmental Priorities for the Future*, edited by Peter Borrelli, *Environmental Action* (September–October 1989), 33.
5. Dave Foreman, "Making the Most of Professionalism," *Whole Earth Review* (March 1985): 34–37.
6. Philip Shabecoff, "Environmental Groups Told They Are Racist in Hiring," *New York Times* (February 1, 1990): A16.
7. Peter Borrelli, ed., *Crossroads: Environmental Priorities for the Future* (Washington, D.C.: Island Press, 1988), 10.
8. Howard Youth, "Boom Time for Environmental Groups," *WorldWatch* (November–December, 1989), 33.
9. National Governors' Association, "Economic Realities in Rural America: Recent Trends, Future Prospects," in *New Alliances for Rural America* (Washington, D.C.: National Governors' Association, 1988), 1.
10. John Osborne, *Laboratories of Democracy* (Cambridge, Mass.: Harvard University Press, 1990).
11. Jonathan B. Cook, "Managing Nonprofits of Different Sizes," in *Educating Managers of Nonprofit Organizations*, ed. Michael O'Neill and Dennis R. Young (New York: Praeger, 1988), 103.
12. Ibid., 105.
13. Ibid., 110.
14. Peter F. Drucker, "Managing the Public Service Institution," *The Public Interest* (1973): 33, 43–60.
15. Conservation Leadership Project, *Final Report* (Arlington, Va.: The Conservation Fund, 1989), 13–14.
16. Ibid., 17.
17. John Gardner, *On Leadership*, 121–37.

CHAPTER 5 *Academic Training*

1. Samuel P. Hays, *Conservation and the Gospel of Efficiency: The Progressive Conservation Movement, 1890–1920* (Cambridge, Mass.: Harvard University Press, 1959), 2–4.
2. American Association of Fund-Raising Council, *Giving U.S.A., 1990* (New York: AAFRC, 1991).

Bibliography

American Association of Fund-Raising Council. *Giving U.S.A., 1990*. New York: AAFRC, 1991.

Bennis, Warren, and Burt Nanus. *Leadership*. New York: Harper and Row, 1985.

Bogue, Donald J., and Stanley G. Hudson, eds. *Personnel Management of White-Collar Employees*. Chicago: Community and Family Study Center, University of Chicago, 1976.

Borrelli, Peter, ed. *Crossroads: Environmental Priorities for the Future*. Washington, D.C.: Island Press, 1988.

Boulding, Kenneth E. *The Economy of Love and Fear: A Preface to Grants Economics*. Belmont, Calif.: Wadsworth, 1973.

Commoner, Barry. "The Environment." In *Crossroads: Environmental Priorities for the Future*, edited by Peter Borrelli. Washington, D.C.: Island Press, 1988.

Conservation Leadership Project. *Final Report*. Arlington, Va.: The Conservation Fund, 1989.

Cook, Jonathan B. "Managing Nonprofits of Different Sizes." In *Educating Managers of Nonprofit Organizations*, edited by Michael O'Neill and Dennis R. Young. New York: Praeger, 1988.

Davies, J. Clarence, Frances H. Irwin, and Barbara K. Rodes. *Training for Environmental Groups*. Washington, D.C.: The Conservation Foundation, 1983.

Drucker, Peter F. "Managing the Public Service Institution." *The Public Interest* (1973): 33, 43–60.

Foreman, Dave. "Making the Most of Professionalism." *Whole Earth Review* (March 1985), 34–37.

Fox, Stephen. *John Muir and His Legacy: The American Conservation Movement*. Boston: Little, Brown & Co., 1981.

Gardner, John. *On Leadership*. New York: The Free Press, 1990.

Gottlieb, Robert, and Helen Ingram. "The New Environmentalists." *The Progressive* (August 1988), 14–15.

Gray, Sandra. *An Independent Sector Resource Directory of Education and Training Opportunities and Other Services*. Washington, D.C.: Independent Sector, 1987.

Grossman, Richard. Review of *Crossroads: Environmental Priorities for the Future*, edited by Peter Borrelli. *Environmental Action* (September–October 1989), 33.

Hansmann, Henry B. "The Role of Nonprofit Enterprise." *The Yale Law Journal* 89 (1980): 835–901.

Hays, Samuel P. *Conservation and the Gospel of Efficiency: The Progressive Conservation Movement, 1890–1920*. Cambridge, Mass.: Harvard University Press, 1959.

———. *Beauty, Health and Permanence: Environmental Politics in the United States, 1955–1985*. Cambridge, England: Cambridge University Press, 1987.

Jaques, Elliott. *A General Theory of Bureaucracy*. London: Heinemann Educational Books, 1978.

Koontz, Harold. *Toward a Unified Theory of Management*. New York: McGraw-Hill, 1964.

Kramer, Ralph M. "The Future of the Voluntary Agency in a Mixed Economy." *The Journal of Applied Behavioral Science* 21 (1985): 377–91.

Kuriloff, Arthur H. *Organizational Development for Survival*. New York: American Management Association, 1972.

Larson, Magali Sarfatti. *The Rise of Professionalism: A Sociological Analysis*. Berkeley: University of California Press, 1977.

Litterer, Joseph A. *The Analysis of Organizations*. New York: John Wiley & Sons, 1965.

McAdam, Terry W. *Careers in the Nonprofit Sector: Doing Well by Doing Good*. Washington, D.C.: The Taft Group, 1986.

Majone, Giandomenico. *Professionalism and Nonprofit Organizations*. Working Paper no. 24, Program on Nonprofit Organizations. New Haven: Institution for Social and Policy Studies, Yale University, 1980.

Mason, David E. *Voluntary Nonprofit Enterprise Management*. New York: Plenum, 1984.

National Governors' Association. *New Alliances for Rural America.* Washington, D.C.: National Governors' Association, 1988.

O'Connell, Brian. *Effective Leadership in Voluntary Organizations.* New York: Association Press, 1976.

O'Neill, Michael, and Dennis R. Young, eds. *Educating Managers of Nonprofit Organizations.* New York: Praeger, 1988.

Osborne, John. *Laboratories of Democracy.* Cambridge, Mass.: Harvard University Press, 1990.

Schein, Edgar H. *Organizational Culture and Leadership: A Dynamic View.* San Francisco: Jossey-Bass, 1985.

Tucker, William. *Progress and Privilege: America in the Age of Environmentalism.* Garden City, N.Y.: Anchor/Doubleday, 1982.

Weber, Max. *The Theory of Economic and Social Organization.* Translated by A. M. Henderson and Talcott Parsons. New York: Oxford University Press, 1947.

Wilson, Edward O. "The New Environmentalism." *Chronicles of Contemporary Culture* (August 1990), 16–18.

Youth, Howard. "Boom Time for Environmental Groups." *WorldWatch* (November–December 1989), 33.

Zucker, Lynne G., ed. *Institutional Theories of Organizations: Culture and Environment.* New York: Ballinger, 1986.

Conservation Leadership
Project Personnel

Staff

Patrick F. Noonan	President, The Conservation Fund
Donald Snow	Project Director and Editor
G. Jon Roush	Senior Associate
Laurie L. Hall	Project Assistant
Jean W. McKendry	Project Associate

Consultants

Joe W. Floyd	Eastern Montana College
Victoria Bomberry	Private Consultant
Dorceta E. Taylor	Yale University

Advisory Council

Lamar Alexander	University of Tennessee
Wallace Dayton	The Conservation Fund
Thomas Deans	New Hampshire Charitable Fund
George F. Dutrow	Duke University
George T. Frampton, Jr.	The Wilderness Society
Jerry F. Franklin	University of Washington
Ralph E. Grossi	American Farmland Trust
David F. Hales	Michigan Department of Natural Resources
Jean W. Hocker	Land Trust Alliance
Charles R. Jordan	City of Portland, Oregon, Bureau of Parks

Jack Lorenz	Izaak Walton League of America
Gerald P. McCarthy	Virginia Environmental Endowment
Lyle M. Nelson	Stanford University
Donal C. O'Brien	National Audubon Society
John C. Oliver, III	Western Pennsylvania Conservancy
James Posewitz	Montana Department of Fish, Wildlife and Parks
Nathaniel P. Reed	1000 Friends of Florida
Henry R. Richmond	1000 Friends of Oregon
Daniel Simberloff	Florida State University
Hubert M. Vogelmann	University of Vermont
Norman K. Wessells	University of Oregon

About the Author

Donald Snow is executive director of the Northern Lights Research & Education Institute and founder and editor of *Northern Lights Magazine,* in Missoula, Montana. Since 1976, he has worked as a volunteer and staff member of several environmental organizations in the American West. He completed the Conservation Leadership Project as an associate of The Conservation Fund, based in Arlington, Virginia.

Index

Policy-development centers, 17–18, 131, 147
  regional, 177–78
Political activism:
  lobbying, *see* Lobbying by organizations
  of organizations with volunteer leadership, 101, 111, 130–31
Political weakness of conservation movement, 142–43
Politicians, responsiveness to staffed organizations of, 34
Pollution, 13, 137
Preservationists, 12
  environmentalists vs., 13
Professional conservation societies, 20
Professional development:
  of staff leadership, 45, 56, 69–73, 188
  of volunteer leadership, 103
Professional leadership, *see* Staff leadership
Programmatic evaluations, 216
Public education, 43, 56, 77, 82, 102, 110–11, 183–85
Public lands management, 109–10
Public relations function of staff leaders, 42, 56, 58, 165

Questionnaire:
  academic programs, 195–96, 263–71
  commentary of leaders on, 136
  staff leadership, 40–41, 227–43
  volunteer leadership, 98, 247–60

Race of conservation leaders, 42, 213
Racial limitations of conservation movement, 23, 27, 138, 155, 180, 213
Reagan administration, 146
Real estate conservation groups, 19–20
Recommendations, 212–21
  to academia, 218–21

to funders, 217–18
movementwide, 212–15
to organizations, 215–17
Recreational and sporting clubs, 16–17
Recruitment by organizations:
  of board of directors, 58–59
  recommendations, 214
  of staff leadership, 43, 73–76, 214
  volunteer leadership's attitude toward hiring staff, 125–29
  of volunteers, 113, 214
Referenda, 56, 102, 131
Regional advocacy groups, 17
  policy centers, 177–78
  regions lacking conservation advocacy, 141–42, 157–58
  small, staffed groups, 159–61
Regulators, opportunities for collaboration with, 119
Research in environmental ethics, 102
Research organizations, *see* Policy-development centers
Research staff, 116
Resources of organizations:
  external, *see* External resources, evaluation and use of
  internal, *see* Internal resources, evaluation and use of
Responsibilities, 164–68
  editorial, 42, 48, 165
  fund-raising, *see* Fund-raising function
  time divided among, *see* Time, utilization of
  writing, 42, 48, 165
Rod and gun clubs, 16–17
Rural membership of conservation groups, 154–55

Sabbaticals, 70–72, 82, 103, 119, 190–91
  recommendations, 216–17, 218
Salary, *see* Compensation

Staff leadership (*cont'd.*)
  viewed as positive development, 46
  volunteer leaders "graduating" to,
    113–14
  volunteer leaders wishing to join, 113
Staff of organizations:
  difficulty recruiting, 170–71
  evaluations, 44, 216
  relationship with boards of directors,
    35, 36, 102, 216
  relationship of volunteer leaders
    with, 115
  with staff leadership, 43, 51, 53–54
  turnover of, 141, 161, 170
  with volunteer leadership, 107
  attitude toward hiring staff, 125–29
State-based conservation groups, 17,
  107
  gulf between large institutional orga-
    nizations and, 28, 145–49, 151–
    54, 155–57, 162–64
  small, staffed groups, 159–61
  strengthening, 215
  states lacking conservation advocacy,
    141–42, 156, 157–58, 176, 215
State grants and contracts, 59, 62
Statewide coordination of efforts by
  staff leadership, 34
Strategic planning, *see* Planning by organizations
Strategies of organizations:
  comparison of responses of staff and
    volunteer leaders, 130–31
  with staff leadership, 43, 55–56, 57
  with volunteer leadership, 110–11,
    112
Student conservation organizations,
  220
Support and service organizations,
  20–21

Technical education, 192
Technical experts, 28
Texas Center for Policy Studies, 160
Time, utilization of:

management and fund-raising tasks
  as dominant, 144–45, 168, 169,
  170, 186
  recommendations, 216
  by staff leadership, 42, 44, 56–59,
    82, 168, 169, 186–88
Toxic waste accumulation, 136
Training, 11, 30–32, 125
  in-service, 31–32, 81, 103, 179,
    205–207, 216
  lack of opportunities for, 144, 145
  organizations with staff leadership,
    31–32, 81, 90, 161, 179
  organizations with volunteer leader-
    ship, 102, 103, 111
  see also Academic natural resource
    programs; Education
Trustees, *see* Boards of directors
Types of environmental and conservation organizations, 15–21
  education, research, and policy-
    development centers, 17–18
  large national and international
    membership groups, 19
  law and science groups, 18
  professional societies, 20
  real estate conservation groups, 19–
    20
  recreation and sporting clubs, 16–17
  small, all-volunteer, issues groups,
    15–16
  small national and international
    membership groups, 18–19
  small, quasi-volunteer naturalist
    groups, 16
  state-based or regional advocacy
    groups, 17
  support and service organizations,
    20–21

University of Michigan, School of
  Natural Resources, 200
Urban membership of conservation
  groups, 154–55
User fees, 59, 62

Vermont, 175
Volunteer leadership, 25, 95–132
  all-volunteer operations, 11, 15–16
  as board members, 102, 105, 115
  comparisons of responses by organization size, scope, and geographic orientation, 121, 129
  comparisons with responses from professional staff, 121–32
  Conservation Leadership Project study of:
  gathering sample of volunteers, 97–98, 99–100
  method, 96–100
  portrait of distinguished NGO volunteer leaders, 101–104
  questionnaire, 98, 247–60
  in early conservation movement, 4–5, 6, 150–51
  key findings, 104–21
  attitudes, 121, 126–28
  evaluation and use of external resources, 116–19, 122–24
  evaluation and use of internal resources, 116, 117–18
  issues and programs, 109–10
  management tools, 115–16, 117
  organizational attributes, 115–16, 117
  organizational characteristics, 104–109
  organizational strategies, 110–11, 112

  volunteer leader characteristics, 111–15
  limited training of, 11
  negative attitudes about business and money, 125
  nurturing, 6–7
  organizational design, weaknesses in, 125
  see also All-volunteer, small, issues groups
Volunteers:
  cooperation with staff leadership, 35
  desire for greater participation of, 73
  evaluation of use of, 216
  recruitment and training of, 214
  see also All-volunteer, small, issues groups; Volunteer leadership

Washington Environmental Council, 29
Water pollution, 137
Wilderness Society, The, 5, 138, 158
  founding of, 6
Wilson, E. O., 136, 185
Women as organizational leaders, 214
World Watch Magazine, 148
World Wildlife Fund, 148
Writing responsibilities of staff leaders, 42, 48, 165
Wyoming Outdoor Council, 29

Yosemite National Park, 6

Also Available
from Island Press

Ancient Forests of the Pacific Northwest
By Elliott A. Norse

Balancing on the Brink of Extinction: The Endangered Species Act and Lessons for the Future
Edited by Kathryn A. Kohm

Better Trout Habitat: A Guide to Stream Restoration and Management
By Christopher J. Hunter

Beyond 40 Percent: Record-Setting Recycling and Composting Programs
The Institute for Local Self-Reliance

The Challenge of Global Warming
Edited by Dean Edwin Abrahamson

Coastal Alert: Ecosystems, Energy, and Offshore Oil Drilling
By Dwight Holing

The Complete Guide to Environmental Careers
The CEIP Fund

Economics of Protected Areas
By John A. Dixon and Paul B. Sherman

Environmental Agenda for the Future
Edited by Robert Cahn

Environmental Disputes: Community Involvement in Conflict Resolution
By James E. Crowfoot and Julia M. Wondolleck

Forests and Forestry in China: Changing Patterns of Resource Development
By S. D. Richardson

The Global Citizen
By Donella Meadows

Hazardous Waste from Small Quantity Generators
By Seymour I. Schwartz and Wendy B. Pratt

Holistic Resource Management Workbook
By Allan Savory

In Praise of Nature
Edited and with essays by Stephanie Mills

8227